OP 6a

THE WORLD OF
PATIENCE GROMES

THE WORLD OF
PATIENCE GROMES

Making and Unmaking
a Black Community

Scott C. Davis

THE UNIVERSITY PRESS OF KENTUCKY

A portion of this book appeared in *The Christian Science Monitor* and is reprinted here, in revised form, with the permission of the publisher.

Copyright © 1988 by Scott C. Davis

Published by the University Press of Kentucky.

Scholarly publisher for the Commonwealth, serving Bellarmine College, Berea College, Centre College of Kentucky, Eastern Kentucky University, The Filson Club, Georgetown College, Kentucky Historical Society, Kentucky State University, Morehead State University, Murray State University, Northern Kentucky University, Transylvania University, University of Kentucky, University of Louisville, and Western Kentucky University.

Editorial and Sales Offices: Lexington, Kentucky 40506-0336

Library of Congress Cataloging-in-Publication Data

Davis, Scott C., 1948-
 The world of Patience Gromes : making and unmaking a black community / Scott C. Davis.
  p.   cm.
 Bibliography: p.
 ISBN 0-8131-1644-9
  1. Afro-Americans—Virginia—Richmond—Social conditions. 2. Afro-Americans—Virginia—Richmond—Social life and customs.
3. Richmond (Va.)—Social conditions. 4. Richmond (Va.)—Social life and customs. I. Title.
 F234.R59N43 1988
 975.5'4510049607—dc19   88-98

To the memory of
LILLIE MAY GILLESPIE

CONTENTS

1

PATIENCE GROMES

February 1971

I WANT to tell the story of a black community: its birth in the country at the end of the Civil War, its move from country to city, its disintegration during the war on poverty.

This community began with black men and women who belonged to the first generation after slavery. They were young, blessed with strong families, and in a position to make a life for themselves. They had been children during the Civil War, had seen the end of slavery, and had become convinced that history was working in their favor. They developed an idea of who they were and what they could accomplish with their own hands. They and their descendants passed this idea down from one generation to the next. Sometimes it became stronger, sometimes it weakened or was lost altogether. At the turn of the century, members of the third generation carried the idea to the city, to the run-down neighborhood of Fulton, a working-class district of Richmond, Virginia, where wooden shacks and tenements and brick row houses stood at the edge of the James River.

I arrived in Fulton in February 1971.

The wind came strong down the river, moved into the hollow at the river's edge, and flowed through the streets and alleys of Fulton. It was a cold wind, and it moved across granite curbstones, filling fenced front yards, encircling houses and holding them, wrapping them in cold. The houses on State Street looked out through windows covered with sheets of plastic. I saw doors closed with rags in them to keep out cold. I saw smoke drifting up from houses, black coal smoke, and I smelled coal. No one was around. No one came out to speak with me. I had never known such a world before: empty streets, old houses, the smell of coal.

A woman on State Street opened her door to me and offered temporary lodgings. Mrs. Frank Gromes was black, eighty-three years old, and owner of a wooden house. She led me upstairs. The back bedroom was warm from the heat of the kitchen below. The front bedroom was cold. I chose it for the dormer window that looked down on the street.

In the morning when I awoke I sat on a leather hassock in the cove before the windows, listened to doors slamming and gates latching, and saw neighbor women walking to work. People on this block lived close. Houses were hunched together, facing each other across the narrow street. Walls were thin, windows and doors loose fitting. Sounds carried and penetrated the dwellings.

One night after going to bed I lay in darkness, waiting for sleep and listening to the neighborhood around me. Long after all human sounds had ceased, I heard a car racing down narrow, cobbled alleys, skidding and sliding like some unholy visitation. My neighbors and I were tight in our beds, like children, and I imagined some unseen spirit of the night running loose in our village, encircling us all.

War and conscience brought me to Fulton. When I graduated from Stanford in 1970, the Vietnam War was in progress. Facing the draft, I filed for conscientious objector status and eight months later arrived in Richmond to begin two years' alternative service. I found a position as community worker with the Bethlehem Center, a Methodist-sponsored institution that had offered arts and crafts, sports, and summer camp to Fulton youth since 1937. The Bethlehem Center was private and therefore could not avail itself of VISTA (Volunteers in Service to America) workers. I was the equivalent. For the first few weeks I lived with Patience Gromes.

The life of Mrs. Gromes was intricately ordered and did not appear to have yielded even slightly to the spirit of the times. In the kitchen, for example, there was a place for everything, no matter how small or incidental. Patience Gromes offered an unsparing reproof if I were so careless as to return boxes, pots, and frypans to incorrect positions after a meal. Occasionally I made the mistake of leaving a cabinet door ajar by a quarter inch, a dimension that was imperceptible to me where kitchens were concerned. Mrs. Gromes, however, never failed to notice. "You left that kitchen a mess," she told me. "Go back and clean it up!" My landlady had eyes like a hawk.

The middle room was seldom used for dining now that Frank and the children were gone, and the front room was never used except on formal occasions. Yet they were organized with no less precision than the kitchen. The front room was dominated by the mantel above the fireplace. Here photographs of Patience Gromes's forebears were displayed alongside those of her descendants.

The poorest Fulton residents (many of whom I would visit during my work here) displayed portraits of Martin Luther King, Jr., and John F. Kennedy on their mantels. Many of them felt incapable of altering the circumstances of their lives. They lived in fear that they would be unable to pay their bills at month's end. If calm and order were to be established in their lives, they seemed to think, it would have to happen through a miracle, the return of lost sons, or an unexpected gift of talent and good fortune from the two dead heroes whose pictures were displayed on their mantels. Mrs. Gromes was different. The photographs on her mantelpiece honored the line of strength and accomplishment in her own family. The men and women pictured here had been bearers of talent and good fortune themselves. To Patience Gromes success was not an impossible dream but a continually unfolding reality.

A family wreathes itself in an atmosphere of thought, developed over the years, that confronts a visitor and belies or sustains formal words and gestures of greeting. When meeting Fulton's poorer families, I often sensed their desperation before they voiced their woe. When I first met Patience Gromes, on the other hand, I sensed that she was strong and self-sufficient and regarded her not as a low-income person who needed help but as one who could help me.

Patience did not wait to be asked. In the evening she trapped me in the corner formed by the refrigerator and the kitchen wall. "When was the last time you've gone to church?" she said. "When was the last time you've written your mother?" I mumbled a reply, then she looked me full in the face, paused, and said, "Don't forget your Maker, now, and don't forget your mother, either."

I later talked with her daughter. "My mother used to corner me too," she said, "—corner me and talk straight at me." A successful cornering maneuver required precise choreography. After rearing eight children Patience Gromes was a master of the art.

I enjoyed living with Mrs. Gromes. On Friday evenings she fried small fish called "spots" and served them with spiced potatoes and greens. Mrs. B, who lived two doors down, came over, and Patience kidded her by saying, "Here comes the Signification" (meaning, here comes the neighborhood gossip). We sat and ate, and afterward Mrs. B and I walked on the back porch to rattle our bones. After we were loosened up and our meals had settled, we sat in the middle room where Mrs. Gromes read the newspaper and "signified" a little while the events of the day came and went over the television in the corner. The old set was broken and the new one was stacked on top of it. No one paid any more attention to the new one than to the old.

Sundays were special on State Street. I did not hear doors slamming early, for this was a day of rest. Only later did women come out, dressed in black coats, and walk slowly toward Rising Mt. Zion Baptist Church, two blocks away.

I remember one Sunday in particular. The cold had abated and the sun shone faintly. Ever the optimist, Patience Gromes donned a long white dress and a wide-brimmed white hat, as though by dressing for spring she could induce that season to arrive six weeks early. There was still time before church, and she stood in the back yard poking a flower bed with a stick. I suppose she was looking for signs of life, but I could not help thinking that she was working over the flower bed much as she had worked me over in the corner of her kitchen, prodding it to do its duty, to bring up flowers the first day of spring if not before.

Mrs. Gromes was a vigorous woman who appeared to have grown past the feebleness of old age: ten years earlier her hands were crippled with arthritis, but now she could use them freely. She was articulate, quick-witted, and well versed in the difference between right and wrong. She seemed in control of her world.

Patience had troubles but kept them to herself. After I had known her a while she told me about her husband, who was dead, and her children, who had moved away. She grieved for one son, killed in an explosion at a loading dock, and for a grandson who had been injured in a car wreck. Although I wouldn't know these facts until later, I guessed that there were hard memories in her life. My one clue came in the middle of the night.

At bedtime Mrs. Gromes added a large lump of coal to the kitchen stove, then slowly climbed the stairs to the second floor. Her bedroom was adjacent to mine, and the connecting door was jammed so that it did not shut tightly.

One night I awoke in darkness. I was disoriented and at first did not remember where I was. I heard a sound: a moan, a sound of loneliness and frailty. Was I hearing my own dream sounds? Or was it the old woman, just a few feet from me? It's her, I thought. I listened for a few minutes but heard nothing more. Would she pick this night to die?

In the morning I awoke to the jabbering of a radio: quips, songs, hard sells. I was relieved to find that Patience Gromes had not died. Apparently her sounds in the night were due to a vague ailment of old age. Perhaps it was no more than the burden of loneliness, the pain of separation from those she loved. I knew other Fulton women who preferred to lie in bed while their children cared for them. They seemed to draw strength from their children's lives. But Patience Gromes had a mission of her own. In a few minutes, I knew, she would slowly climb down the stairs and resume her duties as commander of her household. A visitor never would suspect what it cost her to maintain civilized life in her small corner of the world.

Fulton occupied a site of about fifty blocks in a hollow running back from the James River and was located just within the Richmond city limits. It had about 2,500 residents, 700 households.

In the section of Fulton where Patience Gromes lived, most houses were well maintained, surrounded by neat yards and white picket fences. But at the edges of the neighborhood, especially in the section near the river called Rocketts, houses and tenements were in poor repair. Many had been abandoned and were slowly being dismembered by vandals and woodcutters. Over the years whole blocks had been demolished and their footings now were hidden by shoulder-high brush.

Wandering through Fulton, I had the feeling that the decay of the neighborhood's edges was beginning to affect its core. Two blocks away from Mrs. Gromes's house a row of houses stood shoulder to shoulder with windows like eyes looking out on the street. But the row was interrupted. A single house was missing, and the whole block looked wrong, like a man missing a front tooth. In the gap where the house had been, nothing showed but raw earth, bent water pipes, and a sign that read: M&M Wrecking Co.

At the time I arrived, Fulton was under urban renewal. Bulldozers owned by M&M would be the ones to demolish Fulton. Vacant houses scattered across the neighborhood had plywood nailed across windows and yellow signs tacked beside their front doors: Property of Richmond Redevelopment and Housing Authority. The signs referred to the renewal agency which, in addition to overseeing urban renewal, ran public housing projects. When they were being polite, Fulton residents referred to the renewal agency as the housing authority. The authority maintained a site office in the old liquor store on Fulton's main street. The irony of this location wasn't lost on local residents who admired the sophistication of the urban renewal planners but thought their occupation suspect, a way of getting paid without having to work—a lot like bootlegging. In Fulton, needless to say, work meant heavy physical labor or mind-numbing factory tasks, tearing up track for the railroad or sorting immense piles of tobacco leaves. As far as Fulton residents were concerned, people who dressed in Sunday clothes and sat in an office all day talking on the phone were not working, they were enjoying a temporary suspension of reality.

Two or three nights a week community leaders came to the old liquor store to meet with the renewal planners. The planners pointed to charts and maps and explained the intricacies of federal funding. The residents looked and listened. Once a week or so they met during the day among themselves. They were convinced that the housing authority was trying to do them wrong and were fascinated with the possibility that they, poor folk from the wrong end of town, might in some way outwit the planners and bureaucrats and put federal money where it would do some good.

Fulton residents were good schemers. Neighborhood politics placed a premium on imaginative scheming; and, as blacks, Fulton residents had often been forced to use subtle means to influence the white world. Urban renewal initiated a world series of scheming that was to last for nearly a decade.

Not all this scheming passed back and forth between the housing authority and the residents. By the time I arrived community leaders had split and then papered over their differences in order to present a united front. One faction was composed of neighborhood civil-rights leaders who had met at the Bethlehem Center to plan their registration and voting drives for the previous fifteen years. Their rivals were neighborhood anti-poverty leaders who met at the RCAP (Richmond Community Action Program, pronounced are-cap) center on Louisiana Street. RCAP was the Fulton manifestation of the war on poverty. Civil rights was in decline by now, black power was in vogue, and RCAP supporters took pride in their independence from white society. The Bethlehem Center received most of its money from white churches uptown, but RCAP got its money straight from Washington— nothing white about it.

Community leaders of both factions were certain that this neighborhood could be revitalized. Fulton's ministers, urban renewal consultants, anti-poverty lawyers, social workers, and VISTAs agreed. How could we fail? Few people lived here, yet millions of dollars were coming in through anti-poverty programs and urban renewal.

My job was to rattle the bureaucracy uptown a little, to dislodge benefits for Fulton's poorest residents so that they would survive to see the neighborhood's salvation. I helped old men and women shuffle through shoe boxes full of utility receipts for their food-stamp applications and gave them rides uptown to the welfare office. I called in the City Health Inspector to force landlords to repair broken water lines and exposed wiring that gave off sparks. Once, during the Nixon price controls, I caught a landlord cheating on rent increases. In those days we were all experts, by our zeal if not our training, and we saw a professional challenge in Fulton.

Halfway through my second year in Fulton, the James River flooded and fifty families were forced to move. Suddenly everyone knew that Fulton would suffer a far different fate than we had imagined. I realized that this neighborhood needed something other than the intellectual and technical help we had been prepared to give.

Over the next two or three years, Fulton residents would be relocated by the housing authority. Dozens of yellow signs would be tacked beside the front doors of Fulton dwellings that now were vacant. Before long the houses, stores, churches, trees, streets, and sidewalks would be broken apart, loaded into dump trucks, and hauled away. Half the old people who moved would die from the strain. In the fifteen years that followed, some of the land would be rebuilt in subsidy apartments and a few former residents would return. The rest of the land would wait for industry.

Fulton began in colonial times as a seaport called Rocketts Landing where sailing ships tied up, tobacco and hemp were taxed before export, and Irish dockworkers lived in shacks near the water. Nearby, on higher ground, stood the fine houses of sea captains.

After the Civil War the port lost business to Norfolk and Newport News and went into decline. But during these years factories were built here. The Richmond Cedar Works manufactured cedar cigar boxes. Millhizer Bag Company produced tobacco pouches for Bull Durham and "crocus bags" of burlap used to hold potatoes, onions, and pig feed. The tobacco by-products plant, called the "stem factory" by Fulton residents, extracted nicotine and other chemicals from the waste portions of the tobacco leaf and sold these chemicals for use in fly spray and other products. The largest employers were the Chesapeake & Ohio Railroad, which hauled coal from the West Virginia hills to the docks in the Tidewater, and the Philip Morris and Lucky Strike tobacco factories located nearby on Main Street.

Blacks didn't come to Fulton in any numbers until after the Civil War, and many of these early arrivals left during the Panic of 1893. I knew of only one family who had survived in Fulton until my arrival. The senior members of the black community I found in Fulton had come from the country at the turn of the century and found that Irish immigrants, attracted by factory jobs, were already crowding into tenements, bedroom apartments, and three-room shacks built on swampy ground near Gillies Creek.

Many of the neighborhood's oldest white families were members of the Fulton Baptist Church and looked down on hard drinking Irish. They didn't like the blacks either, but at least the blacks were Baptists. At this time Fulton was known for its drinking and gambling dives. One minister of the Fulton Baptist Church is remembered for saying, "A preacher in Fulton needs to carry a Bible in one hand, a gun in the other."

The twenties were prosperous, and the older white families, many of them members of the Fulton Baptist Church, moved from Fulton. A church history comments that every white family who could "afford a barrel of flour" moved out. Irish newcomers and blacks stayed in the hollow but moved into better blocks. White merchants who now lived on the bluffs above Fulton nevertheless returned each day to work. By 1929, Fulton's oldest families were black, and blacks were a slight majority of the population as a whole.

After World War II Fulton's factories began to close. White families who could afford to do so purchased houses on Fulton Hill (which they called Montrose Heights) and along with their deeds signed covenants forbidding the sale of their houses to blacks for 100 years. Poor black families moved in from the country, then the last whites began to move from Fulton. By the late sixties this neighborhood was almost entirely black and housed half as many people as it had in the years before World War I. Although many Fulton residents still worked and brought home paychecks each Friday, the larger part of the neighborhood's income was in welfare and retirement checks that came in the mail each month.

Fulton is a place that has seen several different communities come and go. The Powhatan Indians were camped on this site when the first whites, members of John Smith's expedition, landed in 1607. After independence a waterfront trading community grew up here that relied largely on Irish labor. Following the Civil War Fulton became a populous factory town with German merchants and Irish saloon keepers.

Fulton has a long and varied history of its own, but my interest is in the community that Patience Gromes and others of her generation brought with them from the country at the turn of the century. Although they did not know each other before they arrived, Patience and her contemporaries shared a way of looking at the world and a belief in old virtues. Theirs was a community of the mind and spirit that gained authority within Fulton and held it for sixty years.

An idea comes to a place, gives that place life and character. Later the idea is gradually diminished and lost, and the structures it inspired begin to sag and crack and after a time come down. So it was in Fulton. The community of Patience Gromes transformed this neighborhood, gave it a distinctive tone and vitality. When this community weakened and was lost from Fulton, the place was changed, never to be the same again.

The idea was enriched by the place. Patience Gromes and her friends lived for forty to sixty years next door to a variety of people. Most were convivial, but some were angry, ornery, or dead drunk. Patience and her friends couldn't afford to move away from their problems but were forced to rethink their ideals, to accommodate, to love people they could not bring themselves to like. They confronted their own prejudices, worked through moral quandaries that many of us can avoid.

The idea also interacted with the larger society. Urban renewal and anti-poverty programs were the payoff for twenty years of civil-rights activism. Yet these federal efforts carried with them concepts from the wider culture that portrayed individuals as victims, a notion that did not sit right with people like Patience Gromes who had spent their lifetimes exercising self-sufficiency. Patience and her contemporaries tried to deflect these intrusions from the world beyond, tried to bring the power of their ideals to bear. But the anti-poverty mentality was too unexpected and aggressive.

In their day Patience Gromes and her neighbors couldn't call a doctor or lawyer every time someone sneezed. If they thought of themselves as victims they became just that—and had no recourse. Forced to rely on mental and moral resources, they discovered a universe that responded to their needs. They found that events and conditions of daily life embodied good or evil.

Obstacles were evil and therefore could be overcome by an individual who was willing to develop skills or strengths of character that were good.

As a culture we face a number of dire threats, most of which appear to be beyond an individual's control. We can benefit from the experience of people who found themselves in a similar position a century ago at the end of the Civil War. Blacks had no money, no property, no government help, and were set in a hostile world where they were preyed upon by the Ku Klux Klan, vindictive former slave owners, and shysters carrying carpetbags. Commentators of that day charged blacks with biological inferiority and gave them no chance of beating the odds. But they did, and we would do well to learn how. We would do well to understand the idea they brought with them from the country and put to the test in city neighborhoods such as Fulton.

In the following pages I want to tell the story of the community that came to Fulton, stayed for sixty years, then was lost. I want to tell about men and women such as Patience Gromes who possessed an idea of grace through history, an idea for want of which a culture is broken, scattered, and unable to find its way.

2

FIRST, SECOND, THIRD GENERATIONS
1865-1929

DURING my two years' work for the Bethlehem Center the fragments of an old culture were all around me. But I did not see them. Neither did I perceive the efforts of Fulton's first citizens and of their sons and daughters to reassert this culture. It never occurred to me that a distinct way of seeing and living once governed this neighborhood with unquestioned authority. I never thought to query Patience Gromes about her origins or about the setting in which her conception of life had taken shape. One afternoon she told me, in anger: "As a girl my grandmother was a slave. She was in the house. Her job was to open doors for the white ladies, to save their little, white hands."

Patience Gromes and her contemporaries in Fulton were the third generation since slavery: their grandparents had been slaves. Their parents had been born at war's end. This third generation grew up in the same cabins and fields and woods that their grandparents had lived in as slaves. They reached adulthood only forty years after the war. Their line of attack on the world was formed in response to slavery itself.

Patience Gromes and her contemporaries came to Fulton in the first years of this century. They established a culture here that took slavery as its unspoken point of reference. Decades passed, the culture weakened a little but remained largely intact until urban renewal arrived in March 1968. The controversy over renewal shook Fulton residents as nothing before. Fulton's old culture had thrived on adversity. Two depressions, *de jure* segregation, and the continual affronts of white-controlled press and schools and city government had only drawn residents closer together. But renewal was different. It promised benefits far beyond the ability of an individual family to obtain by their own work. It promised power and prestige to neighborhood leaders. It was not government oppression but government help, a quantity that Fulton folk and their progenitors going back a hundred years had never before confronted and did not know how to defend against. It was like a small explosive charge placed at the precise point where the forces of an immense structure converge. Urban renewal shattered the patterns of public life in Fulton.

The old culture of Patience Gromes and her peers embodied lessons taken from slavery. In 1968 it gave way before the assaults of urban renewal, but these events are the climax of a story that began a century before at the end of the Civil War.

Following Lee's surrender in 1865, most of the former slaves of Virginia and North Carolina stayed in the country and pursued familiar farm tasks. Putting down plows in the fields, the freedmen walked from their plantations and gathered in temporary settlements—free towns—on the outskirts of country villages. They rejoiced in their freedom. In the days of idleness and hunger that followed, however, they began to consider how they could survive. They knew they had to own land in order to lead independent lives in the country, for land was the primitive source of wealth. The planters had drawn their carriages, grist mills, and mansions from the land, and still it was the planters, the owners of land, who gave orders and paid wages. The blacks were free in law, but they knew they would never be free in practice until they held title to the land.

The freedmen worked as farm laborers, plowing, hoeing, and harvesting in gangs, living in slave haunts, following the rhythms of slave life. They arose early and walked into the fields, cut furrows in the ground, sowed wheat and corn, transplanted tobacco seedlings. They received bacon and corn meal as rations each week, and at season's end were paid with cash or a share of the crop.

In other cases they rented land and worked it as tenants. It was the same land and the same crop but a new routine, for they were out from under the white man's eye. They hauled a shanty from the old slave quarter or built a cabin of their own, bought rations on credit in the whitewashed building where the slave commissary had been before and the county store was now, paid rent on the land and on the tools with bushels of corn or the loan of a son to plow the owner's field. They paid in odd combinations of produce and labor, wheat and tobacco, ditching and fencing.

In some instances the land they tilled was enclosed by thickets of oak and scrub pine and surrounded by abandoned fields overrun with briar and broom sedge. The soil was thin, and the creeks ran red when it rained. Men plowed the ground behind mules, women cut back grass in the fields and worked around the stables. Cabins were made of logs, rough-hewn on three sides and chinked with red clay. At one end were stick-and-mud chimneys, and inside was one room with a wide hearth and a floor of packed earth. Peaked cabin roofs were made of hickory or oak split into shakes and fastened to a frame of pine saplings. Carts were homemade, built of split logs set on city-made wheels and axles.

In spring the freedmen burned off neighboring fields. When broom sedge began to grow and was tender and pale, they pastured livestock on the blackened land. The last days of summer they hired out to large farms in the district. The reapers moved first through the fields, swinging long-bladed scythes into the grain. Behind them moved binders, raking the wheat into piles and tying it in bundles. In autumn they put in dried corn husks and tassels for winter forage, packed their season's crop of tobacco into hogsheads and rolled it down country roads to market.

There were a few dirt roadways cutting through the countryside, and where three roads met there was likely to be a store.

No one had cash money, so everything was credit and barter. On Saturdays freedmen came in hauling corn and hogs, cut wood, chickens and eggs: the mule pulled the cart and took hours to reach the store, even longer when spring rains came and roads ran mud. The trip home was equally slow. Produce was gone and in its place were work shoes and a Sunday suit, pewter plates and coffee, ginger cakes, calico, a hooped skirt. If the store man did not have what they needed in stock, he sold them some other item they probably would need someday.

Day after day the freedmen carried water from the spring in the ravine until there was a trail of dirt where grass had been, and in rain the trail was slick and wet. Day after day they dragged pine logs from the forest, cut and split them to size, stacked them against the side wall. They knelt upon the hearth to kindle a fire, cover potatoes with ashes, turn meat on the griddle. On summer evenings they sat out front and watched the colors of the evening sky and the pattern of blackened trees, listened to familiar night sounds, waited for the first bright stars.

The freedmen put a lien on their coming year's crop to purchase fertilizer and seed. When the crop was carried to market and sold, they paid the rent on the land, the lien on the crop, and the store bill. It was sometimes a struggle to even out accounts with the storekeeper, and often there was little left to tide them over until spring. A few fell into debt followed by deeper debt. Others came out ahead and stashed their money away, burying it in the ground, as in slavery times, or depositing it in the county bank.

Many of the freedmen learned to manage their farm operations, saved a little more each year, and looked forward to the day when they could purchase farmland of their own.

Lewis Armistead, the grandfather of Patience Gromes, advanced more quickly toward land ownership than most freedmen. He was unusually resourceful and had the good fortune to settle in a district that was linked to growing northern cities by rail and steamboat. After the war, tobacco markets were depressed but city dwellers needed vegetables: a family could earn a living by truck farming and, if they were clever, could even put money aside. Unlike blacks in Virginia's landlocked counties, Lewis Armistead was in a position to benefit. He also started early: five or six years before Lee's surrender he had escaped from slavery.

Lewis Armistead was born around the year 1845 and lived on a plantation near Eastville on Virginia's Eastern Shore. As a child he worked in his master's house and very likely was taught to read and write in secret by master's children. One of master's sons was a deaf mute. Lewis learned to speak sign, the hand language used to communicate with the deaf. Presumably he occupied a position of prestige within the big house due to his ability to translate for master's child and, quite possibly, to understand this child better than master could.

As a teenager, Lewis was given the task of carrying water from the river to the quarter. The work was repetitive and tiring. It removed him from the activity of the big house and drove home the point that he, who had grown up with master's children, would not share their future. He would become a laborer like those crude folk who toiled day long at simple, deadening work in the fields.

Needless to say, Lewis bridled at his task. Master responded by whipping him until the blood ran. It was then that Lewis vowed to escape. He would have known that the odds were heavily against him, and that slaves who were caught were severely punished.

Lewis was fourteen years old, and the year was about 1859. He hid dry clothes on the other side of the river. One morning he laid his water buckets aside, swam the river, changed clothes, and walked away from the plantation. When suspicious whites stopped him, he gestured to them in sign, as though he were a deaf mute, and showed them a pass he had forged.

Most likely Lewis chose to escape by water. Virginia's Eastern Shore is a peninsula dividing the Atlantic from Chesapeake Bay, and Eastville is located only a mile from the bay, which at this point is fifteen miles wide. Once he crossed the bay Lewis would still be in slave territory but could pass as free. If he traveled another twenty-five miles to the south by water he could reach Fort Monroe at the tip of the Williamsburg Peninsula, where Union troops were stationed at this time. In 1860 a slave named Harvey Jarvis followed a route such as this to freedom. As recounted in an early publication of the Hampton Institute, Jarvis stole a canoe and sailed it from the Eastern Shore across the bay to Fort Monroe.

When the war commenced thousands of blacks crowded into Fort Monroe seeking asylum. They lived in tents, lean-tos, and hastily built cabins situated among the ruins of Hampton. The Yankees gave out certificates that blacks could use to prove their free status and encouraged them to return to the countryside, which was nominally under Union control.

Plantation owners in the area were sympathetic to the Rebel cause but needed laborers: their own slaves had escaped to Fort Monroe. Such was the case at Cherry Hall, a plantation located about thirty miles up the peninsula from Fort Monroe. It had a brick mansion that looked down a long drive to the county road. According to legend, the owners fed Rebel troops at the kitchen door all through the war. The missus stood lookout on the deck atop the front portico and signaled by playing her violin when she saw a Union patrol approaching.

By 1865 Lewis Armistead was married to Grace Anderson and living at Cherry Hall. Grace came from Portsmouth and, as a slave, worked on a farm in a neighboring district. In that year she gave birth to a son whom they christened William. Lewis worked the land as a laborer or rented land from the plantation on which to grow his own crop. His wife supplemented their income by working as a midwife on outlying farms and in the villages of York and James City counties.

As the years passed, Lewis and Grace kept money coming in from every possible direction, grew their own food, and spent little cash. More children came. The couple saved what they could toward the purchase of land and the education of the children.

Lewis sent his sons and daughters to War Hill School. After graduation the girls went to Claremont High School, located some distance to the south on the other side of the James River. They had to live near the school and may have performed domestic work as partial payment of room and board to the families with whom they stayed. Professor John Smallwood was the principal of Claremont. He was a graduate of nearby Hampton Institute, as was Booker T. Washington who later founded the Tuskegee Institute in Alabama.

In 1887, twenty-two years after the birth of their first child, Lewis and Grace purchased fifty acres of farmland in James City County for $500. The property included a frame house and adjoined the land of Grace's former master and mistress. Lewis and Grace had thirteen children by now, and they worked the farm as a family, raising peanuts, potatoes, and turnips which they shipped to market in Richmond, Newport News, and larger cities to the north.

As his daughters graduated from Claremont School, Lewis sent them to Tuskegee. Even though Tuskegee was devoted to education of a practical nature, it was only a teacher or preacher who could benefit financially from such formal schooling, to Lewis Armistead's way of thinking. In Virginia's country districts other positions that drew on clerical or managerial skills were reserved for whites. As his sons came of age, Lewis sent them to the northern cities of Washington, Harrisburg, and Baltimore, where they became apprentices and learned skills that would enable them to support their families.

After finishing their schooling and apprenticeships, ten of Lewis and Grace Armistead's children chose to live in northern cities. Of the three others, one was a daughter who married a minister in Hampton and taught music. Another daughter taught at Chickahominy School, the black primary school near her home. After learning the trade of butcher, William Armistead returned to James City County. In 1888, at twenty-two years of age, he married Sarah Jones and built a log cabin on his father's land. Their first child was a daughter whom they christened Patience.

Like his father, William raised vegetables for sale in the city. But William's primary markets were the larger northern cities of Baltimore, Washington, and possibly New York and Boston. William's main crops were watermelons, cantaloupes, and potatoes, although he also grew tomatoes and beans and his children gathered chestnuts and blackberries. William sold some produce in his butcher shop, but most of the melons and potatoes went to produce buyers, either the buyer from Richmond who came through early in the year, or C.C. Branch, a local man who also ran a large farm of his own. Normally the buyer from Richmond would offer a price for produce delivered to the Toano siding where he kept a freight car waiting. He required that the melons be packed in wheat straw and paid ten to fifteen cents each for the highest grade of melon.

C.C. Branch preferred to purchase the crop when it was still in the field. He offered a price for an entire patch of potatoes, for example, then hired local and transient laborers to plow up the crop, place the potatoes in barrels, load the barrels on a wagon, and drive them to the Toano siding. The potato barrels were specially made by Branch. Before loading the potatoes, the laborers "put a head" on each barrel by covering its open top with burlap and nailing a metal band around it. Most wagons were drawn by a single mule and carried sixteen or eighteen barrels containing three bushels each. Usually barrels of potatoes would be carried to the road a few at a time to enable the wagon to travel easily across the soft ground of the field. From the Toano siding the produce traveled north in ventilator cars. As an alternative, buyers would ship their produce north on the steamboats that loaded at Croaker on the York River.

In addition to raising fruits and vegetables, William worked as a butcher in a rented storefront shop in Toano. Alongside his shop he added an ice house with double walls filled with sawdust for insulation and stocked it with ice cut from the Chickahominy or York rivers. He took orders for his beef in advance so that he could sell all that he slaughtered while it was still fresh. There was little waste, so his prices were low, and for taste his was considered the best meat in town. He also secured contracts to keep the local hotel and hospital supplied with beef. He bought calves and raised them on his father's farm or pastured them at King's Mill for one dollar per season. William slaughtered one cow a week, except during the hottest part of the summer, and sold chickens every week, relying on his sons and daughters to do the fine plucking. Four times a year he butchered a hog.

William and Sarah Armistead worked hard. Sarah took in washing and ironing for white families and canned fruits and vegetables for her own family to eat. They saved their money or invested in tools. Over the years William bought three horses, a wagon, and a buggy. He rented his buggy to traveling insurance men who rode down from Richmond on the train, then traveled the back roads collecting premiums. When William did not need his team on his father's place, he hired it out to neighboring farms for two dollars a day, or three dollars a day including the services of a son as teamster. During the off season he found temporary work with the C&O Railroad as an "extra force" employee.

By 1897 William and Sarah had saved enough to purchase fifteen acres of their own and a frame house near Toano. The house was painted white and had a large sycamore tree in the front yard. Their land included a well with a hand pump, stables, a fruit orchard, pasture for cows and horses, and several acres of woods. In April the peach trees bloomed, signaling William to plant potatoes.

William and Sarah had nine children by now. When a neighbor woman died and her drunken husband pushed his daughter into the fire, William and Sarah gave the girl a home. That made an even ten. The buggy wasn't large enough to carry them all, so William bought a surrey with lights on the side and fringe around the top.

William sent his children to Chickahominy School, located

next door to Chickahominy Church, where Lafayette had quartered his troops during the Revolutionary War. Each day the children walked two and a half miles to school. When it was raining, their father drove them in the surrey with the side flaps down. The older boys arrived early to set a fire in the wood stove. Even so, in winter the school room was cold until noon. Some years the minister of the church served as school teacher. The Reverend Mr. Gerf preached from the Bible on Sundays and taught from it during the week. His favorite text was the Twenty-third Psalm: "Yea, though I walk through the valley of the shadow of death, I will fear no evil. . . . "

Once a month during the summer, a black church near Toano held a dinner meeting and invited the membership of neighboring churches to attend. When it came time for Chickahominy to host, Sarah Armistead worked all day Saturday cooking ham, rice custard, cakes, pies, and chicken, which were kept cool in the well overnight. After the morning service, tables were set beneath the oak trees and food was served. Afterward a second service was held. During one of these services, William saw a young man slip back to the tables and pick up a piece of chicken, take one bite, then throw it in the dirt. Growing angry, William left the service for a moment to deliver a sermon of his own. "Time comin'," he said, "when you will want food and not have it."

William and Sarah expected the younger generation to learn from the past. They didn't lecture Patience or her brothers and sisters about slavery. They didn't have to.

The children knew that their grandfather, the tall, gaunt man who stooped to keep from hitting his head when he walked in the door, had escaped from slavery at age fourteen. They remembered their father saying that as a boy he loved to scratch their grandfather's back because of the ridges and furrows that ran across it—the scars left by master's whip.

The vestiges of slavery were all around the Armistead children. The larger farms had employed slaves forty years before. Virtually all the old people had been slaves or lived as "free issue" (the offspring of free black women) during slavery. The children all knew George Crawley, the newspaper writer on Chickahominy Road, who was the secretary of their church and a deacon. He told stories to everyone who would listen about the cruelty of slavery, about slave whippings he had witnessed. Following the war George was appointed judge in James City County and served for many years, administering the law for whites as well as blacks. A man with George Crawley's confident, outspoken manner most probably was free issue.

Patience and her brothers and sisters heard that their mother's uncle had killed his master during slavery and lived to tell about it. Their mother's father was a proud man, a fisherman on the York River and owner of prime riverfront property. They guessed that a man with his arrogance must have been free issue.

Their mother was arrogant as well and quick to detect a racial affront. Patience's sister had been promised a new dress and accompanied her mother to the store in Toano, where the white proprietor measured, cut, and folded their cloth. Before totaling their bill he walked toward the back room to get their thread. A white woman entered. The proprietor came forward to serve her, expecting Sarah Armistead to wait. But Sarah led her daughter from the store, leaving the cloth sitting on the counter. Patience's sister grieved for the dress she would never receive, but apparently her mother felt this lesson in pride would hold her in better stead.

Patience's grandparents and parents were proud but nevertheless forgave whites for the injustices of slavery. After the Civil War Patience's grandmother continued to work as a domestic for her former master and mistress and cared for them without pay when they became old. Patience's grandmother did not teach her children or grandchildren to hate, nor did she instill in them a sense of the injustices blacks had suffered at the hands of whites. She and her husband focused their energies on the goal of becoming landowners.

Although Patience's mother was a proud woman who did not forgive easily, she and her husband knew they could not change the past. They did not forget it, but neither did they fret over it or allow it to interfere with the steady progress they were making. When Patience's father was run out of business by white competitors at the turn of the century and forced to take up butchering as the employee of a white man on the other side of the street, he knew he had no practical recourse and decided, nevertheless, to protect his peace of mind. "There are times when a man can't speak the truth," he told his daughter, "so he'd better just keep his mouth shut."

James City County was a much safer place for blacks than counties in North Carolina, where the Ku Klux Klan was more active. Although eighty-eight lynchings occurred in Virginia between the end of the war and the passage of a state lynching law in 1930, the Armistead children never heard of a lynching in their county. On the other hand, a certain element among the white population harbored ill feeling toward blacks, prompting Lewis Armistead and his son William to anticipate conflict and avoid it. Lewis, for instance, would not let his daughters go out to service, as they longed to do. Neither would William. As William put it, "The white man don't know how to restrain himself, and I don't want to have to kill somebody." Using similar reasoning, William forbade Patience and her sisters to work at the Stansbury cannery.

Neither did William and Sarah permit Patience's brothers to work on board boats at the Croaker or Chickahominy waterfronts. They knew of young black men who had been tricked on board ship, worked involuntarily for six months, then thrown overboard to drown. One day two of Patience's brothers caught a white youth of bad reputation trespassing on their land. The youth began to shake with fear, for he was outnumbered and expected, apparently, to be shot for trespassing. Is that what he would have done had the situation been reversed? The young Armisteads calmed him, then lectured him on the wisdom of staying out of the Armistead woods.

The law was important to blacks. Only a generation earlier the law had been entirely in favor of the white man. But now

William Armistead possessed legal title to his land, and his sons didn't hesitate to expel whites from their woods. Legal marriage had been an urgent request among the thousands of contrabands—blacks who escaped from slavery and flooded Fort Monroe and other Union encampments during the war. Legal marriage was a protection to the family, legal deeds were a necessity to protect the ownership of land, legal wills were sought to safeguard the passage of land from one generation to the next, and legal contracts were used to govern the sale of labor. Freedmen had standing in law and savored the spiritual implications of their legal status even while they applied the law as a practical defense in their day-to-day lives.

William Armistead seems to have shared his father's attitude toward education. He supported Patience and her sisters while they attended high school away from home and while at least two of them pursued higher degrees. On the other hand he allowed his sons to take laboring jobs when they came of age. The wider black community judged education as the key to advancement, even though they could not show how, in practical terms, an education could help a black man support his family. It was widely remarked of William Armistead, for instance, "If he had had an education, he would have been a genius." It must have been only too clear that even a genius, if he were black, would be forced to till the soil to earn a living.

William took satisfaction in the complexity of his farm operations. He could conceive of dozens of ways to make a farm pay for itself. He and his family were as self-sufficient as possible and made themselves indispensable to their white neighbors.

Patience's father and mother knew how to count their pennies. Still, they were generous people. They were saving to purchase land, but to them land was something more than property. Land was proof of the dignity and intelligence of their race. William gave freely of his time and money. He was a Trustee of Chickahominy Church and a member of Oddfellows Lodge. He didn't hesitate to take in a child who needed a home. Patience's grandfather displayed similar generosity: if he hadn't spent so heavily on the education of his sons and daughters he undoubtedly could have purchased land more quickly. Savings and land were at the service of education and family, so that giving in these respects was not a loss but part of the goal.

The Armistead family gave to one another, helping young and old alike. When Patience Gromes's grandparents grew old they moved to Phoebus, a small town on the outskirts of Hampton where they lived with a daughter, the music teacher, and her husband. After Patience graduated from Chickahominy School, she attended high school in Hampton, the local high school being reserved for whites. She lived with her aunt and cared for her grandparents in exchange for room and board.

Patience grew up with a clear sense of what she was missing in education and opportunities by her country upbringing. Her cousins in the cities had access to good public schools and were advancing far more quickly than she could. After graduation from high school, she attended Virginia Normal and Technical School (later named Virginia State University) in Petersburg for two years. Returning to Toano, Patience fell in love with Frank Gromes, a young man whom she had known in school. Frank was gentle, steady, and hard working, though not well educated. They would have a good life, a respectable life together.

In the last years of the century, federal troops withdrew from the South, the political gains of Reconstruction were eroded, lynching and Klan violence became common, and the ground was prepared for de jure segregation, which Virginia enacted in 1898. Yet during these same years blacks made striking economic gains, reflected most prominently in the purchase of farmland.

Among the first generation of Virginia's black citizens following the Civil War, few attained land ownership. Among the second generation, however, land ownership became common. And concurrently, as the third generation reached adulthood, blacks in large numbers began moving to the city, to small cities nearby such as Portsmouth and Richmond, and later, around the time of World War I, to the larger, northern cities of Washington, Baltimore, and New York.

Black men and women who moved to Richmond could choose to settle in Jackson Ward, Seventeenth Street Bottom, or Fulton. Most chose Jackson Ward. Those at the top and bottom of the scale, however, preferred Fulton. Its shanties and two-room shacks rented for the lowest rates in town and attracted the downtrodden, those who had had little success in the country. But Fulton also had detached houses and duplexes which could be purchased for a few dollars down. These appealed to upward-moving men and women whose families had striven to acquire farmland in the country.

Black men and women came to the city because they were tired of the dirt and boredom of country life. Many wished to escape the depressed economy of the region where they lived and came to the city looking for jobs. Some of the most capable members of the third generation already had left agriculture to work for the railroads because it paid better. A few individuals such as Patience Gromes, whose father and grandfather had succeeded in purchasing farmland, knew that if they stayed in the country their minds would atrophy. The skills and confidence their forebears had developed would be lost. The farm task had been mastered or at least successfully endured in their families. The challenge of their time and generation lay elsewhere than among fields and pine woods. It lay in the city.

In 1906 Patience Armistead married Frank Gromes. Frank wore a blue serge suit. Patience was eighteen and her skin was brown against the white of her dress. They recited their vows at Chickahominy Church and that evening boarded a steam train to Richmond. The following day they were in Fulton.

Fulton was a factory town. Frank and Patience could hear the streetcar bell and the sharp sound of horses' hooves on Denny Street, which had been cobbled in honor of its streetcar tracks. On the hour they heard the firehouse bell, the whistle at the

C&O Railroad's Fulton Yard, and the whistle at the Richmond Cedar Works. Later they heard the shrill steam whistle of the five-thirty train hauling coal from the mountains and bound for Newport News.

Frank and Patience saw women sitting in chairs on front porches. Beside them crocus bags were folded and stacked in piles, and their hands worked quickly, methodically as they threaded drawstrings. They saw corner stores run by Jews from Poland where homemade pies sold for two cents. Grills and bars were scattered among the houses. Crowds of men came home from work wearing rough clothes, talking and laughing, walking on sidewalks and in the streets. Women in aprons stood on front porches waiting. Voices carried gently.

Frank and Patience rented an apartment in a wooden tenement on Denny. Within a week Frank began work as a laborer for the C&O. A year later they paid ten dollars down on a house of their own up on Denny near Charles Sessom's ice house. Within a year Patience gave birth to their first child.

Frank worked graveyard shift, eleven in the evening until seven in the morning. Patience would have his breakfast ready for him when he came home. After eating, Frank would sit in a rocking chair in the living room drinking his toddy, smoking his pipe. At two-thirty in the afternoon he would go to sleep. At ten in the evening he would rise in time for work. As required by the C&O, Frank worked seven days a week.

The road crew on the C&O—the stokers, engineers, conductors, and foremen—were white. The yard crew included carpenters, pipe fitters, machinists, and mechanics who were white. Brakemen were black, since whites were unwilling to walk between the slowly moving cars to pull the link pin. A few hostlers and mechanic's helpers were black. But nearly all of the 125 black men employed in the Fulton Yard were laborers.

Black men worked in the roundhouse, in the yard with its labyrinth of tracks, in the brick buildings where brick and earth were black from years of coal and soot. Laborers swarmed over

an engine when it came in off the line, gave it water, stoked the
fires, put dope and oil in the wheelboxes, shook furnace grates
to remove the clinkers. Black section hands from other parts of
the state lived in the yard in shanty cars. Each week day they
replaced track and rotted ties, working as far up as the Seventeenth Street Yard, where the next section began. On Saturday
evenings they boarded trains for the trip home and a day of rest.

The C&O owned a tool car and a 150-ton derrick that went
after wrecks. Sometimes Fulton residents heard the loudspeakers
at the Fulton Yard: "Thomas Arrington, Thomas Arrington,
report immediately." Thomas Arrington worked on the tool car,
so everyone knew a train had crashed. One time the wreck was
past Charlottesville, where a hundred cars and an engine had
ripped down a cliffside and coal had spilled into the river so that
it ran black and then clear again, swirling around overturned
cars: Thomas Arrington and his co-workers were out eleven days
for that one, winching broken cars back onto the tracks, hoisting
them on flatcars for scrap, or bending them back into running
order for the trip to the company shop in Huntington.

The laborers for the C&O never had a union. Although the
mechanics and other workers were unionized, it was union activity in the coal mines of West Virginia that affected railroad
employment. Every three years, when contracts came up for ne-
gotiation, there were threatened or actual coal strikes. Since a
principal business of the C&O was carrying coal from the coal
fields to waiting ships at Newport News, the railroad laid off each
time there was a strike. One day a man would come to work
only to see the five-day notice posted on the shop wall. There
was no explanation, no questions were answered. When the
strike was over the railroad did not rehire immediately but waited
for the freight to pick up, preferring to be short than to pay idle
hands. Among Frank Gromes and his fellow workers the saying
was that the railroad operated "according to the business."

Fortunately for Frank Gromes, business was good in the first
years of the century. Although the railroad did not pay well, it

paid better than anything else available to blacks. Frank enjoyed a quiet camaraderie with his black fellow workers. Patience was grateful that he had a steady job.

Frank and Patience lived in the section of Fulton called Foxtown. Theirs was a four-room house, two bedrooms upstairs, a kitchen and sitting room downstairs. Across the front was a porch and in the rear a dry toilet. Every so often men came by to dig out the toilet. They were called "city scandals" and only worked at night, perhaps because of the stench that followed their dung truck wherever it went. When Patience needed water she walked five blocks up Fulton Hill to the spring or eight blocks to the water trough at Williamsburg and Louisiana. At night she lit oil lamps. With the passing years Frank and Patience were blessed with more children. Before long Patience was able to send her sons to draw water in five-gallon lard buckets.

In the twenties city water and sewer lines were put in and a siphon toilet replaced the dry toilet. Although located in an outbuilding as before, the toilet now was connected to the sewer. Patience still did not have running water, but the new hydrant in her side yard was a considerable improvement over the trough on Williamsburg Avenue.

The Gromes house was a cut above the other dwellings occupied by Fulton's blacks, the tenement apartments, and the shacks that still stood near the river in the old port settlement of Rocketts. On Hague Street Mrs. Grant, an Irish woman, rented two-room cottages that offered a scenic view of the neighborhood dump from their front stoops. Fulton lacked city water, sewer, and gas during the first years that Frank and Patience lived here. It also did without city garbage pickup.

The streets of Fulton were dirt except for Denny, which was paved with cobblestones in the blocks where the streetcar ran. Unfortunately for Patience, the streetcar did not run in her block. There were no sidewalks and the rains created wet red mud on Denny St. hill that made difficult going for wagons and the occasional automobile. In dry weather the ruts baked and hardened, making the street rough and troublesome for vegetable and fishmongers to negotiate. Between winter mud and summer dust, Patience found it difficult to keep her house properly cleaned.

Patience cooked and washed for her husband, went to market to "make groceries," changed diapers, reared children. She also carried on two business enterprises: lunches and laundry. Each morning she cooked vegetable or bean soup and made chicken or ham sandwiches. She packed them in wicker baskets which she carried, one under each arm, to the tobacco factories on Main Street. She charged five cents for a bowl of soup.

Patience took in laundry for white families living nearby on Fulton Hill or on the other side of town in Highland Park and Ginter Park. She boiled the dirty wash in kettles on her coal-fired, cast-iron stove. Her secret ingredient was a lye soap which she made herself, mixing fat and lye and pouring it into pans to cool and harden before she cut it into oblong cakes. She dried the wash on the line in the backyard. In winter the clothes froze stiff like boards. Her sons walked or rode the streetcar to deliver the fresh laundry and pick up the soiled. They carried the laundry in a wicker basket with a newspaper folded over the top. Patience charged one cent for each diaper.

Patience worked hard, and one year out of every three she worked while pregnant. Fulton had two midwives. A stout, brown-skinned woman named Mary White was the better known of the two. When Patience was in confinement, Mary White came to visit carrying a small, black leather satchel. Patience waited for Mary White and for her newest child in the bedroom upstairs. As the years passed and children continued to come, Frank and Patience found their house on Denny growing crowded and looked forward to the day when they could afford more spacious accommodations.

Patience was an advocate of the old virtues of religion, education, and thrift. She and Frank belonged to Rising Mt. Zion Baptist Church and, although neither rose to prominence within the church, both attended regularly. Patience supported church groups such as the Candlestick Club (which raised money for church projects and looked after those who were sick or in need) and saw to it that her children never missed Sunday School.

Frank Gromes never had gone far in school, since his labor had been needed at home and in the fields. Patience taught him to read and write. She was thrifty, whereas Frank had a tendency to spend money quickly and freely, but her habits prevailed. They applied his earnings to their living expenses; hers were saved. "Earn a dollar, save fifty cents," said Patience. From the time her children were small, Patience taught them to save their money. "Rainy day comin', sick day comin', hard times comin'," she told them. Before long Frank began to set aside money toward the purchase of a car.

In 1927 Frank and Patience paid off the mortgage on their Denny Street house and made a $500 down payment on a larger house on State Street. It was a two-story house with indoor plumbing and a gas range. The previous owners were white as were all the neighbors but one. Frank and Patience did not sell their Denny Street house, but rented it and put their rental income into savings. Within a year Frank purchased a used Model T Ford.

Frank and Patience worked hard, saved their money, enjoyed simple pleasures. They were building a family, a church, a home.

Fulton was a zone of entrance. Country folk arrived with little money. They "pinched their backs and pinched their bellies" and "scrambled" the best they could. Some had a difficult time, but neighbors were quick to share money, food, tips on jobs. Although individual families had slender resources, a larger group acted as an extended family that carried hot rolls to those who were sick, cared for their children, collected money to pay their rent. The churches of Fulton took collections to help residents in need, whether or not the individual in question was a church member.

Fulton's adults shared responsibility for rearing the young. If a child misbehaved, he received two reprimands, two spankings:

one from the adult who caught him in the act, the other from his parents. Everyone in Fulton knew everyone else, and at times it seemed as though everyone was related to everyone else. In a cold and anonymous city world, Fulton was like a country village. It had closeness. As one resident put it, "Fulton was a little paradise."

Only menial work was available to blacks. Squire Dowd, who worked as a section hand for the Seaboard Railroad, pointed out to his foreman a dangerous error in the placement of a switching device. "The man called me down and fired me on the spot," Dowd told me. Railroads didn't hire laborers to think or talk. Although Dowd later appealed to higher-ups and had the satisfaction of being rehired and seeing his foreman fired, he still looked forward to a line of work where his ideas were valued.

The younger generation had a similar experience. In the early thirties Manny Gromes, the oldest son of Frank and Patience Gromes, decided to try for the Navy. He solicited letters of recommendation from his pastor and teachers, then submitted his application. The Navy thought things over for a while, blacks not being entirely welcome at this time, then accepted him. Manny was a Navy man now. How many of his high school classmates could say the same? When he reported, the Navy gave him a job as a cook.

The position of Fulton's blacks as the descendants of slaves and as people who were prevented from rising above menial jobs lent a special quality to public life, for only in Fulton was their native worth allowed expression. In Fulton they could demonstrate their growing mastery of managerial skills.

Ambitious men and women who belonged to Rising Mt. Zion Baptist Church could aspire to the positions of usher, deacon, or trustee or could become superintendent of the infant department of the Sunday School, as the nursery was called. And Rising Mt. Zion also had a dozen or so clubs, such as the Willing Workers, the Busy Bees, the Missionary Circle. Each club had its own president, secretary and treasurer, kept its own minutes and books, and ran its own meetings with varying degrees of adherence to *Robert's Rules of Order*. Aside from church, there were lodges, social clubs, PTA.

The emphasis on ranking and titles was a natural response of people whose administrative and managerial skills were not recognized in the workaday world. Those few who did succeed in the world beyond Fulton confirmed the abilities of those who had stayed behind. Tossie and Gregory Whiting were two such heroes.

Born and raised in Fulton, Tossie and her younger brother Gregory graduated from Richmond's Armstrong High and took degrees from the University of Chicago, Columbia, and Virginia Union. In 1914 Tossie began a teaching and administrative career at Virginia State University. Gregory served as a high school principal before assuming an administrative position with Bluefield State College in West Virginia. Tossie and Gregory Whiting took jobs in black institutions and were not considered to be people of distinction by the wider, white culture. But within Fulton they were giants. In an age when only the elite among blacks could become porters or waiters, they showed the heights to which an individual could rise.

Fulton's churches applauded the advancement of their members. They were strict, as one would expect of Baptist churches in those times. The oldest white church in the neighborhood, Fulton Baptist, adopted a manual of rules in 1883 that assigned punishments for dishonesty, theft, intoxication, and gossip. Several members who frequented the skating rink or attended card parties found themselves publicly reprimanded in church meetings. One member of a white Baptist congregation uptown who danced all night found himself in serious difficulty. Fulton's black churches were equally severe. Rising Mt. Zion, for example, held special meetings at which the membership considered charges against individual members. A woman who bore an illegitimate child was automatically expelled from membership. To gain reinstatement after a probationary period she had to make two appearances, one before the deaconess board, a second before the deacon board.

The moral stringency of Fulton's black churches was part of the discipline by which their members sought to advance. These churches judged slave morality to have been lax and unbefitting a free people. In the present day white critics pointed to the drunks, thieves, prostitutes, and deadbeats among the black people as justification for race laws. Upward-moving black men and women felt that strict morals would do justice to their free standing, answer their critics, and at the same time assist them in achieving tangible goals that were the visible evidence of free status: houses, gardens, families. Energies that could have been dissipated in social or sexual indulgences were gathered into a single focus.

Apologists for slavery argued that blacks lacked discipline, punctuality, and the ability to defer pleasure in the present moment to the attainment of a distant goal. Jack Mosby and Doc Edwards left for work at precisely 2:45 each day and walked the same route to work at the Fulton Yard seven days a week for year after year. Fulton residents set their watches by Jack Mosby, and he took pride in his extreme punctuality. So too did upward-moving Fulton folk take pride in their exacting morals. They were certain they could match or exceed the standards of their times in morals, as well as in industry and thrift.

It could be argued, of course, that strict morals were honored more in the breach than in the practice, and many a neighborhood wag devoted his or her career to elaborating this thesis. Yet among those who took pleasure in rearing and educating their children, making payments on their houses, and building their churches, strict morals did not require a great effort of will. In any case, I suspect that the moral standards expounded in church were largely intended as statements of aspiration. Fulton residents, whose grandparents once had been denied churches or any other ethical institutions, were characterized by their moral aspiration.

By the late twenties some of Fulton's blacks had advanced farther than others. At the top were patricians like Patience Gromes who owned their houses and were working to advance themselves and their race. At the bottom were bootleggers, gamblers, and their regular clientele who were going nowhere in particular. In the middle was a large, sympathetic group of working people who were respectable but not as ambitious or successful as some of their neighbors. Some were tenants, many of whom would move in search of work with the onset of the Great Depression. Others were homeowners who would stay in Fulton when factories shut down and eke out a living by any honest means.

Fulton residents did not analyze their neighborhood's class structure, but they loved to chart the social standing of individuals and families. This was not always a simple matter. Squire Dowd, for example, might have shared the striving and aspiration of Fulton's patricians, but he did not own his house and was not properly married. Charlie Barbour, on the other hand, was steadily employed, yet he purchased illegal whiskey from bootleggers on weekends. Judging by his employment he was a citizen of ordinary respectability, but his sympathies seemed to lie with Fulton's low life.

The difference between private and public status further complicated the issue. Even the most sodden members of Fulton's underclass were allowed to assume a dignified public posture in church, were addressed respectfully on the street, and were properly mourned at their funerals. Fulton folk accorded one another great respect in public, a tendency that is understandable among a people who were given little respect in the wider culture and whose great-grandparents had been given even less respect as slaves.

The men and women of Fulton were sophisticated in their perceptions of status, yet the very complexity of classifications and the lack of simple, rigid class lines encouraged them, as blacks living in a white world, to be conscious of the experience they held in common. The striking characteristic about Fulton during this period was not the social stratification of its residents, but the compression that brought black people of very different tastes and tendencies into close relationship.

Although I met ten or twelve of Fulton's patricians during my work for the Bethlehem Center, it was not until several years later that I realized they were of a class. They were homeowners. Many of the men worked for the C&O, the women for tobacco factories. They had been married for decades to the same spouses, had raised large families. They were church members and served as deacons or deaconesses. Many of the men belonged to Odd-fellows Lodge, the women to its auxiliary, the Beneficial Society. Most had moved here from the country during the first twenty years of this century and had quickly acculturated to city life.

Peggy Howell was a soft-faced woman who sat on her porch watching her street and singing quietly to herself. She and her husband had moved here from Powhatan County in 1903 and rented an apartment in the hollow at the edge of Fulton called Sugar Bottom. He found work with Albemarle Paper Company, she with American Tobacco. During her lunch break, Peggy walked home to nurse her girl baby. As the child sucked, Peggy sang old songs she had learned from her grandmother. Three years after arriving, the Howells "stood" for a house of their own on Orleans Street.

In 1922 Thomas Arrington moved to Fulton from Halifax County, where he had worked in a country sawmill. In Fulton he landed a railroad job on the tool car, married, joined his wife's church, and made a down payment on a house—all within a few weeks. Unlike the young men who hung out at Fulton's pool hall during my time in Fulton, Thomas Arrington did not need to spend months in moody consideration of his place as a black man in the scheme of things. The thoughtful preliminaries to action had been taken care of years before.

Squire Dowd had a grandmother who was sold as a slave from a flat-topped rock on Fulton's waterfront. He did not attend our civic meetings with the frequency of Thomas Arrington, seemed rougher, did not own a house, and was divorced. Yet his striving to improve himself recalls the spirit of this class of aristocrats. Squire Dowd had been raised on the family farm near Char-

lotte, North Carolina. At eighteen he took a job with the Seaboard Railroad as a section hand, and in 1925 his work brought
him to Richmond and Fulton, where he met a young woman
who had recently moved in from Butterworth. They married and
were happy for several years until they began to grow apart. He
valued the things of the spirit, longed to quit his railroad job and
work carpentry part time, devoting himself to studying his Bible.
He had become a deacon since their marriage; perhaps he could
become a minister. She valued the objects of the world. How
could she ever own the fine clothes and furniture she had promised herself if her husband quit his job? "I want a man who will
make a dollar," she said. "I don't want no preacher for a husband." And so they parted ways. She moved to Nicholson and
took up residence with a high-living man. He quit his railroad
job and began to do carpentry for a living.

Dowd liked the feel of rough-sawn pine in his hand. He liked
to work it with his plane until its figure was plain to view. What
other people regarded as rough lumber he knew as beams, joists,
plates. Where they saw smooth wood, he found jambs, casings,
sills. He liked his material for what it could build.

Squire Dowd stored his tools in the front room where neighbors
would have placed their family albums. He spent evenings and
weekends filing his saws, setting their teeth, rubbing them with
oil. His chisels had good steel. He kept them sharp and oiled
and wrapped in cloth. Dowd was not a master builder. But in
this neighborhood of aging wooden houses his services were in
demand. He worked quickly, was a genial person to deal with,
and his prices were low.

Squire Dowd lived alone and, as the years passed, grew more
confident. No longer did he grieve for the loss of his wife or
condemn himself for having fallen short of her expectations.
During free hours he read a small carpentry book that explained
secrets of building that would keep a house strong and true, never
weakening through the years. More often he read a Bible, which,
he once told me, explained secrets of the human soul. His neighbors noticed that his disposition had improved. He did not brood

as before. Occasionally the members of a storefront church asked
him to preach, his neighbors began to call him Reverend.

Patience Gromes, Peggy Howell, Thomas Arrington, and their
peers came in from the country during a span of twenty years.
This was their first permanent residence after leaving home. They
constituted a patrician class.

Jack Mosby and Cicely Tallman, two of Fulton's patricians,
explained to me their prescription for the good life. Jack was
born and raised near Chase City, Mecklenburg County, on a
farm where his father had been a slave as a child. Although I
was a slow notetaker, Jack was happy to repeat every line several
times:

"People in the old days planned ahead, looked to the future.
There warn't but little then, and people learned how to live on
a little. Everything's big now, and young people expect to carry
it on big.

"The more cars and things you get, the more you want. You
gonna die and leave it all. If money is all you got on your brains,
then you ain't goin' where Jesus Christ is.

"Some people pray for a fine house and a fine automobile and
like that, but I pray for God to open the way for me. Every night
I get down by my bed and pray. I take my burdens to the Lord
and leave them there. If you doubt noway, you can't get nowhere.

"I say honesty is the best policy. People ain't goin' to agree
with me, goin' to cuss me out and point at those drinking and
gambling all day and all night. But I say that's all right, you do
your part and you's in the clear. Every tub stands on its own
bottom.

"I've never beat a man out of a dime in my life. I've never
craved after money and if I ain't got a dollar, I feel satisfied. I'm
always thanking God for this day.

"If you have two things you can be poor and happy: good
religion and a good wife. But ain't neither one of them easy."

Cicely Tallman lived alone in a high, wooden house. From
the street I saw an upstairs window where garments pressed upon
the glass from within as though the entire room were packed

tight with clothes. Her husband, who worked as a railsetter for the Seaboard Railroad had retired, then died. Now Cicely spent her days embroidering religious mottoes on slipcovers for her chairs and her sofa and on dozens of pillows. The words were peculiarly spelled and some letters faced the wrong direction. Where the course of a Biblical line was interrupted by the edge of a slipcover, it casually doubled back on itself, wandering crookedly upside down until its message was complete.

Cicely Tallman's father had been a well-known preacher in Atlanta, and she was quite a talker herself. A person could lose the better part of a day by stopping to greet her. She spoke to me as though she were an evangelist, stamping her foot on the floor to keep time, occasionally breaking into song, and pausing every so often to spit tobacco juice into a vase.

"Jesus says, 'Be ye also ready.' You can't get ready by cutting the fool and raising hell. Is I right or is I wrong?

"Ain't no need in lying about things. A liar shall be hung in hell by his tongue.

"I don't care how much money or how many houses you got, you leave it with the living and not with the dead. I don't care how much clothes you got, you only wearin' one suit to the grave. Have you ever seen a funeral car with the body inside and a house on top?

"Satan knows the run of heaven just like if you been in a house you know the run of that house. Satan is bookin' down everything you do. He knows the run of heaven and will try to keep you out. Am I lyin' or am I tellin' the truth?"

> Well, this old world is not my home,
> Oh, I'm living in a borrowed land.
> Someday my name goin' to be called,
> I got to answer at the judgment bar.
> I'm goin' home where Jesus is,
> Some of these days.

Mrs. Tallman claimed to have lived in the West Indies, and told stories of that land. In West India, she said, a man was punished for murder by having the victim's corpse strapped to his back until it rotted off. Cicely Tallman was something of a curiosity in Fulton, for she was Deep South.

Betty Norton, for instance, thought she was crazy. "She's not from the West Indies," said Betty. "She's from Georgia." Of course Mrs. Tallman had lived in Georgia, but Cicely insisted that she had been born across the water in West India, and no one could actually prove her wrong. Once Betty saw me talking to Cicely Tallman. "Telephone, Scotty," she yelled. "You got a phone call." I ran across the street to Betty's house. There was no phone call. She was rescuing me from Cicely Tallman's unending conversation.

In the corner of Cicely's living room, amid stacks of forty-year-old newspapers, stood an upright piano. I often wondered why she and her husband had invested in it, since it was not used to make music, perhaps never had been. Instead it served as a display stand for family photographs. Why had this woman and her husband invested in such an expensive yet impractical object? I think now that it was a statement of family dignity. Cicely Tallman performed menial work in a tobacco factory, lived in the wrong end of town. But she thought of herself as a woman of value, an equal of white ladies uptown who performed music for guests after dinner.

Fulton's patricians moved in from the country with a sense of their own power. Their parents had struggled to purchase farmland as a way of anchoring their lives, and now houses provided an equivalent opportunity in the city.

Country dwellers of necessity paid cash for farmland. Thus the purchase of land signaled an achievement that was complete. But city houses were available on twenty-year contracts. A Fulton family that signed a mortgage was putting its ideals and its savvy to the test in full view of their community.

As a factory town Fulton possessed sharp memory of factory layoffs. The Panic of 1893 hit Fulton hard. And in the first three years of the Great Depression, one-fourth of Fulton's residents, both black and white, would move. Fulton always had given shelter to people who did not expect to stay permanently. These residents operated on the margins of the city economy and were constantly moving to find work or escape creditors or both.

Every three years residents waited to see if there would be a coal strike. Railroad employees were well aware that at any time they could receive the five-day notice and slide from the ranks of Fulton's working class to join its transients. Fulton residents knew the risks. Yet by 1929, 40 percent of them were paying on houses of their own.

Patience Gromes and her neighbors took pride in their houses and yards. As blacks they were excluded from politics, yet they knew that the simplest elements of domestic life had political implications. Patience and her friends intended their perfectly maintained houses and yards as a political statement, a ringing contradiction of the reasoning behind segregation laws.

Patience Gromes and her neighbor Ophelia Whitley seldom missed a meeting of the Fulton Garden Club. They tore down the rough, wooden fence separating their backyards and installed an attractive wire fence that allowed them to admire one another's flowers. Later Patience built a fish pool and installed a bird bath.

Although the houses on State Street were some of the best in Fulton, there was still room for improvement. Ophelia Whitley's back room was divided into a bathroom and a bedroom in such a way that one had to walk through the bathroom to get to the bedroom. Ophelia enclosed the side porch, moved the bath to this new room, and restored the back bedroom to its full size. They hired a neighborhood man to paint their house, covering the old gray paint with creamy yellow, chocolate brown on the trim. "We thought our house was the most beautiful in Fulton," her daughter told me later.

Patience added a third bedroom upstairs over the kitchen and modernized the bathroom. She painted one room every year, the tin roof every other year, and the exterior as needed. Although Ophelia hired Mr. Hill to do her painting, Patience preferred

Mr. Jones, a tall, dark-skinned man who lived on Denny and made his living painting and repainting Fulton's houses.

Peggy Howell installed asphalt siding in a red brick pattern on her house. Thomas Arrington painted his house inside and out whenever necessary, took particular care to paint the roof every other year, and later installed asphalt siding in a gray brick pattern.

If Fulton residents were drawn together in sympathy for the project of racial advancement, then it was the houses of Fulton that provided the most tangible expression of that project. In church, the minister put ideals into words. But after church, in silence, the houses still stood, a testament to all that Fulton's upward-moving folk had risked, all they hoped to prove. At home, parents lectured their children on respect, honesty, charity. But when children were out of earshot, traveling abroad in their neighborhood, it was the houses that continued to speak, surrounding the young like pillars of conscience. New residents, fresh from the country, listened to neighbors expounding the ethos of this neighborhood. But when talk ran down and the physical routine of life reasserted itself, they were left to judge by the bare, physical statement of buildings and streets. They walked to market each day, walked to the job. They stood with feet in the dirt and saw the shacks of transients, the wooden tenements, the vacant lots. They saw two-story houses with porches, fenced yards, and gardens and knew they were owned by black men and women who had been born in the country. Newcomers did not have to be told; they could see for themselves.

During the first years of this century, Fulton residents were demonstrating their ability to stand on their own. It was a simple challenge, yet it offered its own rewards. Frank Gromes attached special importance to his role as a family man. Thomas Arrington took pride in his position as deacon. Jack Mosby found satisfaction in his status as neighborhood timekeeper. They understood that the quality and pattern of their lives were the prime instrument, perhaps the only instrument, of the black race in its struggle for advancement and recognition.

3

THE NEW POOR
1930-1972

NOT ALL the blacks who moved into Fulton at the turn of the century were as high-minded as Patience Gromes. Waddy Crowder, for example, arrived in the twenties from North Carolina, rented a house, and quickly established himself as a bootlegger and police informant.

Others who arrived during these years were not as self-sufficient as Patience Gromes or as quick to acculturate to city life. In many cases the poor and weak who came in from the country were descendants of families that had been broken and dependent since slavery. Social workers reported finding country families raising chickens in upstairs apartments and using bathtubs to store coal.

These rough, country folk were stomp-and-shout evangelicals who favored one-room churches such as Shiloh Baptist in the hollow near the swamp. Others preferred equally boisterous activity at neighborhood gambling and bootlegging dives, such as the Riverfront Social Club on East Main. Some of these country folk stayed in the neighborhood until my arrival (enough for Waddy Crowder to earn a living selling illegal whiskey). But most of those who were least fitted to survive in the city, who might have become discouraged and bitter and have changed the tone of life in Fulton, were dislodged during the first hard months of the Depression. It was not until the years following World

War II that the poor came en masse and made permanent homes in Fulton.

During the thirties, hard times came to Fulton. The brick works slowed down, laid off workers, then went out of business. The cedar works cut back to a three-day week. The market for coal was down, and the railroad was laying off. The tobacco factories weren't laying off, but they weren't hiring either; in any case much tobacco work was seasonal.

In 1932, Cary Nettles moved to Fulton from his family farm in Ridgeway, North Carolina. He was eighteen years old, away from home for the first time. He looked for work: "Won't no jobs in Fulton. I came up Seventeenth Street. Won't no jobs. You couldn't find jobs, couldn't buy jobs, won't no jobs nowhere."

Cary supported himself by walking the streets and picking up paper ("newspaper, cardboard, any kind of paper") and selling it for thirty-five cents a hundred. I asked him what the poorer Fulton residents did to survive. "People would double up in houses together," he said. "One would pay the rent, one buy the groceries, all went and got in the soup line."

"I did anything I could get to do, not one particular thing, and I can't name the things I ain't done. I had to work or starve and I won't about to steal nothing."

In the first years after the 1929 crash, dozens of Fulton families moved, presumably in search of work. Cary Nettles and others on the margin of the economy might not have survived without soup lines and the city trucks that brought rotted cabbages and other food to the needy in Fulton. But those who had seniority at the C&O or at the Philip Morris, Lucky Strike, or Liggett & Myers Tobacco factories continued life much as before. Forty years later they looked back on the thirties as a stable time. Billy Dismith, neighborhood barber, told me, "Fulton was solid in the thirties." Patience Gromes's youngest sister lived with her in Fulton for several years. "In the thirties," she said, "a new face in Fulton was the talk of the neighborhood." Hard times seemed to bring Fulton residents closer together, strengthening the authority of ideals that were designed to carry them against the opposition of the world.

Changes came to Fulton in the years following World War II, and little by little the old order was weakened. Patience Gromes and her contemporaries had taught their children well. And in the fifties, as jobs and houses became available beyond Fulton, their sons and daughters took advantage of them. Those who were best schooled in the old ideals were the most likely to move out. In 1953 the C&O switched from coal to diesel, laying off younger employees who did not have seniority. In 1957 the cedar works shut down. Fulton did not have jobs for the younger generation, and neither did it have houses.

Before the war, speculators like William Dupree had begun to purchase houses in Fulton and operate them as slum rentals: they kept rents at two dollars per week, which was low, but spent little or nothing on maintenance. Each year the properties became more decrepit, gradually consuming the investment made at the time of construction. Thus there were few decent houses available in Fulton after the war. Although banks would lend for the purchase of slum rentals by investors, they hesitated to provide mortgages to homeowners for new construction. Even if financing could have been arranged, the younger generation saw that a new house in Fulton would be a trap, not an opportunity. If they ever needed to sell they would be unable to get their money out.

At the turn of the century, the Dupree family had operated a store in Seventeenth Street Bottom that offered furniture for rent and for sale. They employed several men to make the rounds of low-income neighborhoods to collect rent on the furniture, and after a time they began to collect rent on the houses and apartments as well, acting as agents of the owners. Later the firm began to rent furnished houses, then unfurnished houses until their business in houses outweighed their business in furniture. According to legend, the Duprees owned a majority of the houses and tenements in Seventeenth Street Bottom, and I would guess that they ended up with a third of the dwellings in Fulton. Neighborhood residents thought William Dupree spent all his time carrying their rent money to the bank, but it was not so simple. Dupree was always fighting the city health inspector, paying to board up houses he could not afford to demolish. Once I asked him to demolish a wrecked house he owned on Orleans Street. "Who destroyed this house," he said. "Did I tear it apart, or was it the colored people who live here?" Dupree knew that time is money, and when faced with complaints from one city department or another he dragged his feet for months. Sometimes I thought his motto was: "Delay until they carry you to court, then fight like hell!"

William Dupree rented his houses and flats to the poor, fresh from the country. Billy Dismith calls these people "drifters." Although Billy (as a member of an old Fulton family) is prejudiced, there is some truth in his description. They were latecomers who had stayed in the country forty to sixty years longer than Fulton's founding families and tended to come from the poorest and most isolated country districts. If Patience Gromes's generation had come to the city as young men and women looking to make their mark on the world, these folk arrived in middle age looking for sanctuary. They were beaten, behind the times, and trying to improve their position without going through the slow process of working hard and saving pennies. They drifted from one shack to another whenever slightly better circumstances became available. Some moved to equally decrepit housing in Southside Richmond, only to return to Fulton again a year or two later.

Although a few newcomers established stable families and integrated themselves into the fabric of traditional life, most kept to themselves and regarded the neighborhood's first citizens with suspicion and scorn.

The growing isolation of Fulton's poorest families was held in check during the civil rights movement. One person equaled one vote; every resident was important. Neighborhood drifters and low life made common cause with proper, fourth-generation leaders and ran voter registration and get-out-the-vote campaigns every year following the Montgomery bus boycott in 1955. Dignified residents went door to door in the roughest sections of Fulton, urging the poor to take pride in themselves and their race, to pull together for the common good. Civil rights brought Fulton residents together.

When urban renewal began in Fulton in 1968, registration and voting drives continued, but renewal supplanted them as the compelling neighborhood project. It soon became apparent, however, that renewal would divide Fulton residents along class lines. As a housing program it drew a sharp distinction between homeowners and tenants. And as a technical subject it emphasized small, educational meetings aimed at homeowners over mass meetings with greater appeal to tenants.

In the early renewal controversies, neighborhood leaders rallied the new poor along with everyone else they could get their hands on. Leaders still possessed a civil rights mentality and held mass meetings patterned after those in Montgomery thirteen years before. The press was invited, as were public officials and urban renewal planners. The theory was that the words of neighborhood leaders would have power if they were backed by the bodies of their troops. This tactic had been effective in civil rights where the issues were simple and a powerful emotional appeal by masses of demonstrators struck at the nub of the problem. In those days public officials stated their prejudices and encoded them in segregation laws. Villains wore black hats and crowds had something identifiable to complain about.

But urban renewal was different. The planners hired by the housing authority were black, and even Mr. Fey, the white man who served as director, professed to have the best interests of Fulton residents at heart. Thus renewal did not present easy targets for mass denunciation. What is more, urban renewal was a sea of technicalities. Any action, good or evil, would be subject to the will of technicians and bureaucrats. Federal regulations governing renewal were three feet thick and changed a little every month. The flow of money from one government jurisdiction to another was abstract, the meshing of the city budget with construction requirements even more abstract.

To give one example, the City of Richmond was required to match federal renewal money: one-third from the city matched two-thirds from the feds. Like most cities, Richmond already spent tax money on an engineering department whose employees parked their trucks in the street, jackhammered holes in the pavement, and repaired storm sewers, sanitary sewers, and water lines. If the timing was right the engineers could send their trucks to Fulton, do some jackhammering down there for a few weeks, and claim that work as their one-third match. "That's called in-kind money," one planner told me. "The city doesn't have to spend money that it wouldn't have spent somewhere in town anyway. But if the city has to come up with cash money to make its match, has to raise taxes or something to get that money—this project will be dead in five seconds." An angry crowd might fry some public officials for an hour or two, but when the meeting was over and a week had gone by and neighborhood leaders met privately with these officials, they ran into the same technicalities they had faced before. The crowd might demand immediate action, but when the planners explained in private session the need to mesh federal fiscal year and local fiscal year so that the city would be able to use in-kind services for its one-third match, what could leaders say? More than that, what could they take back to that angry crowd?

Before long neighborhood leaders found that mass meetings weren't helping matters and, to the contrary, put them in the position of explaining the technicalities of renewal to their constituents, a posture that seemed a lot like siding with "the Man" to angry folk who wanted yes or no answers and wanted them right now. Simply as a matter of self-preservation neighborhood leaders cut down on mass meetings in favor of small weekly meetings with the planners and their bosses.

As mass meetings grew fewer and farther between, Fulton's new poor became less and less involved in renewal. These folk could get excited about angry speeches and villainous officials sitting on stage, but weekly planning meetings, they said, caused a person to bleed from boredom. Who really cared about the progress HUD was making in writing the administrative interpretation to the recent laws passed by Congress?

Homeowners could get big money for their houses or they could get nothing: it all depended on the fine print in HUD's administrative interpretation. Homeowners cared about such matters, but Fulton's new poor were tenants who had little to gain one way or the other. Neighborhood homeowners attended meetings, learned a little more every month about the complexities of renewal, and gradually got hip to the situation. But Fulton's new poor preferred to sit on their front porches and exercise their skepticism. Housing authority officials and neighborhood leaders had made promises in the early mass meetings. But the wisdom of the front porches held that none would come true, that the planners were liars, that neighborhood leaders couldn't deliver even if you dropped the thing in an envelope and put a stamp on it.

Neighborhood riff raff had been angry and skeptical about renewal when it began in 1968. They were still that way four years later when the James River washed fifty families out of Fulton. After the flood renewal once again became a hot topic, and mass meetings resumed. In the meantime neighborhood homeowners had learned some things and their sympathies had shifted. They were experts themselves by now, but that fact did not ingratiate them to poor people who were still sitting in the same rut, didn't feel too great about their lives, and resented the fact that their neighbors, who already had houses of their own, might parlay their new-found expertise into federal cash.

Stepney Waterman was a member of the fourth generation, owned his own house, and belonged to an old family that had long been prominent in Rising Mount Zion Baptist Church. As urban renewal got under way, he and an ally challenged neighborhood civil-rights leaders and soon found themselves official representatives of Fulton for urban renewal. Waterman was capable but unrecognized. He had a high school diploma and sold insurance for a living, whereas his brother had a PhD and held a high-level job with the Pentagon. Another brother had a good job and a nice house in another part of town. Stepney and his second brother had married sisters, and Stepney's wife could not help but admire the clean, modern house where her sister lived. I probably shouldn't have been sympathetic toward Waterman. In neighborhood political controversies he was allied with RCAP, whereas I worked for the Bethlehem Center. Even so, I thought that life owed him more than a run-down house and the reflected glory of his brothers' success. If he got a little prestige and respect from his position as leader, so much the better.

But Fulton's new poor didn't see it that way. To them, Waterman enjoyed his status too much. Sometimes I visited them to talk about food stamps. When the conversation turned to renewal they ripped into Waterman and the other citizens who were helping to plan this project. Their attitudes filtered down to their children. Waterman told me how he was walking on Denny Street one day when a child on the sidewalk cussed him out. "I looked up on the porch," he said, "and the child's mother was laughing at me."

No longer did the adults of this neighborhood assist one another in disciplining the children. After the advent of urban renewal, Fulton's new poor let their kids run loose on the playground until ten or eleven at night, and now, in the opinion of Fulton's first citizens, this was not a good place to raise children. Each year a few more fourth-generation families came to the same conclusion and began to save toward down payments on houses in better neighborhoods.

Patience Gromes and other members of the third generation came to Fulton at the turn of the century, applied their ideas to city life, and learned more about themselves and the notions they had brought with them. Self-reliance was their credo, but they seemed to hold that this capacity was best nurtured and most convincingly demonstrated in group activities, in family, church, social club. The self-reliant individual used his or her talents to benefit the group. If the ideas of Patience Gromes began to lose their hold after World War II, they also found their most visible expression in the registration and voting drives of civil rights. It was later, after the introduction of urban renewal in 1968, that the break between Fulton's poorest residents and its neighborhood patricians came into the open.

Fulton's new poor are important to this story, for they illustrate the decline of traditional values. Neighborhood patricians and their sons and daughters of the fourth generation failed to transmit their vision of good and evil to these newcomers. Still, the failure was uneven. Matte Curtis, the welfare chiseler and political activist, went out of her way to reject the old ideals and to let the world know about it. Candis Goodwin, on the other hand, accepted the old ways but was getting on in years and was not capable of bolstering her neighborhood. The thinking of Fulton's poorest residents is revealed in their choice of enemies and of heroes. They despised Fanny and Chub Mordecai, two Jews who owned a corner grocery, and adulated Richard C. Moring, a slick operator who became Fulton's first millionaire (Waddy Crowder, the bootlegger from North Carolina, was its second). Although the old virtues may have been simple to conceive, their loss from Fulton was complex. The neighborhood's poorest residents illustrate this complexity.

Quite a few recent arrivals to Fulton would not have identified themselves as members of a class. But Matte Curtis took pride in her status as a poor person. She arrived with her husband in 1953 from a farm near Darlington, South Carolina. Matte's husband decided to continue north, but she had family here and chose to stay. At the time Matte arrived, her son Grunt was one year old.

Matte Curtis never cared much for established Fulton society. The old families of this neighborhood looked down their noses at her, disapproved of the way she kept house and raised her children. Matte never missed a chance to return their contempt. She did not spit on the sidewalk whenever she passed a house owned by an old Fulton family. She did not teach her children to throw cigarette butts and beer cans into their fenced front

yards. But she did something they considered worse: she received
welfare and bragged about it. And, as a member of the National
Welfare Rights Organization (NWRO), she bragged about it on
the evening news.

I met Matte Curtis at the beginning of my career as a community organizer. At the time I was working in Fulton, community organization was chic among social activists. Saul Alinsky
inspired us with his political guerrilla warfare in Chicago's notorious Back of the Yards (recounted in his book *Reveille for
Radicals*). If low-income people in Chicago could fight City Hall
and win, think what we could do in Richmond.

As a novice, however, I was assigned the less-than-crucial job
of organizing the local NWRO group. My boss and assorted other
dignitaries attended meetings at which they discussed the future
of Fulton and the fate of its inhabitants. But I stood in the
bombed-out kitchen of Matte Curtis trying to get together another meeting of the Poor People's Club, as the NWRO group
called itself. "Food stamps are big right now," I said. "What
about a meeting next week?"

Matte Curtis continued to work as I talked to her. She placed
a galvanized tub across the top of her gas range, dished it full of
water from the tap, and lit all four burners. The living room was
sectioned off with blankets to create sleeping quarters close to
the kitchen. A child gathered soiled clothes and heaped them
on the kitchen floor. Matte sat and waited for the water to heat.
A neighbor boy came in to purchase cigarettes for his mother,
and Matte pulled a carton from a pile in one corner. Her oldest
daughter wandered in wearing dirty night clothes. She was re-
tarded and held her baby under one arm. A younger daughter
looked at me cautiously from the doorway. Light-colored skin
was stretched over her face and shoulder, the scar from a burn.
Matte dished steaming water from the tub to an old round washing machine with the wringer missing and no motor. I had seen
better appliances than this rusting in the trash heaps on Fulton's
vacant lots. She placed a scrubboard in the machine, added soap,
and began to wash her clothes by hand, placing them in the sink

for their rinse cycle. Her kitchen did not have a drain for the washing machine, so Matte used a section of old garden hose to siphon dirty water into her backyard.

Matte was a clever woman. She collected welfare from the city and ran a flourishing business in bootleg whiskey on the side. All night long, low-slung cars drove down her alley, stopping momentarily to transact business before rumbling off in the darkness. She also had connections with the federal elements of the war on poverty. She was paid by RCAP to house VISTAs during their training period. One VISTA, a white woman from New York, was not unduly surprised by the dreary aspect of her temporary lodgings. The rusted siphon toilet situated in the back yard merely amused her. But there were practical difficulties. Where, for instance, could she hang her coat? Always eager to provide for paying customers, Matte grabbed a hammer and pounded a nail into the plaster of her living room wall.

At length Matte agreed to a date for a Poor People's meeting. I spent the intervening days canvassing the neighborhood, putting up announcements in corner stores. When the designated morning arrived, I drove the Bethlehem Center's station wagon from house to house to pick up those who had agreed to attend. No one seemed to be home. I saw a group of middle-aged men standing on the street corner. They agreed to attend, but declined my offer of a ride. I arrived at Matte's without passengers.

Matte and two of her friends were waiting for me. My boss arrived and several more women, friends of Matte's, came in. We talked about food stamps and NWRO. Matte told about a dinner given by the NWRO for local welfare officials who were served a typical welfare meal, very small. Next year she and Laura Bell, a younger woman who was vice president of the Poor People's Club, would attend an NWRO convention in Detroit. They would stay in a hotel, listen to speeches, sing songs, present and receive awards. Matte encouraged those of us who worked at the Bethlehem Center to help them pay for their bus tickets and lodging by purchasing chicken dinners at two dollars a plate.

Few members on the club's official list were active any more, and neither Matte nor Laura was interested in recruiting new members, perhaps because that meant possible competition for the positions of president and vice president. Why should Matte and Laura risk losing their status as Poor People's Club delegates to Detroit? On such considerations a social movement founders. Laura was younger than Matte and more citified. "I come from the baddest part of town," she told me. She had moved to Fulton in 1964 from Seventeenth Street Bottom, or Hell's Kitchen, as it was sometimes called, when that district was demolished for urban renewal. Laura had no husband and six children, but eased the burdens of motherhood by arranging to have her own mother raise five of them. Laura lived above a bar in a clean, modern apartment. At night she could hear the tump tump tump of the bass line coming from the juke box downstairs.

An hour in Matte Curtis's living room, which was poorly heated, was long enough even for Matte's friends. We closed with a prayer, and everyone left. I am not sure what I hoped to accomplish with this meeting, but afterward I felt that I had failed. In our war on poverty the imponderables were great. We could never be certain, for example, that procuring food stamps for a family would actually help to make them more stable or would even help them to eat better each month. Perhaps the food stamps were used for gambling or traded for drink. In a situation this nebulous, we fell back on numbers to measure our effectiveness. I thought my work a success if I signed up a large number of residents for food stamps. And I judged one of my community meetings a success if a large number of residents attended. In the case of our first Poor People's Club meeting, too few attended.

What about all those who promised to come, then never showed up? The week following our meeting, I visited them again. They claimed "death in the family" or reported that they were overcome by illness on the morning in question. After a while I began to understand that the chronically unfulfilled promise was one ploy that residents used to defend themselves against the demands of activists such as myself. How else could they preserve some measure of coherence and custom in their lives? Apparently Fulton residents considered it rude to give a flat "no." What I would naturally regard as phoniness or dishonesty, they thought of as civility and diplomacy.

I learned that the neatly dressed middle-aged men couldn't be expected to attend meetings, for they were alcoholics who had little interest in civic affairs. I had been deceived by their appearance. Unlike white skid-row alcoholics in Seattle and other cities, these men had not been disowned by their families and did not sleep under bridges.

Our next meeting was better attended. Betty Norton came, along with two friends. I had no idea that Betty, as a fourth-generation member of an old Fulton family, was departing from her normal practice by entering Matte's hovel. Food stamps had piqued the interest of Fulton's bourgeoisie, people who would have nothing to do with traditional forms of welfare.

Matte Curtis stood and opened our meeting. I delivered a speech on food stamps. One of Matte's friends, a sweet looking elderly woman named Miss Sarah, interrupted my spiel with earthy comments to keep things from getting too serious. When business was completed, Matte brought out potato chips and ginger ale, and Laura Bell told a story.

"My caseworker come to visit one day," said Laura, "like they do from the welfare. And I opened the door and she come in and ask all kind of questions. Then she gets up to leave. But she can't get out, cause she don't want to touch my door knob—me being a little unclean to her mind—and I sure won't about to open that door for her.

"So she keeps on talking about the weather and what have you, hoping that I'll take the hint—but I don't take it—and after a time when I had her cooked pretty good I opened that door and let her out." Laura always seemed to have the welfare department at her mercy. She thrived in a welfare economy.

Although Laura was one of the more sophisticated welfare recipients of Fulton, and was perhaps typical of younger welfare mothers, Miss Sarah gloried in her status as one of Fulton's coarsest welfare recipients. At one point in the proceedings she pounded her chest, spat tobacco juice in the corner, and said, "They call me the 'Pig of Fulton.'" Miss Sarah loved an audience. Once she stood on her front porch giving Matte's VISTAs a training session. At the climax of her speech she pulled a switchblade from beneath her skirts, then danced the shimmy and waved the knife in the air. Miss Sarah made a point of being disrespectful of authority. Above the mantel in her front room she displayed the speech, written in crayon on a continuous piece of butcher paper, which she had delivered on the front steps of city hall. In the most picturesque passages, Miss Sarah's speech compared the president of the United States to several common and unappealing objects. This was a formal speech, no dancing, no knife waving, but Miss Sarah was playing to the larger audience now—cops and TV cameras as well as VISTAs—and didn't want to be taken for a complete fool.

Not everyone thought Miss Sarah funny. Betty Norton, for example, thought Sarah to be worse than a fool. After Matte made her closing remarks, Betty offered her own living room for the following meeting. No one objected, so it was decided, and I adjusted my plans accordingly.

The third meeting of the Poor People's Club was well attended, and Betty Norton proved a gracious hostess. But Matte, Laura, and Miss Sarah were absent. Death in the family?

I did not yet understand that in Fulton the meeting place of a club or civic group determined that group's character. If we were to gather in Matte's shell of a house, the group was certainly a chapter of NWRO. But if we met in the comfortably furnished front room of Betty Norton, the group was a civic club, a ladies aide society along traditional lines, never mind the decidedly untraditional benefits that food stamps promised to confer.

Without the slightest knowledge on my part, I had participated in a coup d'état. Betty Norton's offer of her living room actually was a motion to censure Matte Curtis. The lack of discussion was not consensus, as I assumed, but deadlock. Later I would understand that Fulton folk rarely fought with enemies in public, no matter how much they ripped one another in private.

Matte, Laura, and Miss Sarah belonged to an underclass. They gloried in what, to Betty Norton, were gross elements of circumstance and character. Matte Curtis had turned the tables on traditional Fulton society. If she was excluded from the best circles because of her rough manner and reliance upon welfare, she would transform faults into virtues. She would become known all over Richmond as a tough welfare mother who did not fear arrest. She would get her face on the evening news. Perhaps she would develop a national reputation. When was the last time Betty Norton had attended a convention in Detroit?

Once I saw a man at Matte's dancing strange, quick steps to the sound of a record player. I supposed he was teasing Matte a bit for her seriousness about her position as president of her own club while she hurried back and forth to prepare for guests who were due any minute. This man gave me a glimpse into a different culture, a world of hot music, bare pine floors, old dance steps, fists, guns, whiskey in the night. As the months passed I began to think of Matte as a rebel who brought vitality to an otherwise drab and compartmentalized workaday world. I was wrong, but I wouldn't know I was wrong until much later when I visited a bootlegger's dive on Orleans Street.

In the meantime the Poor People's Club continued to meet on first and third Wednesdays at Betty's house. The women often joked about Matte's bare floors and unheated living room: they had kept their overcoats on; they had seen their own breath—and that was *inside* the house. The name Poor People's Club dropped from our vocabulary. When the women got around to discussing the need for a name, Betty Norton said, "Any name would be better than Poor People's Club." Then one woman, a friend of Matte's, said, "We can't call it the *Rich* People's Club, now can we?" No one spoke for a few minutes. Then one of the other women introduced a fresh subject. No sense starting a controversy.

By the mid-fifties a few fourth-generation men and women of prominent families were moving out of Fulton each year. Their parents, however, stayed behind. They could not sell their houses for enough cash to purchase houses in other neighborhoods. They would not take out new mortgages which they had little chance of repaying before they died, and they were unwilling to relinquish their status as homeowners simply to get out of Fulton. They stayed on, kept to familiar routines, spent time with old friends. They did not hear too much about their rough, new neighbors, which was unusual in a neighborhood where everyone had always known everything about everyone else. They kept the old life going, but a quality of closeness was gradually being lost. No longer was Fulton the sole arena in which black residents could display managerial or entrepreneurial skills. No longer did working men and women look to church and community to certify and give value to their actions. Success for the fourth generation, both those who had moved and those left behind, was defined by some working of popular culture beyond Fulton itself. Like steam escaping a pressure cooker, the energy of seeking and striving in Fulton, built up over fifty years' time, was lost.

By now the middle group of working people in Fulton—members of the fourth generation—who had never purchased houses or achieved prominence in church, realized that they never would hold white-collar jobs or live in the suburbs or send their children to college. Many relaxed their efforts to better themselves and determined to enjoy life right here. They discovered their liking for corn whiskey and found companions among those of Fulton's new poor and traditional low life who had similar tastes. As the ranks of Fulton's first citizens thinned out, a consensus was forming among the other residents of this neighborhood. Poor folk and failed working folk were creating a new ethos that they judged better fitted to their circumstances in this modern world.

In the past Fulton residents had known the country, known former slaves, and were conscious of the distance they had progressed since slavery. The success of an individual had been welcomed as a victory on behalf of the group. But now the link to slavery was lost, and slavery ceased to be a standard against which progress was measured. Now the success of those who moved to better neighborhoods only underlined the failure of those left behind. James Dewbre ran a diner on Louisiana beginning in 1948 and was in a good position to see these strains develop. "In Fulton you had people who grew up together," said Dewbre. "One of them makes it in life and then won't even talk to the other."

Fultonians who were beginning to succeed didn't want to be reminded of their origins. And quite naturally residents who appeared to be going nowhere resented the strides that some of their neighbors were making and did what they could to trip them up. Mrs. Sparks purchased a corner store from a Jewish woman and operated it successfully until, a year later, news of the sale leaked out to her customers. "They had thought I was running the place, not owning it," said Mrs. Sparks. "When they found out, they held back a little on each month's bill, until they had me in a corner. I couldn't not sell to them, or I'd never see my money." In another conversation Mrs. Sparks returned to this subject. "It's like crabs in a bucket," she said. "One climbs nearly out, the others grab it and pull it back down."

Fulton's new poor paid lip service to many of the old virtues, but charity was not their strong point. In the aftermath of slavery, the family of Patience Gromes set aside their anger toward whites because they knew it would interfere with their progress. Fulton's newcomers, on the other hand, did not believe progress was likely and preferred to cultivate their resentment toward neighborhood storekeepers. Traditional enemies beyond Fulton were yielding, progress appeared to be coming more easily than before, but instead of striving to improve themselves Fulton's new poor found surrogates within the neighborhood to account for their own lack of success. They resented Mrs. Sparks and despised Fanny and Chub Mordecai, who ran a corner store down the street.

For their part, Fanny and Chub complained about the low moral tone of their neighborhood but didn't hesitate to sell quart jars and hundred-pound bags of sugar to bootleggers or to write numbers for those who trusted in chance. Although they were white and owned a business, Fanny and Chub were scarcely better off than their customers. In a sense they were members of Fulton's underclass themselves.

At the time I knew them Fanny and Chub were alone. Presumably they had family in Lithuania, but the ties had been broken years before and now were beyond recovery. In 1906 their mother and father had left Lithuania on a steamboat and traveled to Baltimore. They were looking for a good life but decided that Baltimore was the wrong place, so they traveled south to Richmond and opened a grocery in Seventeenth Street Bottom. Children came, first a son named Mordecai, then a daughter named Frances. The family moved to a grocery on Church Hill, then to a grocery on St. James Street uptown, then to a country store in Seven Pines, then back in town to a grocery on Federal Street. In 1929 they moved to Fulton and set up shop in a storefront that once had been an Irish bar. They decided to make their stand here, to survive or perish, but never to move again.

Mother and father worked hard for six days each week. They knew the grocery was a fragile enterprise, and they nurtured it, gave it everything they had to give. They did not allow themselves favors, did not purchase flashy clothes, did not drink or gamble. They did not expect their store to carry them, but worked to sustain it.

Mother was fair and her son had her fair hair and blue eyes. Father was dark and his daughter had his dark hair and brown eyes. Mother and father took care to teach their children the pitfalls and dangers of the world. As Jews, they felt alone, with only themselves to call upon in time of need. Always they told their children, "Whoever remains, stick together."

The Mordecais were smart about money. They understood how loans work, for example, how interest mounts up over time, and were careful never to borrow, never to be in debt. The Mordecais had little money, but they were their own boss, they had their own key.

Mordecai Mordecai grew up and went into business with a young Italian. They operated a pool room where neighborhood men came after work. Soon Mordecai was known as Chub. A year passed. Chub did well and married. Frances graduated from high school and moved to Baltimore to find her own life. Later, when their mother and father died, Chub dropped the pool room to run the family store. He put a permastone covering over the wood siding, steel screens over the windows, and built a cinderblock wall six feet high around the backyard. He joined Richfood Stores and bought a station wagon with which to pick up his orders.

Chub's wife died, and he was alone. Frances had not found a good life in Baltimore and returned to Fulton to help her brother. He ran the store, and she worked in a tobacco factory, catching cigarettes from a conveyor belt. She had taken creative writing in high school. Several years after returning to Fulton, she completed a novel, *Poor White Trash*, about a Fulton family who lived in a shanty car on a railroad siding. Frances sold copies during break time at the tobacco factory. Unfortunately, some of her superiors were white people who lived in Fulton. They took offense, fired her, and Frances came home for good. Now she worked in the store mornings and evenings, taking turns standing behind the counter ringing up the cash register while her brother put stock on the shelves. Soon Frances was known as Fanny.

When night came Chub locked the doors and Fanny totaled the day's receipts. They spent an hour together in the back room, sitting in the old, soft chairs, looking at the television. Images flashed across the screen, images from all over the world. They climbed the stairs to the low bedrooms above the store. Fanny prayed for their dead mother and father to watch over them, and Chub was happy because he was smart and the store had everything they needed—food and drink, a television, two bedrooms. Fanny and Chub were sticking together as their parents had asked. They were alone with the knowledge of their mission. In their house they were self-contained like an island, a fortress, a ship at sea.

Some nights Fanny and Chub were awakened by the sound of a brick landing on the roof. They listened, then heard another brick, then another. They were under siege, yet there was nothing for them to do but wait. The young boys who attacked them in the night knew every pathway through alleys and vacant lots. They did not have to follow streets the way police cars did, and no one could ever catch them.

Other nights the older boys came, and Fanny and Chub did not hear the sound of bricks. They did not hear anything until, suddenly, they heard a car rev up and tear out into the night. Chub realized their station wagon had been stolen once again, but he did not bother to call the police. "What good are the police, anyway?" he told me. The next afternoon a young man dropped by the store to say where he had left their car the night before.

Chub thought he was smarter than the dark-skinned people among whom he lived. He installed an alarm on his car (a "sireen," Fanny called it) and told his customers, "Anyone opens the door on this car gets his picture taken by a secret camera." Never again was Chub's car stolen.

Fanny and Chub had a few friends among the blacks. Once in a while Chub walked up the street to speak with Mrs. Sparks. Chub thought he was smarter than Mrs. Sparks. He only extended credit to those who were employed, and then, if they didn't pay, he garnisheed their wages. But all too often he was not smart enough. His customers ran up far more bills at Fulton's corner stores than their wages could ever pay off, garnishee or not. Once Chub came to Mrs. Sparks. "Please don't garnishee this man's wages," he said. "I need to put a garnishee on him first."

One or two black residents stopped in to talk, but for the most part Fanny and Chub felt hostility around them and returned it with indifference. Physically they were short and squat. Even twelve-year-old children looked down on them. Fulton people disliked Fanny and Chub because they were creditors and Jews—a little different, a little better off, running their own show instead of begging for their bread from the welfare department or working all day in a factory. Fanny and Chub had never been in debt. They were poor but free, and the residents of Fulton who were poor and in debt resented them deeply. Neighborhood children translated their parents' scorn into action.

Fanny and Chub owned a watchdog, a boxer, who had the run of the backyard on the few occasions when they were both away from home. One day they returned to find their dog whining at the back door, his face split open and glass in his water bowl. Rocks and pieces of brick lay in the yard. They took the dog inside, cleaned his wounds, and bedded him on a burlap sack. Three days later he died.

If Fulton residents did not like Fanny and Chub, the feeling was mutual. "They all look alike," said Chub. "I swear I can't tell them apart." The Mordecais felt as though they were voyaging on a dark sea. They watched black faces come into their store each day but did not recognize them, did not attach names to them. The same people came in day after day and year after year. Always it was like another black wave washing in the front door.

Fanny and Chub were disgusted with the speech of the blacks who said " 'loney" when they meant "baloney," "choicey" when they meant "choosey," "What time it is?" rather than "What time is it?" The blacks even called Coke "dope." What really frightened Fanny and Chub, however, was the change in themselves. Now they spoke in the same rhythms as the blacks, and many of the black phrases came quickly and easily to mind when they spoke. Now it took a conscious effort for them to speak like white people.

Fanny and Chub kept their windows and doors closed. They lived behind the steel screens and fake stone of their house. They never took walks, never mingled in the grills or sat on front porches to hear the news. When the pool hall crowd vandalized Simon's department store and Harrison's Drugstore after the death of Martin Luther King, Jr., Fanny and Chub saw it as a full-scale riot: the debtors were on the rampage. Chub was uptown and telephoned his sister to come out quick, but she said, "I won't leave, I won't leave," and stood her ground. Both of them knew that Fulton was their home. The decision had been made in 1929. Here they would stay to survive or perish.

If Fulton's new poor showed their distance from the old ideals by their choice of enemies, their choice of heroes was equally revealing. In the twenties Fultonians admired strivers such as Gregory and Tossie Whiting. But now, in the fifties, a loan shark and bootlegger was widely esteemed. Although Richard C. Moring did not arrive in Fulton until 1938, nearly a decade later than Fanny and Chub, he possessed a sense of style that would allow him to reach heights that were unattainable to them. He moved to Fulton from Southside and came with money—his wife's money, as Fulton residents were quick to point out.

Moring was as much a racketeer as any of Fulton's bootleggers or gamblers, but he looked and acted like an aristocrat. A man of great physical stature, he was nevertheless refined and mannerly. Occasionally he donned his $75 Florsheim shoes, $300 suit, and $100 Stetson hat. He carried himself straight-backed as he walked down the street to attend Rising Mt. Zion Church. Children became quiet as he approached, women stared at him from their front stoops. He stole the show. How could plain people like Fanny and Chub compete for the esteem of their neighbors with the magnetic, moneyed figure of Richard C. Moring?

Moring was a supervisor at a Liggett & Myers tobacco factory uptown and made personal loans to other employees on his floor on break time. Evenings and weekends he made loans to neighbors in Fulton. On Friday afternoons he rode the pay wagon at Liggett & Myers, cashing paychecks for a small fee and taking payment on his loans before the cash left his hands. In the evening he and a tall, strong-looking man walked all over Fulton on collection rounds, cashing paychecks and taking payment on loans.

Unlike Fanny and Chub, Richard C. Moring did not have difficulty collecting what he was owed. He only loaned money to people whom he knew to be working, and people had heard

about his strong-arm boys. But mainly it was the service he provided that protected him. Everyone needed him. If a man did
not pay Moring, where would he go next time he needed cash?
There were dozens of corner stores in Fulton and a person could
always transfer his or her patronage if credit was cut off. But there
was only one Richard C. Moring.

How do you think Minnie Fulkes got her sons out of jail? She
borrowed from Moring to make bail. How do you think Clara
Jones's mother, Jewel, financed her drinking binges? She borrowed from Moring and bought from Waddy Crowder. If a mother's son faced certain conviction at the hands of a particular judge,
where could she raise the $300 bribe to pay to a certain bail
bondsman who would make sure it got into the right hands?
Welfare did not have a category to cover such contingencies.
On Friday nights there were cars lined up for a block near Moring's house. People needed money to finance their weekends.
How could a person play a card game like skin without cash
money?

Richard C. Moring was a smart man. He charged twenty-five
cents on the dollar per week. Minnie Fulkes explained it to me
in much the same way, I imagine, that it had been explained to
her. "If I borrow ten dollars from him on Friday, I owe him
twelve-fifty the next Friday. If I don't have all that money, I can
just pay him the two-fifty and pay the rest the next Friday." To
Minnie Fulkes and any number of her neighbors, it seemed that
$2.50 was a far more reasonable payment to make than $12.50,
even if they made those small payments every Friday for a year
or more. It was not uncommon for loans to run that long, or
longer, before the principal was paid. Although he was realizing
a 1300 percent return on his investment over a year's time,
Moring kept collecting his $2.50 each week and never blinked.
Some people borrowed so heavily that they handed over their
entire paycheck to him each Friday and then borrowed from him
to buy food and pay the rent. Some died owing money to Moring.

Although most widely known as a financial institution, Moring sold bootleg whiskey on the side, and several times a year

held a sale on discount clothing that had been shoplifted from department stores uptown. Moring's great love, however, was slum housing.

In the years following World War II, many houses in Fulton could be purchased for as little as $300. A man could get a bank loan to cover that amount and the cost of repairs if he had something of value to use as collateral. The house then could be rented for as much as $40 per month. When the house was paid off the owner would use it as collateral to finance the purchase of a second house. In this way Richard C. Moring came to own twenty or so of Fulton's houses. He was a good businessman and did not hesitate to evict tenants who fell behind on rent. "If they can't pay one month's rent," he said, "they can't pay two."

City health inspectors rarely came through Fulton, and inexpensive housing was in demand among recent arrivals. Moring's income from his rentals was modest but his investment grew steadily.

By the time I arrived in Fulton, Moring had made his million, risen high in the Masonic Order, and become a patriarchal figure among Fulton residents. He retired from Liggett & Myers and spent afternoons on his front porch. He loaned money to Minnie Fulkes for free now, and did not press her to repay him.

Unlike most debtors, Minnie always spoke to her creditor. Once she saw him standing on the corner. "Are you tryin' to catch a girl," she asked.

"Let's just say I'm fishing," he replied.

Moring was a generous man. He gave candy to neighborhood children, took them along when he paid courtesy visits to Liggett & Myers, and interceded when they got in trouble with the authorities. He had connections in high places. Moring was exalted as the man who beat the system that was thought to be keeping Fulton folk poor. The fact that he beat the system by exploiting the weaknesses of his neighbors did not occur to his admirers, who preferred to think of him as a good man who provided a valuable service to the community.

By the late fifties many Fulton residents did not pay their store bills. Food was a necessity, and they were tired of working lifelong simply to pay for necessities. Their debts to Fanny and Chub reminded them of their failure to better themselves. But Moring provided them with a good time and enabled them to forget the cares of daily life. Corn liquor and dice gave a sense of mastery and well being, however fleeting, which compensated for a lack of those satisfactions in the workaday world. Those who adulated Richard C. Moring thought of material wealth, in itself, as the prime measurement of success. Yet they also respected Moring as one who epitomized a new approach to life in the city.

The old ideals promised that hard work and thrift could bring a poor black family an independent life despite the opposition of the white world. But many of the people left behind in Fulton were no longer interested in hearing that their fate was in their own hands. They preferred to think that if they had failed, it was because overpowering forces confronted them and had little or nothing to do with their own weakness of character.

Fulton's riffraff felt that the world had not rewarded their virtue, ability, or effort and was, therefore, amoral. They exalted Richard C. Moring because he confirmed their perception. He was manipulative, cunning. He beat the city at its own game. He made thousands, and every dollar he added to his net worth was further proof that the world operated strictly according to power relationships, with little regard for right and wrong. Those who were left behind in Fulton needed Richard C. Moring. He eased the stigma of their failure.

Not all those who moved in late from the country idolized Moring and despised Fanny and Chub, nor were all welfare cheats like Matte Curtis. Candis Goodwin was old and scarcely able to care for herself. Yet she never asked favors. She was childlike, grateful for the simplest blessing.

Although Candis Goodwin had lived in the city twenty-five years, she never adopted city manners but dressed and spoke like women in isolated country districts. Her country home was Amalgro, a small settlement that has since been incorporated into

Danville, Virginia. Her mother died when she was young, and she lived with her father and sister, worked in the Edmonds Tobacco factory, never married. In 1946, ten years after her father's death, she moved to Richmond, rented a house beneath the enormous steel viaduct that spanned Seventeenth Street Bottom, and took a job with Lucky Strike. In 1953 she moved to Fulton, where she stayed after her retirement ten years later.

Candis lived in the bedroom of a row house on Nicholson. Dozens of photographs hung on the walls, and her dresser top held precious objects of porcelain and plastic, tokens of her former life. She spoke to me of Amalgro: hot summer days, dust and flies, quiet evenings with lingering heat and the sweet smell of curing tobacco. She kept house for her father, cooked for him, sat beside his bed when he was sick. She loved him. And now he was gone and her sister was gone. Candis was alone, living out her days among strangers, living nearly undetected in the upstairs room of a wooden row house.

I had the feeling that Candis was camping out in her room. Fry pans, beaten pots, and other utensils hung from nails driven into the walls. The overall effect was one of neatness and clutter and reminded me of a trapper's cabin or the cabins where plantation workers lived. The kitchen proper was downstairs, but Candis did not climb stairs anymore, so she cooked in her room over the sheet-metal stove beside her bed, the "tin stove" as she called it, which had an oval shape and looked like a blackened and partially flattened tin can sitting on short legs. She stoked the fire with wood and coal. When the fire settled and gave an even heat, she fried slabs of fat back and bread, boiled peas and beans and turkey wings, fried shad and salt fish. "I'm crazy about fish," she told me. When she was not cooking, cleaning, or doing wash, Candis sat before her bay window sewing, singing old songs, looking out on the street. Twice a week her nephew came to carry out her garbage and do her shopping.

During my second winter in Fulton, Candis Goodwin's pipes burst in the freeze, and she had no water for the better part of a week. What could she do? She had no telephone. All this time, after the ice melted, water sprayed out downstairs in the kitchen and ran out holes in the floor. When her nephew made his scheduled visit and discovered her predicament, he borrowed a water key and turned the water off at the meter in the sidewalk. He went down to Richard C. Moring's house to see whether he, as their landlord, would make repairs. But Moring told him, "Get on away from 'round here." According to Candis, Moring had "no mind for poor people." Moring, however, had repaired frozen pipes twice before. He blamed Candis for not keeping heat in the downstairs rooms of her house.

Fortunately, Candis had some pickle jars saved. Her nephew turned the water on in the street and, in the kitchen, caught the water as it sprayed out. When the pickle jars were full he turned the water off. Then he carried the jars upstairs and placed them in the bathtub where Candis could reach them. She had water for the commode, water for wash, water to heat over her tin stove.

Like Candis Goodwin, Matte Curtis preserved a country gift for improvisation. Matte's house reminded me more of the shanties I had seen in the country than of city dwellings. But Matte was an entrepreneur. She knew how to manipulate the elements of city life to her advantage and possessed a cunning that could have been urban sophistication, though it may have derived from the darker elements of country life. In any case, Matte's wisdom was in striking contrast to the simplicity of Candis Goodwin. Candis had a good heart, but was never in a position to bolster the neighborhood in which she lived. Unlike younger people whom she and other latecomers replaced in Fulton, she was not prepared to advance the old ideals. Candis had come to Fulton to finish out her days. She had completed her mission in life before she moved to the city. She had made her mark, years before, in a country town.

4

FOURTH, FIFTH, SIXTH
GENERATIONS

1930-1972

FOLLOWING World War II Fulton's old order grew weak because it succeeded in propelling the younger generation into the world beyond Fulton and because outsiders took their places. But Fulton's old culture lost hold also because of a moral decline that occurred over sixty years' time.

In certain first families the wisdom of the third generation was gradually diluted and lost. By the time of the sixth generation, family members had become disoriented, uncertain of the difference between right and wrong, and disinclined to defend the old order against the assaults of Fulton's new poor.

Patience Gromes reared eight children who grew up to be law-abiding citizens, and she was proud of them. But still, Patience knew only too well about her own failure to transmit the old ideals. Her sons became steady working men, much like their father. Some of them completed high school, none attended college, but this was acceptable, for in the Armistead family the men were expected to bear witness to the high standing of their race through hard work rather than education. The daughters were a different matter, however. Roseale, the older of the two, graduated from high school and attended a year of college before dropping out to marry a man below her station. Her husband moved in with the family for some months, then he and Roseale rented a house on Nicholson that had rotten boards in its front porch.

But it was Betsy, the youngest and most promising daughter, who brought home to Patience her inability to interpret her ideals to this younger generation. Betsy, the baby of the family, came of age in the years following World War II. She graduated from high school in 1946, and her mother offered to put her through college with money saved from twenty years of doing white folks' laundry. "Don't throw away your money on me," said Betsy. "I don't want to be a teacher, or be a nurse and dump bedpans for white people. I want to get a job and buy some clothes."

Patience did not deny that the opportunities for an educated black finding work commensurate with his or her training were limited, but she tried to impress upon her daughter the importance of education as an end in itself. How could Patience describe the hunger for learning that she had possessed as a child? Certainly Patience's own education, outstanding for a country girl of her day, had not been a necessary qualification for a life of washing clothes and rearing children.

"Be somebody in this world," Patience said.

Betsy was outspoken about racial prejudice in a way that sent shivers down her mother's spine. Betsy lacked Patience's enduring repose, her ability to find satisfaction in minute progress each day. She was unwilling to wait for recognition, or to wait for savings to accumulate over twenty years' time. Instead of enrolling in college, she took a job serving hot dogs at a segregated lunch counter uptown.

To Betsy, Patience's strict morals were unnecessary, the high-toned moral posture of church-goers dishonest. Gradually the more liberal views of her generation softened some of the stricter practices. Unwed mothers who belonged to Rising Mt. Zion, for example, no longer went up for interviews with the deacon and deaconess boards but simply continued attending church as though nothing had happened. One young woman stayed indoors for her period of gestation, then claimed that the child belonged to her mother.

Articulate young people like Betsy Gromes castigated the older generation for what they saw as cruelty and hypocrisy on the subject of premarital sex. Betsy knew of deacons and deaconesses who had had children before marriage or outside of marriage. "If I'd gotten pregnant," Betsy said to me later, "I'd have gone up and told them about themselves."

The discipline that had seemed life-giving to an earlier generation now appeared restrictive and lacking in compassion. A young woman with a baby and no husband, as Betsy was quick to point out, needed the church more than most. Why should she be excluded? Why should she be asked to beg forgiveness before men and women who had done the same or worse themselves?

When Betsy began to smoke and drink, Patience was scandalized. Smoking was bad, and drinking was worse. They argued for weeks, but Betsy was adamant. "Well then," said Patience, "drink if you want, but you rule it, don't let it rule you."

Betsy and her friends spent their free time at the Bethlehem Center learning to sew and cook and dancing to the "piccolo," as they called the jukebox. Her brother in the navy sent money for a Victrola. Sometimes Betsy invited friends over to listen to records or play the piano. Once in a while they pushed the furniture of the front room aside and danced. The neighbors were aghast. But Patience liked to have her daughter at home instead of "Who knows where?" and Betsy faithfully cleaned the room and restored sofas and the coffee table to their accustomed positions when her friends were gone.

Still, Betsy and her friends were bored and begged the church to allow dances in its basement, citing the precedent of Jews uptown who held festivities in their temple. Their pleas did not avail. One of Betsy's friends owned a '46 Ford club coupe, and she rode with him and six or seven others, enjoying their laughter and speed in the night. Her parents and other church members regarded these as libertine excursions. Patience and Frank advised her to be cautious around young men. "Don't let them pull your panties down," said her mother. "Don't let them big you," said her father. If Betsy wanted to make love to a man, her parents' warnings did not stand in the way.

Sometimes Betsy and her friends stopped in at the more respectable nip joints in Fulton to drink beer, liquor, or corn whiskey. She always wondered in the back of her mind whether the "purity squad" of the Richmond Police would pull a raid and take her to jail. Then she would be forced to defend her social habits to her parents and the church. She feared this possibility, yet it excited her as well.

Patience Gromes loved peace, avoided controversy, and took pains to keep up appearances. But Betsy loved to confront her enemies and expose their weaknesses. Patience sometimes mentioned to Betsy the criticisms of neighborhood gossips. Betsy became angry and demanded to know the names of her accusers, but Patience refused to say. "I won't have you embarrass me, Betsy," she said, "won't have you shame me."

After graduating from high school, Betsy fell in love with a Fulton man. He took her uptown to dances at the Mosque and to movies at the Hippodrome Theatre. He was not the kind of man her mother could approve of, however, and much of the time Betsy would meet him around the corner from her mother's house. Nevertheless the neighbors could see what was going on. "Oh, Mrs. Gromes, that daughter of yours is slippin' and slidin' on you," they told Patience.

About the time she was ready to marry, Betsy met another man, somewhat older, light-skinned. She did not love him, but he had a motorcycle and took her for rides. Before Betsy decided for one suitor or the other, Patience took her aside. "Forget that Fulton boy. Marry the other one. He will make you a good husband. He will be a good provider."

Betsy pondered, could not decide, and then followed her mother's advice. She never regretted her choice. Her husband was a building contractor and over the years bought her dozens of cars, several boats, and one fine house down Route 5. The Fulton man later married another woman and took her to his mother's house where they had a bedroom of their own. "He never even bought his wife a bed," Betsy told me.

It may never have occurred to Betsy that her mother might have meant something more than cars, boats, and houses when she stipulated that a husband should be a "good provider." Patience was speaking in the context of a simpler time. Betsy's Fulton beau would not make a good husband, in Patience's judgment, because he lacked the stability, uprightness, and industry that were, in themselves, the substance of a good husband's provision for his wife.

For all her differences with her mother, Betsy loved and respected her. She felt a special quality in her mother that set her apart from other Fulton women. "For one thing," she told me, "my mother loved people."

Betsy respected her father, too, but he was different. Frank Gromes rode the train to Cincinnati on his C&O pass, drove his car to Washington or down home to Toano. His life was enlarged geographically from that of his peers, and he considered himself a man of the world. But Patience's life was lifted up from the world. It had vision, kindness, and strength. It had been shaped by the lives of her forebears going back to Lewis Armistead, who escaped from slavery at age fourteen and set himself to become "somebody" in this world.

In the years following World War II, the children of God-fearing folk who had been reared under the dictum "Don't you ever go into Rocketts" found that the nip joints and gambling dens of Rocketts offered entertainment in an otherwise drab and slow-paced urban village. Nevertheless, as Betsy Gromes and her peers reached their majority, married, and began raising families of their own, it became clear that for all their extravagances they were applying the decency and good judgment of their parents to their own lives in a more complex and faster-paced world. If Betsy's actions did not conform to the letter of the old ethic, her thought nevertheless reflected its spirit. Like her mother, Betsy Gromes loved people.

Although Betsy may have deviated from the straight and narrow in superficial ways, others of her generation did more than entertain themselves occasionally at a nip joint or make quick, furtive ventures into Rocketts. Not only their actions but their thoughts, their way of perceiving the world, broke away from the old patterns. The daughters of upstanding families sometimes went out on the street "doin' their thing," as Minnie Fulkes might have put it. They sometimes fell in love with men of unrefined habits and found themselves following a different path than their mothers would have chosen for them. Such was the case with Analiza Foster, whose mother, Peggy Howell, was a contemporary of Patience Gromes. Analiza was a tall, heavy set woman whose son Snort had a reputation as a fighter. Snort was the enormous man missing parts of two fingers who could be seen on Saturday afternoons shooting craps in front of Waddy Crowder's nip joint.

Analiza was an attractive woman in her youth, and her lover was a big, broad-shouldered man named David Francis. They called him Hammer. According to Billy Dismith, Hammer had "a very good talent at baseball" and played shortstop on the Fulton team. At that time the baseball diamond was located in the nearest corner of the field separating Fulton from the C&O tracks and the roundhouse and rail yard beyond. Against the backdrop of steam and smoke and the sound of engines coming in off the line, Hammer and his teammates hit and fielded and argued with the umpire. Thanks to Hammer, the Fulton team won many of its arguments and even more of its games. Folk traveled from all over to see Hammer play. They said he was good enough to be in the majors, and to judge from his swagger he knew it.

Analiza thought Hammer to be a fine figure of a man. He did not have a job and spent his days on the street drinking and rolling dice. He was uneven in temperament, stubborn to a fault and sometimes quick to take offense. But Analiza did not care. He acted like a king, and she courted him and loved him. People said they were married, although theirs was not the legal kind of marriage that the older generation prized. But for that Analiza did not love Hammer any less. She gave him a child whom they named William Francis. From an early age the child was known as Snort.

People on the street said that Analiza and Hammer were a perfect couple, but perfection, like other things in this world, does not last forever. Eventually they quarreled and separated. Hammer was popular with neighborhood women. Analiza began to court other men. She got pregnant and, after the child was born, parted ways with the child's father and took up with some-one else. The pattern repeated itself until she had six children by four fathers. Nothing she did seemed to perturb Hammer. Nothing brought him back. Analiza was getting older now. She began to attend church more regularly and to value respectability. When one of her swains, surnamed Foster, wrote their child into his will, Analiza reciprocated by taking his name for herself and for all her children except Snort.

Hammer had moved to New Jersey by now, and if he felt the slap when Analiza took another man's name, he never let on. He had been king of the street for years, but had nothing to show for it now. Hammer had squandered his special gift as an athlete, and he knew it. He knew he would never amount to anything. He had failed himself, and Fulton people judged that he had failed them as well. He could have been great, but it didn't work out that way. "He just throwed hisself away," said Billy Dismith.

Analiza lived now in the same wooden house where she had grown up. She cooked and washed and made groceries for eight people, including herself and her mother, and at night she was weary. She loved her children, worried about their future, and began to look with displeasure on those of her neighbors who drank and partied. Surrounded by people, she was nevertheless alone. She had no way of knowing whether Hammer would ever return. As it was, she had nothing by which to remember him—nothing, that is, but her first son. As nearly as I can figure, Snort was fifteen years old when they received word of Hammer's death.

Snort already had a large frame and square shoulders. "He's gonna look like Hammer," said the people on Orleans Street. They were right. And the resemblance would go deeper than looks. Inevitably the mildness of Analiza's mother and the industry of her father were lost in the distance between their generation and that of their grandchild. Snort would become a fine-looking man who had the body of his father and his father's character as well.

There was a mixing going on among Fulton residents of the fourth and fifth generations, a mixing that diluted the ideals of their forebears. The changes were not always so pronounced as in the life of Analiza Foster. More often there was a subtle shifting of sympathy or perception, a coincidence of accident and impulse that brought changes that were not visible until a generation or two generations later. Something like this was the case with the family of Charles Dowd.

Charles Grandy Dowd was a member of the sixth generation whom I met when I came to his house to tell his mother about food stamps. His story properly begins with that of Jane Dunston, his great-grandmother and a member of the third generation.

Jane Dunston was born in 1899 near the town of Clove, Halifax County, in Southside Virginia. As a child she lived with her mother and father on the Woodlawn Plantation, where they worked the land on shares. They lived only a few miles from the Mecklenburg County farm where her grandmother had been born in slavery times. Her grandmother was twelve years old at Lee's Surrender. When she came of age and married, she and her husband worked the Timberlake Plantation on shares.

Jane and her parents lived in a log cabin with a stick and mud chimney and three rooms: up, down, and kitchen. They cooked in the fireplace with skillets and a three-legged Dutch oven, and walked a quarter mile down a hill to the spring. Each year they worked the fields of tobacco and corn. At harvest time the owner separated out a share of the crop which Jane's father sold for cash. In addition they raised their own vegetables, chickens, and pigs, and milked their own cow. Jane's mother had a small ox

that she spoiled as though it were a child. The ox was partial to
Jane's mother and pulled her or her children in their cart, but
never obeyed the orders of any man, even Jane's father. One day
her father chased the ox, which, as Jane put it, "was running so
fast he had to turn sideways to keep from flying." After capturing
the ox, her father took it to town and sold it for butchering. Her
mother was so upset that she left him. Weeks later, her mourning
completed, she returned.

Sharecroppers' cash earnings were low, and another source of
income was a necessity if they ever were to purchase a farm of
their own. Jane's father began to work at a brickyard in Ravenna,
New York. Each autumn after harvest he rode the train north.
Each spring he returned in time for planting. Jane and her sister
were lonely at Christmas without their father, but now their
family was able to save a little each year and felt that they were
going somewhere. By 1918 they had saved enough to purchase
a house and ten acres of land.

The soil was fertile, and the house was a fine, frame building
with pine paneling, a clay pipe chimney with mortared joints,
and a shake roof. One day a spark from the chimney landed on
the shakes and started a fire. Jane heard the fire popping and
remembered the old song:

> When your house catch afire
> Throw your trunk out the window and
> Let the shack burn down.

She ran upstairs, threw her trunk out the window, ran down
stairs, and pulled her grandmother out the door to safety. Their
house burned to the ground, but they collected insurance money
and built a cabin with a tin roof.

Jane's father put a lien on the property to purchase a horse,
a plow, and a wagon with which to work the land. He intended
to become self-sufficient but found that he was not as strong as
he had been in the days before he worked at the brickyard. He
had traded his strength and good health for cash with which to
buy land, and now he lacked the stamina to work it. He gradually

grew weaker. Any hope of quick recovery was lost, and it appeared that they would forfeit the place to their creditors.

Jane could not bear to see her father lose their farm. "If he was going to die," she told me, "I wanted him to die on his own place."

Jane set up a "free account" for her parents at the county store, and moved into Clove, where she worked as a cook in the hotel. She earned five dollars each week, of which she gave three dollars to her parents and put the other two in a savings account under her own name. Jane supported her parents and paid off the lien. When her father died in 1925, he died on his own land.

After her father was gone, Jane lost her feeling for their home place. She married a local man and they moved to New York, where she worked as a domestic. Each week she sent money to support her mother in the country. When Jane's husband died in 1930, she moved to Fulton to live with relatives who had moved there just after World War I. Soon Jane's mother joined her, and within weeks they met Jacob Pinckney, Betty Norton, Thomas Arrington, and others whose families had come from familiar country districts. Jane took a job in the cafeteria at American Tobacco and made a down payment on a two-story house on Carlisle Avenue. Her sister married and moved to Fulton. The family was together once again.

Jane brought two children with her to Fulton, a son and a daughter. The girl was named Judith and grew to be a resourceful, even-tempered woman who married Thomas Angus, a Fulton man whose family had moved here from Mecklenburg County before World War I. Although Thomas's parents were pious and hard working, city life brought out other qualities in their son. Thomas became known for his gallantry: over the years he fathered eight children by Judith, and ten additional children by Jane Upperman, a protégée of Matte Curtis's whom I knew through the Poor People's Club. Judith was a religious woman. She forgave her husband, maintained her household, and waited silently for him to grow into an appreciation of the happiness that monogamy can bring.

Judith's daughter Frankey Angus grew to be an attractive woman who was much sought after by Fulton men. She fell in love with Felix Dowd, the nephew of Reverend Squire Dowd, lived with him for ten years, and bore him a son whom they named Charles. Felix was a tough, handsome man who eventually was arrested on a felony charge. Instead of going to prison, he jumped bail and fled to Maryland, leaving Frankey behind. After Dowd's departure, Frankey had relations with an old flame, who comforted her and gave her another child. Then she fell in love with John Miles.

Fulton folk tell conflicting stories about Frankey's relations with her lovers. According to one, Felix Dowd heard that John Miles was mistreating Frankey. He came down from Maryland, risking arrest, fought with Miles, and carved a fine line across his throat with a razor. "If you ever hit Frankey again," he said, "I'll come back and take that cut clear to the bone."

An altogether different story is told by the supporters of John Miles. According to them, Frankey had always wanted to be free of Felix Dowd, but he was big and tough and wouldn't let her go. Such relationships, they say, were not uncommon in Fulton. Dowd was heading for Maryland when he was caught and sent to prison. In the meantime, Frankey made a life for herself with John Miles. Everything went well until, years later, Dowd was released on parole and returned to Fulton to reclaim his woman. Miles refused to back down and fought Dowd until the latter collapsed. Later Dowd went to Maryland in self-imposed exile.

In any case, Frankey and John Miles were married and lived together in a three-room tenement apartment located on one of Fulton's more exclusive blocks. The tenement was an old wooden structure but the furnishings of their apartment were brand new. On the floor in the front room was a red carpet protected with plastic. Beside it stood a new sofa, also red and covered with plastic.

Miles found a job working for Philip Morris. "Thank God for that overtime pay," said Frankey. They had worries. They owed. Each month they paid on the washing-machine bill, the television bill, the bedroom suite bill, the bill for the Frigidaire. That old Frigidaire frosted up so thick a person could hardly close the door. They had to purchase a new one on top of everything else, and then the furniture store garnisheed John's pay check. At Christmas he took out a holiday loan. "It hurts to pay those loan bills," Frankey said, "but you gotta have a decent Christmas." When the holiday loan was nearly paid off, they received a letter saying that their credit was good, so her husband went back for more. That educated Frankey. Thereafter she took the loan company letters out of the mail box and burned them before her husband got home from work. Even though there were troubles, it was nice to be able to sit down on a decent-looking sofa to think it all through.

Frankey could remember every detail of her wedding. They had held a reception at her grandmother's house: downstairs they ate cake and smiled for the photographer, and upstairs they displayed wedding presents for their guests to admire. After the reception was over, however, Frankey noticed that a silver bowl and a gilded looking glass were missing.

Frankey loved her children and loved her husband for providing them with a stable home. It had not always been easy for the kids, for Charles in particular. He had lived with Frankey's grandmother at various times when Frankey was in the process of upgrading her living arrangements and changing living partners. Charles knew his real father and could never accept John Miles as a surrogate. Still, he and his mother were close. She was trying to give her children what they needed. She still danced on Saturday nights, but nowadays she seldom missed a Sunday church service.

Charles Dowd was a senior in high school when I met him. He was a diligent student and did not hang out at the pool hall. He appeared certain to graduate and was a likely candidate for college if finances could be arranged. Charles had prospects, but he also had troubles. He couldn't find a summer job, and his efforts to find part-time work during the school year were equally fruitless. He knew his mother worried about paying their monthly bills, and he found it difficult to ask her for money. He was quiet and well mannered, yet he had seen things that I, as a child of the suburbs, seldom even imagined. When he was young his great-grandmother's second husband sent him around the corner to a bootlegger named Pinto. The men at Pinto's were strange and coarse and obeyed different rules than those his mother and great-grandmother taught him. The bootlegger bragged to young Charles and flashed an enormous roll of bills. They would meet again.

November 20, 1972, was a Friday evening. Charles Dowd left the apartment on Denny where he lived with his mother and stepfather and met three friends. They walked into Rocketts and came to Pinto's. When Charles and his friends got inside, the bootlegger was alone. He was old and weak. One of them held him from behind, another hit him in the head. He had only one dollar. They ran. Several blocks away Charles learned that one of his friends had stabbed Pinto in the chest.

Charles was at home the following morning when the police came for him. He did not feel like a criminal. A counselor from the Bethlehem Center visited him and his companions in jail that afternoon. Charles freely admitted his guilt. He was bored sitting in jail and asked for his school books. He could not explain his involvement in the crime, but later a young woman who lived nearby explained the whole thing to me. They didn't have money that night and didn't mean to kill him, only he recognized them. But even then they didn't mean to kill him. They were in a hurry. "You know how it is when you are in a hurry and just aren't thinking," she said.

Charles Dowd and his friends were the sixth generation since slavery. They had never known former slaves, never lived in the country, and did not see their lives as part of an upward journey from slavery. They committed the first decisive act of their adult lives by mistake, as it were, and found themselves transported in the opposite direction, from city streets to the country work farms of Southampton and Mecklenburg counties. Now they lived in the same country districts where slaves had lived. They worked as slaves had worked, in gangs under the eye of a man with a gun.

Charles's family had lived in Fulton for decades, were known as genial folk, and had distinguished themselves by the purchase of a house. If Charles was uncertain as to the right and wrong of stealing a dollar from a bootlegger, perhaps his hesitance should be traced not to his family proper but to an outsider who joined his family late. As a child, Charles lived with William Dunston, the man who introduced him to the bootlegging underworld and its conception of right and wrong. William Dunston had moved to Fulton in middle age from Charles City County.

Before the Civil War, Charles City County was the site of Virginia's largest and most prosperous plantations, whose big houses still stand along the banks of the James. The owners, men like William Byrd and "King" Carter, were among the elite who controlled Virginia's politics from colonial times. It is tempting to speculate that the black immigrants from Charles City County who rolled dice and drank bootleg whiskey on Fulton's street corners following World War II were exhibiting the sorrier heritage of those grand plantations, the logical counterpart to the fine statesmen who dignify accounts of Virginia's history.

If William Dunston was part of the human wreckage of slavery, he did not let that fact keep him from enjoying life. A few months after arriving in Fulton in 1946 he married Charles Dowd's great-grandmother Jane (who had lived alone since her mother's passing) and before long became known as one who preferred the "sportin' life." By now Jane had grown into an appreciation of the convivial pleasures of Fulton's clubs and beer gardens. William led the way, she followed. As the years passed, she maintained her propriety and sense of grace, for she did not need drink. She had been at peace with herself ever since the day she put the last dollar down on her father's mortgage.

William, on the other hand, seemed to deteriorate a little

every year. He drank steadily and drank to excess. He could not escape the consequences forever, and neither could those around him. William Dunston is the man who sent a child, young Charles Dowd, around the corner to purchase whiskey from a bootlegger. And late one Friday night in the winter of 1972, it was William Dunston who visited the bootlegger himself (they were to go uptown together), only to find him lying face down on the sofa in a puddle of blood.

By the time I arrived in Fulton, William Dunston had become a raving alcoholic. Once a co-worker of mine from the Bethlehem Center visited to give Jane a ride to the clinic. William mistook him for a hoodlum from the pool hall and waved a butcher knife in the air until he retreated. Later Jane laughed about it. "Crazy old Will, crazy, crazy Will," she said.

One day, at Jane's invitation, I visited to explain the food-stamp program. William met me at the door, no butcher knife this time. He was wearing his Sunday best in anticipation of a visit from his priest. He ushered me into the cool interior of their house. Jane Dunston motioned for me to sit on one side of a polished dining table. She sat directly across from me in a straight-backed chair. I lectured on the subtleties of the food-stamp application while her husband, convinced that I was the Catholic priest, clutched at my clothing. "Pray for me, Father. Pray for me."

He smelled of spirits and drooled on his sport coat. I could not ignore him, and, although I was not a priest, I thought I still could comfort him. I stood and placed my hand on his head. "Let us pray: E Pluribus Unum. Veni Vidi Vici. O Tempora, O Mores," I said. I lifted my hand from William's head. "My son, thy sins are forgiven thee. Go in peace."

William Dunston calmed as I spoke, his eyes closed and a peaceful expression, a slight smile, came over his face. When I stopped talking, he opened his eyes and tears streamed down his cheeks. He thanked me repeatedly. From beneath his shirt he pulled a bottle of scotch and offered me a hit.

William Dunston cut a farcical figure, but I think there was something truthful about him, as though a drunk had been chosen to express the secret longing of this neighborhood. His words transcended the Bible sayings of the old women and the quick jive-talk of the young men. His words reached out for sustenance and comfort in what had become a difficult world.

5

STREET YOUTH

1960-1967

PATIENCE GROMES and other patricians were unsettled by
the new poor and dismayed by what they saw as moral decline
within some old families. But nothing shocked them more than
wrongdoing among Fulton youth. In the thirties Fulton residents
did not have locks on their doors. In the fifties they had locks
but didn't use them. By the late sixties they had two locks and
used them both.

Break-ins began in 1961 or 1962. Fulton was bursting with
black country folk at this time, and the last white families were
moving out. In 1964 or 1965 heroin came to Fulton from New
York along new channels, independent of traditional supply lines
of illegal whiskey. Break-ins became more common, especially
in Fulton's business district, as the desire for heroin slowly spread
among Fulton youths. In my work for the Bethlehem Center I
talked with Robert Lumpkin, the white grocer; Billy Dismith,
the barber; and Grace and James Dewbre, who ran the short-
order restaurant on Louisiana. These folks were suffering under
the new youth culture, and they let everybody know it.

On my way to Lumpkin's Supermarket I walked through Fulton's eighty-year-old commercial district. Most of the brick storefront buildings were closed, their windows thick with soot. Fulton
Hardware was still in business, but broken plate glass in front

had been patched with plywood and gave the impression that the business was operating from behind a barricade. An enormous German shepherd lunged at me from behind the windows of another building that was now used for storage. Down the street was a cement-block building of comparatively recent construction, its windows covered with steel screens. This was Lumpkin's, the most active retail business left in Fulton. I spoke with Robert Lumpkin, who was born in a row house across the street. As soon as I introduced myself he cut in:

"You at the Bethlehem Center. With the colored. They steal from me all the time, the little kids, the mothers, even the ministers. I caught a minister in here one time stealing from me. Police picked up a boy one night with an ax chopping a hole in the wall, tryin' to break in. They even cut holes in the roof. What does the judge do? Nothing. The next day they let him out and he comes walking by my front door, laughing at me, and the cement dust from my wall is still on him, on his shoes."

Later I would figure out that Lumpkin was far from the stereotype of a racist storekeeper taking advantage of poor folk who did not have the transportation to shop anywhere else. His store was broken into once a year or so, and it made him angry. But he also had long-standing friendships with the blacks among whom he worked. He played up his grievances because I was white, and he didn't want me to know of the sympathy he felt toward blacks. I would later meet some of the poorest black families, who told me how they turned to Robert Lumpkin for free food in times of crisis. On the other hand, Lumpkin routinely marked up his merchandise the week welfare and Social Security checks arrived.

Around the corner, Billy Dismith's barbershop began losing business in the early sixties. By 1971 Billy was earning enough to pay the rent, not much more, and hardly a week would go by without some small theft. Then things changed for the worse. "One night a guy backed his truck up to the door," said Billy, "and took my mirrors, my barber chair, all of my combs and brushes, my razors. When I came to work the next morning I looked at that place, nothing but bare walls and said, 'That does it. I'm quitting.' "

A block up Louisiana, James Dewbre and his wife ran Fulton's most famous eatery. It was located a few doors from the pool hall and eventually was put out of business by the street youth who frequented the pool hall, stood on the corner, and at night busted into the diner from every conceivable direction. In 1927, as a young man of twenty-one, Dewbre had married his childhood sweetheart in Fulton and moved to New York. Twenty years later he and his wife returned, and he found work as a custodian for a shoe company. The next year they got a $200 loan from the piccolo man, the distributor of jukeboxes in that end of town, and started Dewbre's Diner in a storefront space.

At the time, there was a need for an eating and drinking establishment for blacks. Minter's bar had a corner sectioned off. The whites went in the front door, the blacks came in the side door. Dewbre had seen black men standing shoulder to shoulder and hardly a white man on the other side.

"Our formula was good food and something to drink," Dewbre told me. "Everything fresh. We didn't get nothing out of cans. Our specialty was beef stew. Then we served hamburgers, hot dogs, potato salad, plate lunches. We cooked from rough, wouldn't serve prepackaged food like nowadays. We ate in our restaurant and weren't about to eat junk or serve it to our customers." The diner had tables and booths. It opened at eleven and closed at midnight. The Dewbres bought food, prepared and served it, cleaned up afterwards. They worked long hours, and business was good.

In a few weeks Dewbre had used up his $200 and went back for more, back to the piccolo man, back and forth to any bank that would let him in the door. "I've got the customers," he told them, "but I got to buy the food for them and pay my help." All kinds of money was pouring into their cash register, and they spent every penny on more food, more supplies, more help. Then they got their beer license. Now the customers came storming in. Dewbre went back for more money. "I got the customers," he said, "I need to buy the beer to sell them." More money poured into their cash register. Some months they grossed $50,000, and they spent pretty near every penny on the business. "We had ten good years," said Dewbre. "Then things began to slow down in Fulton a bit." The C&O switched to diesel and laid off, the Cedar Works shut down about that time. But the real difference came in 1961 or so when the break-ins began.

"Now how am I supposed to run a business and work every hour of the day when at any time some punk is going to bust in and make a mess of things?" Burglars kicked in the door, smashed the windows, cut through the roof. Twice they tunneled through the walls from vacant storefronts on either side. "These younger people didn't appreciate what we were serving down there," Dewbre said. "They'd talk trash to you, walk out without paying. Then we'd catch the help stealing from us. It was real work running that business."

Every July the Dewbres shut down and went on vacation. They traveled any direction and went as far as their car would carry them. In their last nine years they had one break-in each year until their insurance was canceled. In 1971 they quit. Dewbre and his wife had run the restaurant for twenty-three years.

Dewbre attributed crime in Fulton to "that dope circulatin' down here." Billy Dismith cites "young kids" and "that crime wave" in all of Richmond's poor neighborhoods about this time. Robert Lumpkin traced crime to the urban renewal program. "There were break-ins down here," said Lumpkin. "Of course the housing authority creates that. They knock things down and the kids think that's what they are supposed to do, break glass.

"The housing authority depresses an area and then undesirables come in, the better people move out. You get a lot of new people down here in these shells, these old houses." In another conversation Lumpkin summarized his experience with Fulton's street youth: "I've been knocked in the head, I've been robbed, cut holes in the roof so many times I've had to put a new roof on. But even then it is better than other sections of town."

The pool room on Louisiana had been a convivial place through the fifties. By the late sixties, however, it had become a haven for young men who were out of school and unable to find work. These were children of families who had moved to Fulton from the country since World War II as well as children of Fulton's traditional low life and, occasionally, a member of one of Fulton's first families who had gone astray.

During the civil rights campaign in Birmingham in 1963 and the Selma march in 1965, the rhetoric of civil rights reached a fever pitch. It was succeeded by the rhetoric of black power during the long hot summers of 1966 and 1967. Fulton's bootleggers and gamblers, like most other residents, were not visibly affected by civil rights demonstrations and the riots that followed. But the youth who frequented the pool hall were changed. They became politicized.

The speeches of black leaders who predicted violence if government did not change its policies were in effect legitimizing violence as a response to racial oppression. A few regulars at the pool hall were like Willy Cozart, a veteran in his late twenties who had seen the world, returned to Fulton, and now was writing a book about his "coming up" in this poor, black enclave. Willy was the philosophical leader of the street youth and a sometime employee of the Bethlehem Center. He preserved much of the intellectual content of black thinking and speaking on the subject of racial oppression and even improvised upon it.

But younger habitués of the pool hall who had been raised in stultifying circumstances and who dropped out before reaching high school were only able to absorb the rhetoric of black leaders in its crudest form. They never considered that a speech could be a specific instrument designed to bring distinct governmental responses. In their lives the angry words of black leaders, together with the bitterness that the civil rights movement brought to the surface among blacks, were transmuted into an amorphous cultural chic: the Afro hair style, rhythmic music with explicit lyrics, an attitude of hostility toward whites, and an even deeper antagonism toward black men in positions of authority. The words of black leaders became to them the street ideal that was the opposite of hard work and thrift: the master street artist was the man who attained riches without working or saving.

The young of the pool hall came to feel that every posture and necessity of their lives was imbued with political significance. If they were poor, out of work, strung out on drugs, that was testimony to the oppression of white society and had little to do with their own weakness. And if violence was an appropriate means of dealing with political oppression on a national level, what could be more natural than breaking the law to deal with the impact of oppression on a personal level? Fulton's angry young men did not reason out these points. They didn't have to. It was all around them on the street. It was inevitable, natural. It was reality and took no effort at all to understand or put into action.

Traditionally Fulton youth had been guided into adulthood by their parents and grandparents. But the houses of Fulton were getting old by now and did not impress city youth raised with television, pop music, and movies. The youth were listening to voices from the world beyond Fulton. Many of them disdained hard work. Willy Cozart noted that slaves had worked hard to please their masters. In Willy's mind hard work was a capitulation to white society even today. "Prison is society's way of forcing people to work," said Willy. "There's no reason to scramble, except to stay out of prison."

The attitudes Willy Cozart put into words grated against the sensibilities of third- and fourth-generation residents who had worked to survive, who had lived through the Depression when a low-paid, dirty job was like a gift from heaven. Fulton's first citizens traditionally distinguished themselves from neighborhood low life by their abstinence from liquor (or at least by their entirely discreet indulgence). Now they distinguished themselves from streetwise young men and women by their hard work in steady jobs. Street youth did not work. Fulton's winos never had worked much either, of course, but there was a difference between failing at a life of hard work, as the winos were thought to have done, and denying the virtue of such a life altogether, in the

manner of Willy Cozart. Winos were content to be low men on
the totem pole. But Willy Cozart and his protégés were attempting to turn the tables on Fulton's first citizens, to cut away the
ethic that gave meaning to everything they had accomplished.
Fulton's fourth-generation leaders might think the neighborhood's dozen or two dozen public inebriates a sad sight, but they
were not angered by them the way they were by the young men,
especially when those young men were their sons.

Unlike the new poor, Fulton's street youth were cohesive and
rejected the old ideals in ways that were fairly consistent from
one person to the next. Sammy Fulkes's experience on the street
is typical of other young dropouts who turned to drugs and crime.
Willy Cozart was typical of the Vietnam era vets who spent some
time in the pool hall but held themselves above street youth like
Sammy. What is difficult to assess is the number of young men
in Fulton who shared the streets with Sammy.

If there were a hundred young people in Fulton sixteen to
eighteen years of age when I arrived in 1971, I would guess that
ten had dropped out to join Sammy on the street and another
ten were still in school or working but spent much of their time
"around the street" with Sammy. That leaves eighty who were
not on the streets, though some of these, like Charles Dowd,
had lost the sense that doings on the street were evil and to be
avoided. Most Fulton youth stayed in school and found steady
jobs after graduation. They were energetic and wholesome. I am
thinking of the Boy Scouts, the Men Who Care, the young men
and women in Fulton's churches, those who performed in local
talent shows or participated in neighborhood cleanup campaigns.
The detail of their lives is not important to our story because
they did not play a decisive role in the effort to shore up the old
ideals. Street youth, on the other hand, provided the most
pointed challenge these ideals would face.

Sammy Fulkes was the son of Minnie Fulkes, who had lived
in Fulton all her life but always associated with the "rougher type
of people," a category that expanded to include Matte Curtis

soon after her arrival. Sammy Fulkes and Matte's son Grunt had been playmates since childhood. A few months before I came to Fulton, Sammy, Grunt, and Sammy's younger brother drove from Fulton down Route 5, then inland to the cement factory. Here Sammy picked up his paycheck for the few hours he had worked that week. Then they returned to Fulton, parked, and entered Lumpkin's Supermarket to cash the check.

A white man who lived down Route 5 in the country also had come to Lumpkin's to cash his check that evening. As he left, he walked toward the liquor store. Sammy, Grunt, and Sammy's brother followed him. When the white man stepped from the curb to cross Louisiana Street, they shot him in the back and, as he lay in the street, stole thirty dollars from his pocket. The following day the police picked up and booked the three of them. Grunt was released from jail after a day or two, and Sammy after two months: insufficient evidence.

The police knew they were guilty, because Waddy Crowder, the bootlegger, had tipped them off. Waddy was the operator of an unlicensed drinking establishment. The middle-aged alcoholics who frequented Waddy's heard and saw everything that happened on the street and traded their observations to Waddy for drink. Waddy in turn informed the police, who reciprocated with tolerance. The operator of a nip joint had to have tolerance. The police began with the criminals, then sought evidence. Waddy's tips helped them locate a young black man who had witnessed the shooting. But he said he would be dead in a day if he testified. Sammy and Grunt were fortunate.

Sammy's brother, however, was not. He was identified by the victim from a photograph and sentenced to ten years in prison. His court-appointed lawyer suggested that he appeal because the photograph of him had been handled improperly: it was presented to the victim as a "throw down" rather than a "montage"— presented individually rather than as one of several photos of possible assailants. But he said no, he would just do his time and get it over with.

Sammy had been arrested in September 1970, and I met him

shortly after his release the following spring. I thought we met by accident, but now I realize that Sammy was looking for help, looking hard, and might well have come to me if I hadn't walked into his life first. I had seen the pool hall as I reconnoitered this neighborhood, but I was afraid of it and steered clear. I sensed that the young men I saw walking in and out had unpleasant things on their minds. My intuitions turned out to be correct. Later a friend of Sammy's told me about a drug user who had begun to sell to support his habit and then came up short on money: he was executed here, run over by a Cadillac until his blood ran in the gutter. I was afraid of the pool hall, but I also resented the fact that I was made to feel afraid. One afternoon, on impulse, I walked in.

The jukebox was loud, but the men I saw were quiet. I sensed that they had stopped talking the moment I came inside. I never considered that the only white men who boldly walked into the black pool halls of Richmond were cops. I felt uneasy and did not realize that everyone was waiting for me to make my move.

I sat down on a bench to the side of the door and looked around. This place was like a cave. The ceilings were high. In the gloom I could make out two rows of pool tables extending to the rear. Above each table hung a fluorescent light, but only the two tables nearest the door were lit and available for use. Behind me in the corner was a round table where men in their late thirties sat playing cards. The other men were young, probably still minors, and stood next to the wall where a rack of pool cues was mounted. In the other direction, deeper into the room, a short, middle-aged man stood, obscure in the gloom. Below his belly hung a chromed change counter, the kind that ticket takers wear. There were no women.

In a few moments a young man walked over to me and sat down. "Hey, brother, shoot pool?" he said. I nodded. We rose, walked to the man in the shadows, and paid him twenty-five cents each. "Don't tell my boss that I'm in here having a good time when I should be out working," I said. He did not reply.

We took cues from the rack and moved to the second table.

I saw a cube of blue chalk dangling on a string from the ceiling and went over to chalk my cue tip. This was my first game of pool, so the chalk didn't help much. My opponent, however, did not seem to savor the prospect of victory. When we finished, he nodded at the door. I walked out, he followed. On the sidewalk, now, I turned to face him. "I need a job, man," he said. "I gotta buy my clothes back out of the cleaners."

As we continued to talk, I learned his name and that he had been jailed for a shooting, even though (he said) he had been nowhere near Fulton at the time. To my surprise, however, he was not bitter about jail. "That jail," Sammy Fulkes said, "cleaned me out—the drugs."

In jail Sammy had gotten up early and divided his time between lifting weights and reading the Bible. He freed himself from drugs. Now he planned to rent an apartment and move in with his girl friend. Nothing could hold him back. "My record is clean," said Sammy. "No convictions."

Sammy's assertion of his bright prospects put me on guard. I sensed his fear. If he was to shore up his life, he seemed to think, he must act quickly. A few days later he joined his mother's church, a Holiness sect, and got saved. Look what the church had done for his mother.

In her youth, Minnie Fulkes gambled, drank, and entertained the men. As she told me later, "I was on the street, doin' my thing." She subsisted on welfare and "love money," while her children wandered about, malnourished and ill-clothed. When neighbors reported her to the city, she was convicted of neglect and sent to the work farm. Her children were given to foster parents. Prison changes a person. Minnie lost her youth. After her return to Fulton, she no longer drank, gambled, or entertained. She grieved for her lost children. "I had got tired of the way I was livin'," she told me later. "I wanted my soul to be right."

After joining the church and being saved, Minnie got her boys back, but not her girls. Perhaps Sammy, with the "prayers of the saints" behind him and a generous measure of divine intervention, could transform his life as his mother had her own.

Sammy knew that he would end up in prison for certain if he was unable to avoid the pool hall or in some way nullify its effect upon him. The young habitués of the pool hall cultivated a contempt for the workaday world and practiced a far easier means of obtaining money than working at a job. Sammy understood the way the pool hall had clouded his intentions in the past, dispelled his finer impulses. "Accept one of the two," his mother told him. "Accept the devil or accept God." He vowed to accept God.

Sammy's girl friend attended high school during the day. The church was open only on Sundays, except for an occasional missionary meeting or revival. The number of hours he could spend with his mother at any one time was limited. Sammy was alone. All the others his age who were headed for a stable, working-class life were in school, preparing themselves for work by mastering the simpler challenge of academics. Sammy had been on the street for six years. And he had no one to be with who was not also on the street.

Sammy returned to the pool hall, but he determined that he would not allow his new life to be tarnished by its atmosphere. He told his "stick partners" that he, as a "sanctified," was going to heaven, they were going to hell. They chased him and shot at him with their guns.

Sammy knew he needed a job, fast. He had worked as casual labor at the guano factory, Miller Manufacturing, the cement company, and Deep Water Terminal. The pay was low, the work hard. Sammy quit because he couldn't stand the regularity, the discipline. He was always forcing himself to be at work, pushing himself, afraid of the consequences of not working. His jobs never felt natural, assured, inevitable.

Sammy asked me to help him find work. I investigated several jobs programs, but nothing was doing. Food stamps and public assistance were easy to get for qualified people. But not jobs. I borrowed the Bethlehem Center's station wagon and drove Sammy and Grunt Curtis uptown to apply for jobs with the Virginia Employment Commission. Innocently enough, Sammy referred to it as the Unemployment Commission. Knowing that their chances of being called to work were so slim as to be non-existent, Sammy and Grunt determined to enjoy the ride as an end in itself. They tuned the radio to a soul station, bounced on the seats in time to the music, shouted, "Hey, Jack!" at everyone they thought they recognized.

On the return trip they convinced me to detour through Church Hill, and I became lost. They directed me along the endless curving streets of the projects. All the buildings looked alike. I slowed, at their request, so they could talk to friends. Riding in a car was status. If the car was borrowed, the driver enlisted against his better judgment, still it was better than waiting for the day when they had jobs and cars of their own. Would that day ever come?

Later Sammy found a job washing dishes in a fast-food restaurant in a suburban shopping mall. The pay was low, the white proprietor was cool toward him, and it took an hour and a half to get to work on the bus each day. But still, it was a job.

Sammy Fulkes lacked a parent or grandparent who had been a bearer of talent or good fortune. Sammy was raised among women, as was his mother. It is not accurate to say that he came from a broken family, for his family, so far as anyone knew, had never been unbroken. Sammy's grandmother had been raised in an orphanage uptown and did not know where she was born or the name of her father, mother, or any other relatives. When she was old enough to support herself she rented a flat in Fulton, found a job with a tobacco factory, and started a family. She never married, but, for the most part, she was able to work and support her family without relying on welfare. Sammy's mother courted a number of different men when she was young, but no one individual for any length of time. Her children had different fathers. Sammy's father died when Sammy was two years old.

Sammy's girl friend was completing her senior year of high

school. Sammy was proud of her and referred to her as his wife, although nothing official had taken place between them. She was bright and articulate. I had difficulty understanding why she was attracted to Sammy, an illiterate who was dull and unexpressive even when his intentions were of the best. I felt differently about her career plans than about his. She seemed to be aiming at the possible. Upon graduation she intended to train for a job as a nurse's aide. She would work at the Medical College of Virginia uptown. She had stayed within the school system for eleven years, and the job of nurse's aide was within her grasp. But Sammy had few, if any, successes upon which to build. He was trying to make it in the world with a single leap.

Several weeks after his release Sammy invited me to attend a meeting at his church. This was to be the crescendo of a week-long revival. And before the meeting closed, I was to learn, the hat would be passed again and again, its contents emptied upon the table in front, until enough money was raised to compensate the preacher for his week's effort. We met in the basement of the enormous brick building with a high bell tower. At one time, staid white Baptists had owned this place. Now the congregation was poor, black, and ecstatic. They called it "Love Temple."

By eight-thirty the low-ceilinged room was crowded. Men, women, and children stood close, sang, and clapped. Reverend Love shouted out prayers. A small woman closed her eyes and recited dozens of psalms. A dark-skinned woman at the piano sang and played while everyone listened. She sang from her guts, her whole body shaking. Reverend Love led us in singing prayers, then asked a deacon to lead us. After a few measures, he asked me to lead. The music never stopped playing, I had to come in on cue. I shouted a line, then waited for the congregation to respond before shouting another:

Lord, we know we haven't acted as we should;
Lord, Lord; Hallelujah.
We've been playing with fire and gotten burned;
Oh Lord, yes Lord.

We've strayed from the flock and gotten lost;
Lord, Lord; Hallelujah.
Help us now to find our way back home.
Help us Lord; Help us.

At last we got down on our knees on the unpainted concrete floor and, in response to Reverend Love's declamations, shouted out our desire to do right, to leave behind us sin of every kind. I could hear Sammy yelling above us all, "Yes, Lord, Yes Lord, Yes!"

Four months later Sammy Fulkes was jailed for breaking and entering. After several months' incarceration he was tried, convicted, and given a suspended sentence. Sammy was jubilant. He told me how jail had put his life in order again. Now he would find a steady job, marry his girl friend, attend church, lead the kind of life he had been attempting to lead all along.

He told me how he had lost his job washing dishes at the fast-food place, had begun to take drugs again, and made raids on Church Hill to support his habit. Once the police surprised Sammy and his crime partners. They ran and were caught, but he crawled under a porch and fitted himself into the hollows of the ground. The police stamped around on the boards above him but never suspected his presence.

Two months later I saw Sammy's girl friend. There were lines in her face and a glazed look, as though she had aged thirty years in a few weeks' time. I asked for Sammy at the pool hall. "He's not here," said a man called Pieface. "You lookin' for a woman?" Sammy had gotten his girl friend hooked on drugs and had become her pimp. Nine months later she gave birth to a child, not necessarily Sammy's. By now her thoughts of becoming a nurse's aide were lost. She lived in the basement of Sammy's mother's house, received welfare for the child, and worked as a whore to support Sammy.

Two months later Sammy was arrested again for breaking and entering. He was convicted, sentenced to ten years, and transported to Southampton Farms, the low-security prison where first offenders are kept. It is located in the countryside of Southampton County, a few miles from the North Carolina line. During slavery times this area was called the Black Belt. Nat Turner's slave insurrection took place only a few miles away. After a month Sammy got in trouble for fighting and was sent to road camp in Mecklenburg County. Each day he worked with a gang of men cutting brush and weeds alongside the highways. Standing above them as they worked was a guard who carried a shotgun.

I do not know what else Sammy did in prison. But I visited another Fulton man in prison who told me that it was common for young black men like Sammy who had never been away from Richmond before to act tough during the day but at night to pull Bibles from beneath their pillows, cry quietly, and beg God to carry them back home. In my imagination I see Sammy as one of these homesick young men.

Grunt Curtis, who pulled the trigger the evening they shot the white man in the back, was more fortunate about prison than Sammy. He went to jail a few times but was never sent up. Grunt could see where he was headed, however, and about the time Sammy was imprisoned he left for New York to start a new life. Several years later I talked to Minnie Fulkes and learned that Grunt Curtis was dead. He had been cut and then shot dead on the streets of New York. "You try to live fast in that big city, try to be slicker than that big city, you get bumped off quick," Minnie said.

Grunt Curtis had been drawn into the vortex of New York street life as certainly as he had been drawn into Fulton's street life. Sammy suffered in prison, but he was alive, still alive.

For the most part Fulton's street youth did no physical harm to the neighborhood's old aristocrats or to their sons and daughters of the fourth generation. The damage they inflicted on the old ideals had more to do with public perceptions. The crimes committed in Fulton received ample news coverage. Everyone in town had heard about the ax murder on Denny, the ski-mask murder on Orleans, the drug murder in the alley behind the Black Spot Laundry. The newspapers and television news gave the impression that Fulton was a zone of instant death. After I moved out of Fulton I stayed for a month in a white neighborhood on the hill above. A white coed from the suburbs was supposed to drive over and give me a lift to a church function, but her mother wouldn't let her go anywhere near Fulton, even at noon. Apparently her reasoning was, "You go down there, you liable to lose your virtue. When you get done with that you'll probably lose your life too." Street youth gave this neighborhood a bad image.

Patience Gromes and her contemporaries had long since relinquished leadership of Fulton to middle-aged sons and daughters, people like Jacob Pinckney and Betty Norton. Upon this younger generation fell the burden of publicly defending their world against evil in general and the transgressions of the pool hall crowd in particular. It irritated them that the quiet, industrious lives of most Fulton residents were forgotten, whereas recent crimes captured the public imagination.

Jacob Pinckney, for example, felt misunderstood and misrepresented as a Fultonian. Pinckney was a short, balding man in his forties who carried mail for the post office. A patriot and an optimist, he was quick to declare his love of God, country, and the Bethlehem Center. He was a member of the center's board and, as a foot soldier during civil rights, distinguished himself for loyalty and steadfast effort. Pinckney could have supported a house in a better neighborhood but chose to stay in Fulton and ride the bus to work each day. So it is not surprising that he found himself pitted against recent arrivals who did not understand the old ideals. He railed against these outsiders and their children, who were, to his way of thinking, the cause of Fulton's problems.

Pinckney was not stupid, but for some reason he would never admit that poverty and crime were part of Fulton. Since these conditions were my reason for coming here, I had a hard time talking to him without becoming irritated at what I then regarded as his denseness. When I brought up the subject of crime in Fulton, he grew angry and attempted to place the incident in its proper context, which, to his way of thinking, was outside Fulton—never mind that it occurred at the intersection of Fulton's two main streets, Louisiana and Williamsburg. Strangely, Pinckney was far more concerned to uphold the reputation of his neighborhood than to protect himself or his family from crime. The criminal acts of Sammy Fulkes and his companions were not a problem in his eyes, but the bad press generated by these crimes was a grievous aggravation.

I had difficulty understanding Jacob Pinckney. What did it matter if white people uptown had the wrong idea about Fulton? For my part, I would have been disappointed if there had been no crime in Fulton. Wasn't Fulton a skirmish in the war on poverty? Crime was a reality of black, inner-city, poverty culture. It was a problem to be solved.

My attitude toward crime in Fulton was much closer to that of Fulton's young men and women than to that of their parents. Willy Cozart, poet laureate of the pool hall, regarded the involvement of Fulton's youth with drugs, crime, and prison as all part of the "Black Experience." This was life in the ghetto. Crime and drugs were not to be denied, overlooked, or excluded when one characterized Fulton. To the contrary, they were touchstones, central elements that structured the random phenomena of life in Fulton. Crime and drugs were central, for they linked Fulton to black communities all over the country.

During my second year in Fulton the athletic coach of the Bethlehem Center was fired, and Willy Cozart was hired, not as a coach precisely, but as a liaison with Fulton's youth. The move was controversial because the coach had worked here for twenty years and was on excellent terms with Jacob Pinckney and other members of the Bethlehem Center board. When the coach's "retirement" was announced at a board meeting, he argued bitterly that his many years' service were being poorly repaid. When he finished his remarks, Jacob Pinckney rose to speak. As a man, Pinckney took pains to preserve the old ideal of public dignity and seldom expressed his convictions in public. On this occasion he chose the most passive language imaginable to express what, for him, was a violent protest. "I really think we are making a mistake," he said.

Fulton residents respected the coach as an upstanding man, a good example for their children. He was their age and spoke their language. They could not say the same for Willy Cozart. Although Willy had lettered in four sports in high school (one had to respect him for that), he had returned home from the navy with heroin in his blood. Supposedly he outgrew his drug habit and took up philosophy in its stead, but his detractors doubted that this qualified him to guide their children.

For his part, Willy Cozart rallied the older youth and brought an element of street life into the Bethlehem Center, perhaps allowing young men to participate in the culture of their generation without being directly subject to its more destructive elements. He encouraged his teenagers to express themselves artistically. At one time, I imagine, the Bethlehem Center had been decorated with drawings of Jesus and his disciples. But now its walls were covered with posters warning about the dangers of drugs, yet in effect celebrating the mystic governance of King Heroin over life in the ghetto.

Betty Norton, who belonged to the same church as Jacob Pinckney, became angry when she heard anyone refer to Fulton as a ghetto. "That ghetto stuff," she said, "is an insult." Betty Norton was a dedicated mother, and her husband made good wages working in a furniture warehouse uptown. Occasionally Betty and several other black women from Fulton served as domestics at the Jewish Community Center. The Jewish women for whom they worked lived in modern houses in the suburbs. Betty felt that she, too, would like to live in the suburbs. Until that day came, however, she would continue to find in Fulton a neighborhood that was just as good as suburban neighborhoods. Although some of Fulton's houses were dilapidated, some of its residents coarse, Betty considered these to be minor defects and bridled at the tendency of the young to enlarge these instances into a definition of the whole.

Still, Betty had to admit that it was getting harder to raise children in Fulton. There always had been unsavory people living here, but in the past they had kept to themselves. Now they were becoming more aggressive, more dangerous. And the city was little help. The city schools, for example, were terrible.

Betty Norton feared that she would lose her son Bubba through the incompetence of the city schools and the influence of the pool hall. Bubba always had received good marks for studies and conduct. Then he entered East End Middle School and developed a personality conflict with the principal. Bubba cultivated the hostile attitude that was then fashionable among his peers. The middle-aged black man who was principal took this attitude as an affront: "You get some respect," he said, "or you leave." Bubba left.

Each morning Bubba got on the school bus, rode to East End, then walked back to Fulton. Why should he honor the principal of East End with his presence? His mother thought he was in school, but actually he was "hanging on the streets," frequenting the pool hall, learning indefinable things from Willy Cozart. The principal expelled Bubba and neglected to notify his mother. If she had known of his absences she would have put him back on the right track, fast. If she had known of his expulsion, she would have taken him back to school the next morning and had him readmitted. As it was, Betty got a telephone call from the city, but it was not the principal's office calling.

That morning Bubba had jumped into someone else's car and driven away. The owner called the cops, who radioed to a squad car in the East End. Instead of chasing Bubba, the police officer parked his car at the intersection of Broad Street and Twenty Seventh on Church Hill. It is a truism among Richmond police that a car stolen in Fulton invariably is driven through this intersection. Fifteen minutes later Bubba drove past. Next thing he knew, he was sitting in lockup.

Bubba was under eighteen and thus went to reform school instead of prison. His mother worried that this was the first step, that her son would spend the rest of his life in and out of prison. She felt thwarted by the spirit of the times. "When I was coming up," she said, "children from good families didn't do like this."

Betty got angry at the mention of Willy Cozart and his conception of Fulton as the ghetto. It was that way of thinking, she reasoned, that had put her child in reform school. In the old days a mother had help. But how could Betty fight the bureaucrats of the city school system? How could she fight the pool hall and the likes of Willy Cozart?

Betty Norton did not feel that Fulton itself was responsible for the plight of her son. This neighborhood always had been a sanctuary from the evils of the world. Fulton was just as solid as ever, to her way of thinking, but its boundaries were shrinking and the influence of the city and the pool hall was growing. Beyond the boundaries of the present neighborhood, in the space where Fulton's tight family structure once had been, the impersonal, structuring institutions of court, jail, and prison were now appearing. It was the city world that was threatening her son. The floating youth culture of the pool hall was, to Betty Norton, in collaboration with the city. It was like the dark heart of the city world, stealing Fulton's children from their families, luring them from the close influence of their parents and Sunday School teachers. As far as Betty Norton was concerned, crimes like that committed by Sammy Fulkes and Grunt Curtis did not take place in Fulton but in a city realm beyond Fulton's boundaries.

The tendency of Jacob Pinckney and Betty Norton to deny that crime was part of Fulton is somewhat easier to understand when we consider that many offenses could be traced to families who had moved here in relatively recent times. If a crime did not involve these newcomers, it was bound to involve their friends, who, as Jacob Pinckney might have put it, came to Fulton whenever they wanted to shoot someone, get shot, or burglarize a store. Jacob did not consider these people to be genuine Fultonians. If Betty Norton judged the members of the pool hall crowd to be in collaboration with the city government, I am sure it was news to Sammy Fulkes and Grunt Curtis, who thought of cops as enemies. Equally strange, Fulton's leaders regarded people like Minnie Fulkes and Matte Curtis as allies of the pool hall crowd.

Sammy Fulkes belonged to one social group in Fulton, his mother belonged to another. Sammy and his "stick partners" were in their late teens or early twenties, preferred weed to hootch, and were violent in a way that affected those outside their circle. Moreover Sammy and his friends took hard drugs that made them immune to normal social restraints. "If you have a child on drugs and they need some money," Sammy's mother told me later, "they'll kill you to get that money. They don't care who they kill. You go in the hospital, and they all busted up and messed up and crazy. See, the dope done get them like that."

Matte Curtis and Minnie Fulkes associated with a crowd who gambled, drank, and fought, but only among themselves. They did not use heroin. According to Minnie Fulkes, gambling disputes had earned Fulton the name Death Valley long before her time. Members of Fulton's traditional underclass were one step removed from the youths who were causing trouble in Fulton. And Minnie Fulkes was two steps removed. For, as a "sanctified," Minnie had severed her ties with the crowd on the street. They were now repugnant to her, as were pushy, loudmouthed women like Matte Curtis. "As far as Matte Curtis," Minnie said, "I don't talk to Matte Curtis for anything."

Fulton's first citizens, however, were unimpressed by these nuances when defending their neighborhood from a white public that in turn did not distinguish between law-abiding Fulton residents and the neighborhood's criminal element. Fulton's leaders did not hesitate to lump together the pool hall crowd and this larger, older, and more passive underclass. Jacob Pinckney regarded them one and all as outsiders, riffraff.

In Pinckney's view, Fulton's rough folk were plunderers who did nothing to build up the neighborhood. They didn't help with voting drives anymore or serve at the Bethlehem Center, the Baptist Center, or even the RCAP Center. All they ever did was give Fulton a bad name, Pinckney seemed to think. Matte Curtis and her associates did not consider themselves to be plunderers, but this point counted for little with Pinckney.

I can sympathize with Jacob Pinckney to some extent. He tried to lead an honorable life but could never achieve due recognition when his neighborhood was held in such low esteem. Fulton's bad name in the media only reflected a deeper public perception. I expected white residents of Richmond to feel disgust toward Fulton, but I was surprised to learn that black residents regarded Fulton with far greater scorn. Blacks from Jackson Ward, Richmond's central district and its largest black neighborhood, always had looked down on Fulton.

In the past such contempt had been parried by Fulton residents with a minimum of agitation or ill feeling, for they possessed a sense of their own worth. But something had changed. It was as though Fulton residents had lost their mental self-sufficiency and now depended upon the good opinion of outsiders for their own peace of mind. A black middle class was forming in Richmond. And I suspect that this wider community was supplanting Fulton society as the arbiter of success. How could Jacob Pinckney succeed in life when the crimes of Fulton youth were getting such play in the media?

Once, when visiting Richmond's public library, I noticed that the check-out clerk, according to her nameplate, was a Mrs. Arrington. I inquired and learned that she was a daughter-in-law of Thomas Arrington, a Fulton resident and friend of Patience Gromes. She lived on Hungary Road, one of Richmond's most exclusive black suburbs. I told her that I worked in Fulton and knew her husband's family. "*I've* never lived in Fulton," she said.

By the late sixties, Fulton's first families and its new poor were barely on speaking terms, and neither group was talking to street youth. The old ideals were merely given lip service by most residents. Still, there was one subject on which all Fultonians could agree: the City of Richmond was out to get them.

Fulton residents did not distinguish the City of Richmond from other government entities run by white people uptown who, according to local wisdom, preferred to keep black men and women under their thumbs. Fulton folk did not like the police, the courts, the schools, the water department, the sanitation department, the power company, the employment commission, or the state medical college, not to mention city welfare workers, food stamp technicians, health inspectors, public housing administrators, and dog catchers.

Traditionally Fulton residents had dealt with the city by keeping it at a distance. They fulfilled their obligations to the city as they did to the companies that employed them. They paid their taxes, mortgage payments, water, gas, and light bills on time, appeared punctually at work, spoke respectfully to the policeman who walked the beat. Yet, as far as possible, they excluded the institutions of the city from their lives.

The city world did provide openings for blacks in the illegal professions, and invariably proprietors of illegal business establishments found themselves in an alliance with the police. But this example hardly encouraged God-fearing folk. What little contact they had had with the city led them to suspect that it would make an unreliable partner. They could accept the idea that the white people who controlled the political machine wanted to keep the highest paying jobs, the best schools, the most modern housing for themselves. But what if there was more than enough to go around? In this case, they argued, the city would destroy something of value rather than let it fall into black hands. The Nicholson Street School was an early example.

Before World War I, Fulton's white children attended school in a modern, two-story building on Nicholson Street. Several years after the war, however, Robert Fulton School was built on the hill above Fulton to serve white families, formerly Fulton residents, who lived there. The old school was closed, used for storage for a number of years, then demolished. The land never was put to any use.

Discussion among black parents grew emotional. The Nicholson Street School was a solid brick building with steam heat, far more up to date than the converted Irish saloon where black children attended school or, for that matter, than the narrow houses where Fulton's black residents lived. How would it have hurt the city to give black children a decent school?

The white people of Fulton also felt short-changed by the city, which had annexed Fulton after the Civil War to raise money for the rebuilding of the downtown and, in the opinion of white merchants on Williamsburg Avenue, had been milking the East End ever since. Fulton's black residents nevertheless thought themselves singled out because of their race. They did not understand the workings of bureaucracies, were unable to distinguish conscious policy from casual blunder, and felt that the motives behind city actions were constantly concealed. They judged the city as though it were a single person, when in fact it was different people who held varying degrees of power on different issues at different times. When the city promised one thing, then did another, Fulton residents judged it to be mean, low-spirited, dishonest: in short, the kind of person they would not want to have for a neighbor. To them, race prejudice provided a compelling explanation for the workings of city government and schools.

Whether from ignorance or from wisdom, Fulton residents developed a conspiracy theory to explain the actions of city government. To their way of thinking the city was inherently less predictable and more easily influenced by racial motives than were companies such as the C&O Railroad that did not hide their discrimination in the allotment of skilled jobs but nevertheless worked largely "according to the business." Fulton residents could accept the explanation that it was a coal strike in the hills, for example, that caused them to be laid off at the railroad, whereas similarly objective explanations in regard to city layoffs would have been regarded as a cover for the real—that is, the political and racial—motives.

As the conspiracy theory evolved, it received encouragement from the few bits of second-hand evidence that found their way

into Fulton. One story came from Billy Dismith, the barber who
faithfully shaved and clipped members of Richmond's white elite
but did not consider it a breach of professional ethics to repeat
the inside information he gleaned from their conversation. One
day the mayor purportedly told Billy, "If I had my way, I'd fire
all the damn niggers on the city payroll."

Almost any city action that touched Fulton fueled the conspiracy theory, for the city did not trouble itself to explain the
reasoning behind its actions, and blacks who were voluble in
their private attacks on the city seldom directed their questions
to city officials themselves. Following World War II, Fulton residents began communicating directly with city officials, and, although the city proved more responsive than in the twenties, it
was too little, too late as far as Fulton residents were concerned.
They commonly cited two examples of the city's continuing in-
transigence: the fight between Snort and the policeman, and the
nonexistent traffic light at Williamsburg and Louisiana.

Although Snort was widely feared in Fulton as a bully and
tough guy, he also was known in the fifties as the neighborhood's
protector. Whenever the thugs from Church Hill pulled a raid,
everyone on the street called for Snort. Analiza Foster illustrated
the ambivalence people felt about her son. She wished he would
settle down, get married, and quit associating with bootleggers
like Waddy and Nell Crowder. Nevertheless, if someone was
doing her wrong, Analiza did not hesitate to say, "Snort will
beat helloutchyou if you keep on like that."

One evening Snort and some friends were rolling dice on the
corner by Smitty's Grill when a policeman walking his beat asked
them to move. Snort's friends walked away, but Snort went into
Smitty's, sat down at the counter, and ordered a beer. The policeman followed Snort inside.

"Don't buy anything," said the cop.

"I can spend my money any way I want," Snort replied.

"Don't sell him that beer."

"I have a license to sell my beer, and he's not drunk," said
the bartender.

The policeman went out the door and stood beside the granite stone that served as a step. Snort finished his beer, walked out, and hit the cop in the face. The two were rolling on the sidewalk when Snort's friends returned, pulled them apart, and called an ambulance for the policeman.

Snort went to court, but the judge did not fine him because he considered it a grudge fight. To the people of Fulton, however, this fight was an incident of more than personal consequence. They identified the policeman as the one who had shot and killed Doc Edwards's son.

A year or two earlier, Snort had been uptown in Jackson Ward when he saw Doc's son running down Second past the pool rooms and restaurants. Edwards crossed Clay and ran toward an overgrown lot beside a Chinese laundry. The policeman shouted at him to halt, then drew his weapon and fired. Snort went to the morgue to identify the body and returned to Fulton to tell Doc and his wife what had happened. Within an hour everyone in Fulton knew that a man from their neighborhood had died. No one ever found out why the policeman shot. As one woman put it, "The city just smothered the whole thing up."

When I first heard about the attempts of Alford Stirling, Fulton's civil rights leader, to get a stoplight installed at Fulton's main intersection I thought this matter an entirely different order of grievance from the complaint about the shooting of Doc Edwards's son. But later, when I learned the consequences of the city's failure to install this stoplight, I realized that I had been wrong. Alford Stirling had displayed a flair for bringing such city favors as street lights, sewer maintenance crews, and the street cleaning machine to Fulton. His supporters expected yet another victory when Stirling declared his intention to have the city install a stop light at the intersection of Louisiana and Williamsburg. As the city's arterial to the airport and to the growing residential area of Montrose Heights, Williamsburg Avenue carried a steady stream of traffic traveling at high speed. How were the elderly of Rocketts to cross the avenue on their trek to Lumpkin's Supermarket? There had been close calls. On a Friday evening one elderly woman got stranded for several hours on the wrong side of Williamsburg Avenue.

Alford Stirling and Jacob Pinckney met with city officials, explained their concerns, and received polite but evasive answers. With the help of white church groups they documented the traffic flow at signaled intersections in white neighborhoods and found them far below that of Williamsburg Avenue. They met again and again with city officials, presented the facts, made their arguments, and went back home. All the city ever gave them was the runaround. The interest of Fulton residents in getting a traffic signal died down. Then an elderly woman trying to cross Williamsburg Avenue at rush hour was hit by a car and killed. Alford Stirling held more meetings with the city fathers, but nothing ever came of it.

Fulton residents privately accused the city of reckless disregard for the life and safety of Fulton's black residents. What could it be, they asked themselves, but some racist conspiracy that motivated the city to gun down a man for "no reason at all" (as a woman from Rocketts put it) or to withhold a traffic signal from people who needed it, had done their homework, and presented their requests in a civil manner?

Patience Gromes and her friends knew that nothing was more foolish than to trust the city. Look what happened to Della Harris, a young woman who lived on Denny. She had been taking treatment at the Medical College of Virginia, where the doctors told her that it was scientifically impossible for her to get pregnant because of her condition. When Della was a child her grandmother had taught her that sin carries penalties and that messing around is a sin. But Della listened instead to her doctors. Next thing she knew there was an uncomfortable swelling around her midriff. Although the doctors were entirely puzzled as to the cause, the grandmothers of Fulton clucked knowingly. A month before Della gave birth, the doctors conceded that, yes, the impossible had come to pass. So much for Della's college education.

One of Analiza Foster's sons had taken the city at its word,

and look what happened to him. He held a good paying construction job when he heard about getting training and work as
a mechanic through a jobs program at the employment commission. The administrator told him that if he wanted to get on,
show up Monday morning at eight sharp. So he quit his construction job, showed up at eight sharp, and the man had him
fill out an application, then go home. "Thanks for dropping in,"
he said. "I'll call you for an interview when your name comes
up." He never called. Analiza's son subsisted on his mother's
food-stamp allotment while he looked for another construction
job.

In the fifties, according to Billy Dismith and other residents,
the local newspaper published aerial photos of Fulton and designated it as a prime target for urban renewal. In 1964 the city
published a master plan that recommended the clearance of
"slums in potential industrial areas." Although this document
did not mention Fulton by name, the implications were clear.
Fulton was the worst slum in town, and it occupied a prime
industrial site: close to the river, the railroad, and the airport.
The city did not provide the same level of services to Fulton as
to more modern neighborhoods. Presumably city officials were
putting the money where they felt it would do the most good.
But the people of Fulton smelled a conspiracy. They accused the
city of withdrawing services to hasten their neighborhood's decline. How else, they argued, can the city justify taking all of
Fulton for industry?

In 1965, at the city's request, Alford Stirling served as Fulton's
representative on a city-wide advisory group that reviewed plans
for demolishing, rehabilitating, or conserving housing in each
part of town. He learned that gobs of federal dollars were coming
down from Washington under new housing legislation admin-
istered by The Department for Housing and Urban Development
(HUD). At monthly meetings of the Fulton Improvement Association he described this largess, but it seemed abstract and
improbable to most. Jacob Pinckney, however, could see possi-

bilities. He and Stirling spent late nights figuring out how Fulton could snag some of this loose federal money.

The following year the city published the "Community Renewal Program," which labeled Fulton a "predominantly blighted area requiring renewal" and suggested that the section of Fulton nearest the river be converted from "residential to industrial use by public action." The Fulton Improvement Association countered by formally requesting city and federal help in restoring Fulton as a *residential* community.

In 1967 the housing authority, with the help of city sanitarians, conducted a door-to-door survey as a preliminary to urban renewal. Fulton residents politely answered the questions the surveyors asked. Still, they were apprehensive. To them, urban renewal seemed unlike the companies and of a type with the city schools, police, water company, welfare office, state employment commission, and Medical College of Virginia—except that the housing authority was worse because, in their opinion, it focused all the ineptitudes and prejudices inherent in the city on the objects they most dearly cherished: their houses.

The urban renewal survey made Fulton folk nervous. Renewal was coming, coming strong. No one family was certain how they would be affected, but most feared the worst. They knew they would have to fight, or at least dodge. The old woman crossing Williamsburg Avenue had been unable to dodge. If Fulton residents submitted to urban renewal where would they end up? Dead on the road like that woman?

6

THE AD HOC COMMITTEE
March 1968

URBAN RENEWAL came to Fulton in March 1968.

In the controversy that followed, Fulton's old order lost its power to govern. It fell victim to events that were swift, unwitting, and irrevocable. In a few days' time the labor of three generations came crashing down. Everyone in Fulton could feel the impact but no one could see what had happened: that which had fallen was too large, and they were too close. No one could see because fear and anger clouded the scene like smoke filling the streets of a burning city. Urban renewal was the instrument, the means, if not in the deepest sense the cause: urban renewal, at once pointed and vague, provided both the death blow and the obscuring cloud.

If the events of March 1968 happened quickly, they nevertheless had been years in the making. The ideals that men and women like Patience Gromes brought from the country had been steadily losing authority since World War II, weakening until a sudden realignment became possible. This shift took the form of a power struggle that pitted traditional civil-rights leaders against insurgents with ties to the war on poverty. Each side had an institutional ally. The civil-rights leaders made common cause with the Bethlehem Center, the insurgents with Fulton's federally funded RCAP Center. This meant that Bethlehem Center employees such as myself would be expected to boost our faction in any public or private forum where we had a chance to speak, while RCAP employees would boost their faction. Each side had its own neighborhood organization. Alford Stirling and Jacob Pinckney were leaders of the Fulton Improvement Association. The insurgents formed a splinter group, ostensibly a committee of the improvement association, which they called the Ad Hoc Committee.

At this time the Fulton Improvement Association and Alford Stirling were official representatives of the neighborhood in the eyes of the housing authority. Bureaucrats in the authority's cinderblock offices uptown had scratched Stirling's name on their obscure forms to bring the situation into conformance with federal law. These particular forms happened to be worth millions of dollars. The federal government required housing authorities to prove that the citizens of a target neighborhood participated in devising a renewal plan and approved the plan. Only then would the feds send money gushing down from Washington. This suggested that the quickest way for citizens to stop a renewal program was to refuse to meet with the housing authority, thereby denying them an official neighborhood group and an official leader to scratch onto their golden forms. And, predictably, one of the key arguments of the insurgents was that Stirling, simply by meeting with the housing authority, had opened up Uncle Sam's checkbook to pay for the bulldozers and wrecking crews that would destroy Fulton.

The insurgents wanted to stop the housing authority cold. If that was not possible they would just as soon have Stirling's name crossed off the federal form and one of their own names written in its place. One insurgent in particular longed for such recognition. His name was Daniel Brady.

Daniel Brady was born in 1916 to a family that was decent though poor. His parents had come in from the country about the same time as Patience Gromes (his mother arrived in 1898 from Mecklenburg County, his father came later from Charles City County), but they had a difficult time establishing themselves. Danny's mother sent her children to church and school, his father worked day-long at the brickyard for a pittance. They saved enough for a down payment on a small house near Gillies Creek and the swamp, but each month they struggled to pay on the mortgage. Whenever it rained or grew cold, the brickyard laid off. Danny's father looked for work, waited, looked again. He did not seem to be making progress. At last he found a better paying job at the stem factory. His wife was expecting another child now. His health began to deteriorate. Three weeks before she gave birth, he died.

Danny's older sister took a job at a tobacco factory and helped to support them until she married and moved out. His mother found a job at the cedar works, but her four dollars a week could not support them. Later she found a better job at the stem factory. They did not starve, did not give up their house, but never had quite enough to cover necessities. Danny's mother worried and seemed to grow weaker every month. Her health was poor, but she didn't dare miss work. There was no one to look after Danny, who didn't get along with his teachers, played hooky, and was sent to reform school for his efforts. When Danny was thirteen, his older sister took him out of reform school one day to attend his mother's funeral.

By 1936 Danny Brady was living uptown, working at a newsstand, and helping to support his younger sister who lived with their aunt in Fulton. Sometimes he surprised his sister with luxurious thin hose for sixty-nine cents from Levine's or with $9.95 Palizzo shoes from Selden's. His sister loved him, was proud of her fine clothes, and never wondered where the money came from. Before the year was over, she found out.

Danny Brady held up a streetcar on Church Hill. The driver pulled a gun, Danny ran and was shot. He lay for weeks in St. Philips Hospital, the black hospital uptown, an armed guard at his door. Each afternoon his sister visited and read the Bible to him. She did not approve of his crime, she told me later, but felt she had to stick with him. "Whatever happens," she told him, "I am your sister, you are my brother." Danny was twenty years old.

Danny Brady's family was not the first to break under the strain of trying to earn a living in the city. Even though blacks looked after one another, city life was still less forgiving than country life. Times were hard, families were destroyed, children became criminals. Yet Danny's sister could not accept the notion that Danny had no control over his fate. "If you pray and pray earnestly," she told him, "the Lord will help you."

Danny served three years in prison before he was paroled and took a job as a salesman at William Clothiers in Seventeenth Street Bottom. He did not want to return to prison, for he knew that he had twenty years "waiting for him at the gate," in addition to the term for any new offense. As the years passed, he didn't seem to be getting anywhere. On weekends he drank and caroused with friends. One night they broke into a gas station and emptied the cash drawer. Brady was so drunk that he passed out while they were counting the loot. His crime partners left him sleeping in the office chair, his share of their take stuffed into a pocket. When Danny came to, he was sitting in the city lockup.

Later, witnesses to robberies of a High's Ice Cream store and a Safeway picked him out of a lineup. They said he had carried a weapon, but his sister insists that he never owned a knife or a gun. "He put his hand in his coat pocket," she explained to me later, "pointed his finger at them, and yelled 'This is a stickup.'" It was 1950, and Brady returned to prison on multiple charges of armed robbery. He was sentenced to forty years for his most recent crimes, and, as a repeat offender, received another twenty at the gate.

Once again Brady took up residence in Spring Street prison. The high walls and guard towers provided a grim welcome to his sister when she came to visit every other Sunday. By now Brady's schoolmates from Fulton had married and were raising families. Some were making down payments on houses of their own. Many joined the military, saw the world, and when they returned par-

ticipated in the great cause of their time, the civil rights movement. They took jobs formerly reserved for whites, sat anywhere
they chose on the transit bus, and sent their children to integrated
high schools. But not Brady. He was thirty-four years old when
he entered prison for the second time and was spending the most
important years of his life there. His contemporaries were making
names for themselves in Fulton, but his name had nearly dropped
from neighborhood memory.

Daniel Brady had been in prison five years when Alford Stirling was elected president of Fulton's civil rights group. Although
neither of them realized it at the time, Brady and Stirling were
destined to become adversaries. They would meet in March 1968.

Alford Stirling was born and raised in the country east of Rocky
Mount, North Carolina. He graduated from high school and
joined the army in 1944, served in Berlin during the Berlin crisis,
and, after leaving the army, settled in Richmond.

Stirling was the son of a sharecropper and had little money.
Unlike others who moved into Fulton following World War II,
however, his family had not always been poor. In the years since
slavery they had acquired 600 acres of farmland, then lost it for
taxes in the Depression. Like Patience Gromes forty years earlier,
Alford Stirling came to Fulton with a self-assurance that promised
success.

Four years after arriving, Stirling was elected president of Fulton's PTA, a position of considerable prestige that he would hold
for seven years. Two years later, in 1955, the Montgomery bus
boycott stirred members of Fulton's Firedome Social Club to form
a neighborhood civil rights group, later chartered as the Fulton
Improvement Association. They chose Alford Stirling as president and met in Patience Gromes's living room.

Stirling, his aide-de-camp Jacob Pinckney, and a dozen other
active members organized voting drives, which they would run
every year for the next eighteen years. For each election they
held two drives: first, get them registered; next, get them to the
polls. When residents complained that they could ill afford to

miss work, Stirling and Pinckney negotiated with the registrar to stay open on certain evenings. When residents complained that they had no transportation, Stirling developed a car pool. When it began to get complicated, Stirling appointed Patience Gromes telephone chairman to coordinate and make certain that everyone knew what to do and when to do it.

Stirling and Pinckney did not have to be told that one body equals one vote, whatever the alcohol content. Their most magnificent achievement was to find a chairman on every block—including the wet blocks of Rocketts. One such chairman was an enormous woman named Mozelle and called Big Mo. On voting day she didn't reason with the drunks on her block, but one at a time lifted them clear of the ground and carried them to the waiting cars: one more vote for our candidate.

In the late fifties (according to Stirling) Fulton boasted the highest percentages of voter registration and participation of any district in town. By 1960 Stirling had become Fulton's prime leader. He served on the board of the Bethlehem Center (where the Fulton Improvement Association had held meetings since outgrowing Patience Gromes's living room). He belonged to the NAACP, the Crusade for Voters, the city's Advisory Group for Neighborhood Planning and attended meetings three or four nights a week, many of them uptown. All neighborhood crises, large or small, were referred to Alford Stirling. Women telephoned him when their children were lost, the trash collector bypassed their block, or a street light burned out.

Stirling was not an eloquent speaker or a great intellect. Yet he was the president of the Fulton Improvement Association, just as Martin Luther King, Jr., had been president of the Montgomery Improvement Association. He became the neighborhood equivalent of Martin Luther King, Jr., through good character, sincerity, and willingness to work.

In 1964 and 1965, demonstrations in Selma and Montgomery succeeded in bringing the Civil Rights Act and the Voting Rights Act into law. Near the end of the Selma and Montgomery demonstrations, isolated acts of violence defied the philosophy of civil-rights organizers but obeyed a logic of expectation, frustration, and anger. This progression anticipated a similar growth within the movement as a whole. King's pacifism was succeeded by the black power rhetoric of Stokely Carmichael, and the pacifistic demonstrations of 1964 and 1965 were succeeded by the hot summers of 1966 and 1967.

In the wake of violence came government money, and civil rights leaders turned their attention to making the most of it. Some leaders sought local political office where they would be in a position to channel government services to black communities. Others took paid positions with Model Cities, CAP agencies (represented in Fulton by the Richmond Community Action Program, RCAP), or other federally funded entities, and lobbied local government from without. George Wiley, who had worked with CORE before founding the National Welfare Rights Organization in 1967, was attempting to create a mass membership group that would provide a permanent lobby for federal assistance to the poor.

Fulton residents followed developments—not interrupting the pattern of their lives, but keeping an eye on national events as for decades they had kept an eye on the street, using these events to gauge their position, as black men and women, in the scheme of things.

Initially, neighborhood civil rights veterans served as leaders of the anti-poverty effort. When RCAP first came to Fulton, Alford Stirling was elected president and meetings were convened at the Bethlehem Center. No one seemed to consider that Stirling's good manners might limit his appeal and make him vulnerable to an insurgent who had ruthlessness and anger to recommend him.

Patricians such as Patience Gromes took pride in the victories of civil rights. They had no idea that the government money that flowed into Fulton following civil rights would undercut their way of life, and that the ability to manipulate government would displace hard work as the primary survival skill. The stage was

set for changes to come, and it would be only a matter of time
before the progress of national events was traced in Fulton. If
Alford Stirling was a rough equivalent of Martin Luther King,
Jr., who in Fulton would become the equivalent of Stokely Carmichael?

In July 1967, summer talk in Fulton dwelt on familiar topics,
and people moved in familiar patterns. Fourth of July was coming
up, but no one was making elaborate preparations. Those who
had lost sons or husbands in the war would fly flags, others would
go down to the river to picnic and fish, walk to the spring at
Chimborazo Park, or stay home and rest. Patience Gromes would
spend the day sitting on her porch talking to everyone who passed
up and down the street, talking about the heat and about who
would become the new pastor at Rising Mt. Zion and about
neighborhood cats who came to the kitchen door looking to be
fed. Daniel Brady was home from prison now, released on parole
after serving seventeen years of his sixty-year sentence. He was
living with his sister and her husband. He would spend the day
with them, eating the ground chuck, biscuits, and coffee his sister
cooked, talking about the food and about the chorus at church
and about people they knew.

This summer, as every summer, neighborhood children picked
berries on Clay Hill, climbed the C&O trestle looking for pi-
geons, and chased rabbits in the field beyond the city-county
line. They sifted through cold ashes at the Fulton Gas Works to
retrieve cinders that were still good for fuel and, come winter,
would be worth money. Patience Gromes's children had grown,
married, and moved, leaving their mother with no one to look
after. Even so, Patience rose at six each morning from force of
habit and from a desire to get ahead of her day.

Nothing was exceptional about the summer talk and movement of those who lived in Fulton. It was a normal summer. But
the times themselves were exceptional and touched all of Fulton's
residents in some way. In July 1967 black men and women in

Detroit and Milwaukee and a dozen other cities were running in the streets, and at month's end fifty-three lay dead. As the summer progressed the rioting died down, President Johnson appointed a "Riot Commission," and the Pentagon drew up contingency plans to deal with mass civil insurrection. In Richmond squad cars cruised black districts ordering young men off street corners, and community block leaders spread the word to stay cool.

The summer of 1967 was different from summers that had come before in another way that aroused notice in Fulton. In February, the housing authority had applied to HUD for money, and now their interviewers were going house to house, asking the number of family members, ages, education, and income, inspecting the houses, and assigning to each house a "structural condition rating." In November the survey was complete. It indicated that 85 percent of Fulton's dwellings had "major and significant deficiencies," a finding that had not been anticipated in preliminary studies based on census data. By February 1968 everyone in Fulton knew of the conclusions the housing authority had drawn.

The public imagination readily supplanted the statements of housing authority officials as to the probable course of urban renewal. According to the news passed door to door, the housing authority wanted to take all of Fulton for industry. No compensation would be given for houses or churches. Both statements were untrue, but this did not dilute their impact on Fulton residents, who long had feared and anticipated this eventuality. They knew that the city and other government entities had bulldozed parts of Jackson Ward and nearly all of Seventeenth Street Bottom, and just now were taking the houses of well-to-do blacks in the West End. It was hard for them, after ten years of civil rights marches and two hot summers, to study the proposals of the housing authority with detachment. A house represented a family's life savings. Three hundred Fulton families had purchased houses, and an even larger number contributed to neighborhood churches. To homeowners, urban renewal was a conspiracy to deprive them of their property. To tenants, it threatened to deprive them of their way of life.

Housing authority employees thought they were planning on behalf of the city rather than conspiring against the people of Fulton. To their minds the facts fully justified clearance in Fulton. Against the anger of Fulton residents they stood their ground: Fulton *was* a poor residential site; the houses of Fulton *were* dilapidated; the street pattern *was* obsolete; the sewer, water, and gas lines *were* old; curbs and gutters, sidewalks and streets *were* in poor repair; clearance *was* the logical course.

Despite the initial opposition that their clearance proposals elicited, the planners appeared to be making progress in winning the understanding of neighborhood residents. Alford Stirling, Jacob Pinckney, and the other members of the Fulton Improvement Association fought clearance. But gradually the explanations of the planners began to sink in. Why put ten dollars into a house that won't be worth more than five dollars when it's finished? At length Stirling concluded that clearance, *per se*, was not the issue. The real question was the continued existence of this neighborhood. After the old buildings were torn down, would the vacant land be given to houses, groceries, and playgrounds where Fulton residents could continue to live? Or would the land go for factories?

Stirling was a leader, but he lacked the instinct for self-preservation to be found in a politician. Because of his earlier experience as Fulton's representative on the city-wide Advisory Group for Neighborhood Planning, he was far quicker to see the implications of the housing authority's survey than were his neighbors, who wondered how he could speak about renewal with such coolness. Wasn't this the latest move in a racist conspiracy going back generations? Before long, conditions were perfect for a palace revolt.

On the first Sunday of March 1968 the Fulton Improvement Association held its regular monthly meeting in the Quonset hut of the Bethlehem Center. Daniel Brady never would have attended but for the urging of his sister. "I wanted him to meet some of Fulton's better kind of people," she said later. "There was talk of tearin' houses down. I wanted him to see could he do anything about it."

The meeting was called to order by Stirling, and an invocation was given by Father O'Connor, priest of Fulton's Catholic church. The reading of the minutes and other business were dispensed with, and the meeting was opened for consideration of the question "What is the future of Fulton?" An Urban League official spoke at length, telling residents how renewal funds could be used to revitalize Fulton. His comments echoed Stirling's approach, a line the Bethlehem Center supported.

The second speaker was Father O'Connor, who tended to side with RCAP in neighborhood political controversies. "Tell the housing authority that you don't want any part of their plan," he said. "No ifs, ands, or buts, you just don't want the program." Father O'Connor pointed out that the federal government required the housing authority to have citizen participation and approval before implementing an urban renewal plan. He charged that Stirling and the Improvement Association had played into the hands of the housing authority and its director, Fred Fey. "Since you have met with Mr. Fey," he said, "this can be used as your participation and approval."

If Stirling simply refused to meet with the housing authority, O'Connor argued, the whole project would be dead—shut down by the federal government for lack of citizen participation. A Fulton woman who worked at RCAP joined the attack on Stirling and the improvement association with a rhetorical question. "Is the Fulton Improvement Association on record in Washington," she asked, "as having approved of Mr. Fey's plan by their presence at his meetings?"

Father O'Connor continued: "Have an ad hoc committee that has not had any dealings with Mr. Fey draw up the whole agenda. Once you give in on one thing, they can take the whole area.

They will use the fact that the improvement association has met with them against you. You have to get about five people that the community has confidence in and make them an ad hoc committee."

At length Daniel Brady stood up. "The Fulton Improvement Association," he began, "is selling us down the river." Brady then moved that an ad hoc committee be formed "to oppose the housing authority's plan." The motion carried, and Brady was voted president, Stepney Waterman, vice president. Brady announced a meeting for the following Wednesday, to be held not at the Bethlehem Center but at the RCAP Center. "We can only accomplish what we need by sticking together, fighting together," Brady said at the meeting's end.

The next Wednesday, the first meeting of the Ad Hoc Committee began with prayer. Then the floor was opened to discussion on the topic "The Salvation of Fulton." Brady gave the first and, judging from the minutes, the only speech:

"I have talked with a lawyer and learned that Fulton has two legs to stand on. First we need to get a court injunction to stop Mr. Fey now; second, we must organize our forces, meet with representatives of the community in a mass meeting.

"I have talked with outside organizations who have promised their support. I am waiting for a report from the Justice Department in Washington. One thing is clear—we must not give the housing authority one square foot of Fulton. If we do, they can take the entire area.

"Even though the committee [i.e., Alford Stirling and Jacob Pinckney of the improvement association] that has been meeting with Mr. Fey did not agree with him, they have not opposed him, either. This has been taken as approval and is on record as such in Washington. If Mr. Fey gets in here, he will take over your problems and tell you what to do. Don't let him do this. Ask the federal government for help. If Mr. Fey has his way, Fulton will become a cinder block city.

"The people of Fulton have not been well enough informed

as to what is going on, but we hope to change this. The press will be brought to these meetings. I hope to get radio and TV coverage as well as newspaper coverage."

Jacob Pinckney defended the work of the Fulton Improvement Association. "We have circulated fliers in the neighborhood," he said. "But maybe not enough."

Brady continued: "We want everybody to know what is going on in Fulton. I have some contacts in Washington that will open doors for me. No individual on the Ad Hoc Committee has individual authority. It must be a body. From now on, no one from this community is to have any dealings with Mr. Fey."

Alford Stirling asked if he should continue to attend advisory committee meetings called by the housing authority. Brady replied in one word: "No."

Phone calls to Washington, D.C., cost money. Leaflets cost money. Who would pick up the tab for these and other Ad Hoc Committee expenses?

"I don't feel it is fair," said a local grocer, "for Mr. Brady to spend his money and not be reimbursed."

"I can't afford not to," replied Brady.

Three Sundays later, on March 24, the Ad Hoc Committee called a mass meeting at Webster Davis School. Brady made certain that the media were invited and circulated a leaflet to residents as they arrived. This leaflet accused the Fulton Improvement Association of making deals with the housing authority behind the backs of Fulton residents, and of withholding information from the neighborhood. Brady couldn't get a key to the building, so he was forced to address the crowd outside on the street. In a speech that was quoted the next day in the *Richmond Times-Dispatch* he played to his audience: "I pledge myself to you now, that as long as I have breath to breathe, those bulldozers will not come into Fulton."

A special meeting of the Fulton Improvement Association was called two days later to question Brady about the wording of his leaflet. After the meeting opened, the paper was read to the group.

Alford Stirling spoke first: "I feel that the paper distributed in Sunday's meeting actually said that all the work of the improvement association was for nothing. Mr. Fey did not give out all the information; therefore the improvement association was unable to pass it on to the people. All information given to the improvement association was passed on to the people through fliers, churches, etc.

"Before this paper was drawn up the Ad Hoc Committee should have come to the improvement association and stated what they were going to do. All the people here [improvement association members] have the interest of Fulton at heart. Whether Fulton was represented adequately, is up to you to say.

"I did my best. I am here to carry out your wishes. If you were not satisfied you should have told me long ago."

Stirling's remarks were seconded by a Mrs. Davis, a long-time member of the improvement association: "Why use us as a stepping stone? It was not necessary to down us. Why say we went along with Mr. Fey? You had a big gathering at this meeting because you played on their emotions. Only those who have labored through the years have attended our meetings."

As Mrs. Davis continued, she pointed out that, to date, Mr. Fey and the housing authority had done no visible harm to Fulton, implying that the improvement association may not have bungled its representation of the neighborhood as badly as Brady was charging. On the other hand, visible improvements had been made in Fulton by the city, which the improvement association had lobbied intensively. "We have worked for years. Why say all our work has been in vain? What has Mr. Fey done? Nothing. What has the city done? Paved the streets, put up lights, traffic signs, etc."

Later in the meeting, Daniel Brady replied to Stirling and his other critics in the improvement association: "Mr. Fey has said he has done everything the Fulton improvement association wanted. What has the improvement association asked Mr. Fey to do? Everybody appreciates the improvement association, but somewhere along the line the people don't feel they have done the job that needed to be done."

One of the founders of the improvement association countered by challenging the legitimacy of Brady's committee. "The Ad Hoc Committee," he said, "has no authority to go out on its own."

Later, under pressure from his own followers, Brady offered a "tentative apology": "I only wanted to do what was best for the people of the Fulton area. I am sorry if anyone is offended. I just can't work under the banner of do this, don't do that. The people will know of every move and every accomplishment that I do. I can't see why anyone would want to take issue with what I did. I'm working for Fulton to the best of my ability."

Although this meeting ended with the improvement association accepting Brady's apology and in turn authorizing him to continue his work of opposing the housing authority, the reconciliation was superficial. The improvement association was a legally chartered organization, the Ad Hoc Committee was not. But that did not deter Brady. His Ad Hoc Committee was acting independently. It had its own meeting place, its own leaders, chose its own members, and did not recognize any obligation to inform the improvement association of its decisions or activities. Before long it renewed contact with the housing authority.

Brady had broken the cardinal rule of conduct in Fulton by publicly attacking other residents, but these were extreme times, and his tactics appeared to succeed. He called more committee meetings, more mass meetings—and Fulton residents attended. He conducted black dignitaries from uptown on tours of Fulton. His sister told me later that he was trying to win their assistance in Fulton's fight against the housing authority. Brady's detractors, however, say he was trying to legitimize his own leadership by association. Before long it was clear that the Ad Hoc Committee had become the official neighborhood representative in the eyes of the housing authority, with Brady the official neighborhood leader.

Jacob Pinckney urged Alford Stirling to counterattack. "Brady can't vote," he said. "How can a man with no civil rights be a leader?" Apparently the director of the Bethlehem Center agreed. According to neighborhood legend, he reported Brady to the state for a parole violation.

As the story goes, Brady got a call from his parole officer, who threatened to send him back to prison if he violated the terms of his parole. Brady was enraged. He lobbied neighborhood residents who were Bethlehem Center board members and initiated a movement that was largely responsible for the director's ouster three years later, at the time of my arrival in Fulton.

Alford Stirling agreed with Pinckney to a point. "The Ad Hoc had acted illegally, so to speak," Stirling told me later, "because you cannot have an ad hoc committee unless you have a parent body." Stirling thought it would be easy to discredit a two-time loser such as Brady. But Stirling also knew that he could no longer unite Fulton behind his own leadership. If he challenged Brady he would create an open split, and the housing authority would be the only winner. "If you start to hagglin' among yourselves," he told me later, "then nothing will get done."

Thus in May 1968, Stirling acceded to Brady's leadership. He really had no choice. As my boss at the Bethlehem Center put it, "Alford Stirling is not the type of person to fight in public."

Daniel Brady was fifty-two years old in 1968 and worked as a used car salesman for Jack DeShazo on Mechanicsville Turnpike. His qualifications as Fulton's official leader, however, had to do with the state penal system. The horrors of life in the high-security prison on Spring Street were legendary here, for many a man had entered, never to be heard from again. Daniel Brady had lived in this prison for a total of twenty years, seventeen of them on the last stint, and had been out in society now less than a year.

Brady was not a pleasant man, though it would be unkind to say, as many did, that he was in a class with Fulton's gamblers and bootleggers. With his sister's encouragement he awkwardly tried to make amends and to find his way into the society of decent folk. He had himself baptized again in the font at the Mt. Calvary Baptist Church following the Sunday service. Most such ceremonies include a number of baptisms, but no one chose to join Daniel Brady. Before immersion he stood alone in front of the congregation. "I want to be reborn again and wash away all my sins," he said.

Few were convinced of Brady's purity, and, according to one report, he was widely feared by Fulton's older generation. But other qualities of leadership were in demand now. Brady occupied a different position than established leaders of his generation. Jacob Pinckney, for example, had built a solid reputation in Fulton over many years' time. He knew that a misstep could take decades to live down, for in Fulton everyone remembered everything. Why should he risk his reputation by resorting to untried and unsanctioned strategies in the current squabble with the housing authority?

Brady, on the other hand, could do nothing to make his reputation any worse. His stay in prison put him twenty years or more behind his peers, and he knew that extreme tactics would be necessary to catch up. Brady wanted a house, a wife, a job. But most of all he wanted to win the esteem of the people of Fulton, the people who had known him from his youth. Brady's deprivations had given him toughness. And his hunger for recognition fueled a rage that Alford Stirling did not possess.

Yet it was more than the Spring Street prison and Daniel Brady's longing for success that accounted for the difference in style between the two men. Stirling was a successful man in the traditional mold. He had a family to support, mortgage payments to make, and a job to hold down. As a federal employee, he feared reprisal under the Hatch Act, which forbade participation in political activities. He had led voting drives and lobbied city hall under the rubric of democracy and civic obligation. But he avoided noise and publicity like that invariably generated by outright confrontation. During the drive for civil rights, when SNCC workers visited an improvement association meeting and pushed for sit-ins at segregated lunch counters uptown, Stirling sidestepped.

Unlike voting drives, urban renewal was undeniably political. It would be impossible for Stirling to wrap himself in the flag on this issue. More to the point, the resistance to urban renewal was striking nerves in city hall. If Stirling led the people of Fulton in the wild confrontation they seemed to desire, he could easily find himself looking for work. Jacob Pinckney, as a federal employee and a family man, was in precisely the same position. But Daniel Brady was not a success in the traditional mold. His job with Jack DeShazo was more of a social pretense than a source of income. He had no wife or family, no mortgage payments to make. If he went crazy before the television cameras, what did he have to lose?

Brady had developed his confidence as a public speaker in prison, where he took a Carnegie course, and had sharpened his verbal skills and manipulative instincts on stray customers who visited Jack DeShazo's car lot. He was at home on terrain where Fultonians traditionally felt ill at ease. Take money, for instance. Fulton residents displayed great reticence on this subject. It had never been considered wise or dignified to come right out and ask a white employer for a raise, for example, no matter how the emotions were churning within. Much better to drop hints and avoid any possibility of open conflict. But Brady enjoyed talking about money. He would say anything to anybody.

In the past, when government had been oblivious to the black community, there was little need to talk about money in public. But now government money was coming down like rain. Would it all go to Jackson Ward? Not if Daniel Brady had his say.

Although Brady was a pariah of sorts, it was clear that he could prove a devastating weapon in this conflict if, like an artillery piece, he was properly aimed. And, allied as he was with Stepney Waterman (vice president of the Ad Hoc Committee and a member of one of Fulton's oldest families), Brady's past was less of an obstacle. Fulton residents would allow Brady to serve as spokesman and rabble-rouser. For all the more intimate and traditional services of leadership, they would turn to Waterman. Brady would play it up before the television cameras, Waterman would visit children in jail and take telephone calls in the middle of the night.

7

THIRD GENERATION

1968-1972

DANIEL BRADY may have been a shrewd choice for neighborhood leader, but he was also a measure of the change that had taken place in Fulton. In years past, Fulton folk considered good character to be the prime weapon against all that opposed them. But good character was not Brady's strong suit. He had never demonstrated hard work and thrift but was schooled in the artful dodging that Fulton's bootleggers, gamblers, and others at the fringes of Fulton society long had practiced.

In the first months of 1968 urban renewal put the houses of Fulton in jeopardy, and instantly the authority of the old ideals was lost. For the houses of Fulton had been proof that hard work and virtuous living—not political power or government money—bring success in this world. The houses were a statement of the essential morality of the universe, a statement which the housing authority bluntly and decisively rebutted. And now public life in Fulton was changed. On the first Sunday in March, Alford Stirling was ousted as neighborhood leader, a position he had held for fifteen years. Four weeks later Martin Luther King, Jr., was shot and killed on the balcony of a Memphis motel, and the youth of Fulton rioted for the first and last time. The old ideals had been discredited. They no longer governed.

Urban renewal broke upon the scene in Fulton in 1968, but it was not until the flood in 1972 that its consequences became clear. For four years Fulton drifted loose from its cultural moorings, and no one knew whether the old order would reassert itself or whether a competing view of the world would become dominant. Under these circumstances events that once had been unthinkable occurred all too often: Charles Dowd, the good child of a good family, collaborated in the stabbing of a bootlegger. Sammy Fulkes, Grunt Curtis, and Sammy's younger brother put a bullet in a white man's back and stole thirty dollars from his pocket. Fulton folk once had been close, like the fingers of one hand. Now rifts appeared between residents of different classes, and closeness was confined to the members of one's own clique.

These four years were difficult for Patience Gromes and her contemporaries. They were well past working age now and survived on Social Security, veterans', and railroad retirement checks. These stipends were the fruit of many years' labor but didn't confer the kind of authority that had come on paydays of years past. Now Fulton's patricians took their living out of the mailbox, just as neighborhood welfare mothers did, and it was hard for the children of Fulton to see more virtue in one instance than in the other. In the competition for the minds of the young, the old first citizens felt themselves losing ground, partly because their numbers were thinning out. Many of their children had moved to other neighborhoods. Some of the older generation were sick, others had died. In many cases a husband had died and left his spouse to face the world alone for the first time in her life.

Frank Gromes worked graveyard shift at the C&O seven days a week for forty-three years. He never changed jobs, never was laid off or fired. He worked through the boom years of the twenties and the big bust of the thirties, worked through two world wars. Frank was steady. The storefront shops he passed on his way to and from the Fulton Yard changed hands over the years, houses changed owners. But he stayed the same, working seven days, working hard.

Frank and Patience paid off the mortgage on their house in 1947, and two years later Frank retired. Now he spent his days sitting on the front stoop smoking his pipe or visiting friends like Thomas Arrington and his wife. He often told Mrs. Arrington of hot numbers he came upon—not that he played the numbers too seriously. Frank Gromes was a simple man, reserved. Silence had been considered a prime masculine virtue in his country home years before. Patience's father, William Armistead, had not been loquacious, and her grandfather, Lewis Armistead had said even less. Patience understood her husband, honored him, and did not fuss at him.

Betsy was the only child still living at home when Frank retired. In 1953 she married and moved to Church Hill. The piano and Victrola were seldom used now that Betsy was gone. Patience sold the piano, put the Victrola in the closet, and placed the furniture of her front room in a formal arrangement that would not be altered for the rest of her life in this house.

Frank and Patience were living alone now for the first time since their arrival here in 1906. Summer evenings they sat together on the front stoop as darkness gathered and spread through Fulton. The nights were resonant. They had been young once, but now they were old. They had reared eight children, paid off two mortgages, supported a church. Years before, they had left the cabins and frame houses of James City County, winter fields rolling away like waves, the bare branches of trees at the horizon.

On Christmas day, 1955, Frank Gromes woke up sick. Ten minutes later he was dead. "Cerebral hemorrhage," said the doctor.

Patience Gromes had expected to support herself adequately after Frank's passing, for he left her two retirement checks, a little savings, and, most important, a rental house.

Patience and Frank had not sold their Denny Street house when they moved into the house on State. Instead they rented it out and saved their rental income. Twenty years later they owned both houses free and clear. I don't think they would have sold the house on Denny even then, but friends needed a place to live and couldn't find anything else. Frank and Patience sold and with the proceeds purchased a row house in Rocketts.

The row house had a front room with a coal grate and a mantelpiece, a kitchen and bath, upstairs bedrooms, and a closet room over the stairway. Although it was small, Patience liked it because it was complete and everything worked. For Patience the house was more than a source of income. It was a way of sharing her notion of life with another family.

After Frank's death Betsy and her husband moved back with Patience to keep her company. Five years later they moved to a house of their own in Henrico County. Patience lived alone on State Street now, although occasionally she took in boarders for varying lengths of time. Betsy stopped by on her way home from work sometimes, telephoned more often, and occasionally took Patience shopping. Betsy was concerned about her mother. "Move with me," she said.

"I don't want to be on none of my children," said Patience, "not unless I'm down and can't do no better."

Patience stayed busy cooking, cleaning, and gardening. A neighborhood man did the heavier yard work under her supervision, and Betsy ran errands uptown when necessary. Once a week Patience and Mrs. B ate dinner together. They joked about the attention that Patience was receiving now as an eligible, single woman of only seventy-eight. One widower had come calling at dinner time. He was a talker, overflowing with self-esteem and oblivious to Patience's hints that he should apply his charm in another direction. At length Patience grew hungry and was forced to invite him to dinner. When she set a plate of food down before him, he judged that he was making certain progress in winning her affections.

It was not uncommon for Fulton residents to eat dinner in one another's kitchens as customers at a "sellin'," a project to raise funds for a club activity by selling dinners of fish, chittlings, or chicken. The going rate for such a dinner was $1.50 at this time. Our widower ate slowly, as though to savor the fact that he was dining in Mrs. Gromes's kitchen not on a business basis, like a customer at a sellin', but intimately, like a lover. When he finished eating, he wiped his lips and leaned back, considering what amorous payment she was entitled to after this fine meal. "Thanks Patience," he said. "What do I owe you?"

"That will be a dollar fifty," she said.

Patience had little difficulty managing her rental property, since her agents advertised, let the property, collected rent, advised her of any repairs that were necessary and made them, with her consent, from the rent money they collected. After her rental agent took his percentage, Patience received about twenty-two dollars per month. Everything went smoothly with the rental house until about 1966. One group of tenants decided to move and carted their belongings away, then returned. They broke out windows, wrenched the kitchen sink from the wall, pulled down the stair railing, and worse. "They took the mantel," said Patience, "and threw it down on the floor. Can you believe that?"

Patience was convinced that her tenants were motivated by pure meanness. Each time she told me this story she began in a calm tone of voice but slowly became more and more angry. When she got to the part about her tenants smashing the mantel, she was shouting at me, as though the violence of her words could effectively repel the violence of their actions.

After the wrecking of her rental house, Patience was in anguish. She spoke of the incident as though a moral transgression had taken place. To her way of thinking, her tenants had desecrated the holiest space in a holy structure when they smashed the mantel on the floor.

One ironic feature of Fulton after 1968 was the way its first citizens were forced to fall back upon the city, their old enemy, to save them from the assaults and transgressions of their neighbors. After her rental house was ruined, Patience Gromes paid a neighborhood man to nail plywood over the windows and doors and resigned herself to paying taxes for the rest of her life on property that did not earn an income and that she could not sell. Patience was angry about her rental house far more than about the transgressions of the pool hall youth. And yet, in the spring of 1971, an event occurred that transformed her anger into a pure, sputtering exasperation. The city sent her a bill for fifteen dollars.

In March 1971 the city council passed a law requiring owners of abandoned houses to bring them up to code, demolish them, or pay a fine of fifteen dollars per month. The law was aimed at slumlords like William Dupree, who owned dozens of wrecked houses in Fulton. Dupree had no incentive to demolish his houses, since the appraisal, which determined the housing authority's purchase price, assigned a given value to the lot and a separate value to the structure. Thus a lot with a structure, even an abandoned structure, would be worth more to the landowner than a lot alone. Naturally, Fulton's leaders and those who worked in its community centers were pleased with the new legislation. What could have been more enlightened?

Patience Gromes thought differently. "That's trash," she said. "Where do I get fifteen dollars a month?" She felt that the city was penalizing her for having led an upright life. "If I had gambled my money away instead of putting it by," said Patience, "would the city be on me now?" She thought the city stupid. Why else would they mistake her for a slumlord like William Dupree? "I don't own a lot of shacks all over town," she continued. "Why don't they get after him, leave respectable ones like me alone?" Patience found herself confronting a dilemma: she could obey the law and bring about her own financial ruin, or she could violate the law and preserve her meager assets. "They can throw me in jail if they want," said Patience, "but I'm not paying."

Fortunately for her, the housing authority agreed to purchase her rental house ahead of schedule. When I informed the city comptroller that the house was in the process of being acquired for renewal, he dropped the fine. Patience was relieved to have escaped this dilemma, yet she was nevertheless frightened by the means of her rescue. She knew that the quickest way to lose one's independence was to ask the city for favors.

The old men and women of Fulton regarded urban renewal as something unspeakable and terrible, like a stroke or convulsions or death. They could never quite understand their children who spent their free time working as citizen planners and who favored renewal as the means of Fulton's redemption. To Patience Gromes and her peers, urban renewal was the calculating, amoral city world breaking into their country village.

Fulton's patricians were skeptical. Their grandparents had told stories about blacks in the country who lost their land to fast-talking agents and salesmen. And Fulton's homeowners knew they could lose their houses. Such happenings, though rare, were not unheard of in Fulton. As a young girl in the twenties, Mrs. B had heard her mother talking about a neighbor who had been unable to keep up payments and had lost her house. The Cottrell family, who were Irish, lost property in the forties for nonpayment of taxes. Billy Dismith purchased one of these lots at a tax sale held on the steps of City Hall.

When welfare was established following World War II, it required a homeowner to give up his or her house to qualify for assistance. Although on paper this would seem a reasonable stipulation, Fulton residents shared the feelings of Corina Dunn, who could not be reasonable about the prospect of losing her inheritance. She would starve rather than betray the years of work and thrift with which her father had founded their family home. The deed to her house made Corina a person of stature and gave her a vantage point from which to look out on the world. If she turned her house over to the city, she would be nothing but a ward of the public, subject to its every whim. Corina had seen plenty of bums and drifters in her day, but she had no desire to join the ranks of these dispossessed. Her family had been poor, but they had never been forced to give up their home.

Jack Mosby was equally concerned that the city might find some excuse to take his house. Jack gave me an earful on this subject when I visited to tell him about tax abatement. In October 1972 the city initiated property tax abatement for homeowners who were elderly and had low incomes. Qualified homeowners could save up to fifty dollars per year, an enormous sum to Fulton's elderly. A more ideal measure could scarcely be imagined, since it rewarded people according to their accomplishments and put money in the hands of those who had demonstrated the ability to squeeze value from each penny. Patience Gromes, Peggie Howell, and Thomas Arrington were receptive and thanked me for helping them fill out and submit their applications.

Jack Mosby, however, refused even to consider such a scheme. He was like a rock. I explained that the city had passed a special law to help people like him. The city was trying to give him money. All he had to do was sign the paper, and I would get him fifty dollars, free. But Jack would not hear of it. I enlisted the help of Mrs. Sparks, the storekeeper who doubled as Jack's financial consultant. But she couldn't budge him. I tried a second visit. Jack sat in a rocking chair in the dim interior of his house. He rocked gently and looked at me with a slight smile, as though displaying great patience with a naive and wrongheaded child. "If I don't pay taxes on this house, the city will take it away from me, sure enough."

Jack Mosby was incorruptible. He knew that a man paid taxes or suffered the consequences. I sensed that this was an axiom that had been formulated years, perhaps generations, before and that Jack consciously used to protect himself from the machinations of a world that he knew to be more cunning and better versed in legal matters than he. It was inconceivable to him that the city could act as his benefactor, for the city was a familiar adversary, lurking beyond Gillies Creek, waiting to snatch houses from the honest folk of Fulton. He looked at me with an expression of great pity that I, a young man of such potential, had been tricked into acting as a dupe of the city.

Since World War II, government bulldozers had joined tax sale and mortgage default as likely means for losing one's house. It was plain to see that when it came to demolition the city of Richmond and other public bodies invested with the power of eminent domain preferred black neighborhoods. In the fifties a

section of Jackson Ward was bulldozed for the interstate, and in
the early sixties the city bulldozed Seventeenth Street Bottom
for the new city jail and an industrial park. In 1968, while the
housing authority was proposing to clear large sections of Fulton
for industry, the transit authority was condemning the solid brick
houses of blacks in the West End for an expressway.

Despite the reassurance of fourth-generation leaders, the old
people were skeptical. They had learned to recognize the bunco
artists of the city, just as their grandparents had the carpetbaggers
of the country. But who were these soft-talking young men, black
men, who carried maps and charts and seemed to know what
they were doing? The old aristocrats of Fulton attended the mass
meetings at Webster Davis School and listened to the plan that
Daniel Brady, Stepney Waterman, and Alford Stirling had drawn
up. But in the back of their minds, I suspect, they considered
whether these proposals were simply one more attempt by the
white world to take their property.

Whether Fulton's elderly residents approved or disapproved of
urban renewal really made little difference. It was here to stay.
Fulton had been like a country village, but now this neighborhood would be intimately subject to the impersonal workings of
a bureaucracy.

Living under the imminent threat of clearance, Fulton's tenants found it difficult or impossible to goad their landlords into
making repairs. Even when the health department cited a landlord, he could argue in court the unfairness of forcing him to
repair units that soon would be demolished. William Dupree was
a master of this tactic. He had helped to write the housing code,
knew it by heart, and, as a lawyer, seldom failed to win the judge
to his point of view. Thus renters, who waited year after year
for the promised demolition crews, were forced to make do with
dwellings that sank ever further below the minimum standards
of health and safety required by law.

In theory Fulton's tenants were free to move to low-cost housing in other parts of town, subject to availability, as they always

had been. But now there were incentives for them to stay, whether or not the roof leaked or the wiring gave off sparks. If displaced by urban renewal, they would receive ample relocation benefits, could qualify for federal help in making down payments on houses of their own, and, most importantly, were given priority for public housing. Why wait for years to get an apartment in the projects when one could go to the head of the line simply by living in the path of the bulldozers? Although some moved from Fulton each autumn just before cold weather set in, most others found that their love for this neighborhood, coupled with the incentives provided by urban renewal, outweighed the inconvenience and discomfort of living in rotten houses. Ironically, the benefits offered by renewal put tenants more or less at the mercy of their landlords. Why should a landlord make repairs when the promise of urban renewal benefits would keep his rental units occupied, broken windows or not?

The landlords now had an argument that stood up in court, and the housing authority had become the slumlords' unwitting ally. But the tenants of Fulton were used to living under imperfect conditions that they were powerless to change. Their situation, though bad, was not much worse than it always had been.

Fulton's homeowners, however, were not accustomed to this kind of purgatory. Renewal planners advised them not to repair their houses. "Every penny you spend will be money down a hole," said one planner. "Our purchase price will be the same, no matter if the paint is new or the paint is peeling."

How could Fulton's homeowners stand by while their houses fell apart? Since slavery they had been able to care for themselves and promote the advancement of their race through the same actions. Houses had been a sound investment as well as good citizenship. But now they were asked to think of their houses as digits on a bank statement and nothing more. This had never been hard for Richard C. Moring, the gentlemanly loan shark and slum-lord who moved easily from his illegal banking activities to real estate deals. To Moring a slum house was strictly an investment. But it was too late for neighborhood homeowners to become investors, elevating the profession as defined by Moring to something consistent with their ideals. On the other hand, neither could they continue to live according to the old definitions of good citizenship and subject themselves to financial ruin.

Fulton's elderly homeowners responded to their predicament in different ways. Patience Gromes's brother, Zachary Armistead, owned a beautifully preserved two-story house situated on a double lot and decided that all this talk of clearance would blow over. He invested his retirement savings in insulation and aluminum siding and took great satisfaction in his low oil bills. But as 1968 passed into 1969 the talk about clearance continued and Zach Armistead grew more and more apprehensive. He could not afford to lose that $4,000. Still, he wasn't overly concerned, since all the houses in his section of Fulton were well built and well maintained, unlikely candidates for clearance.

Ophelia Whitley took a different tack. She was in poor health and requested that the housing authority purchase her house and process her grant application ahead of schedule. Years ahead of her neighbors she was enjoying her new house in the suburbs.

Like Patience Gromes, most elderly homeowners took a middle course, deferred maintenance on their houses, yet resisted the temptation to join Ophelia Whitley in exile. They were not ready to admit in public, as Ophelia had, that the grand renewal scheme developed by the neighborhood's citizen planners was doomed. It was better to await the outcome of events, they reasoned, than to act in haste.

Many of the old folk, however, found it difficult to wait for the coming deliverance, since they were forced to live in an uncomfortable moral posture by the presence of renewal and the other arms of the city that seemed to have descended upon Fulton about the same time. If the question of repairing or not repairing one's house was a dilemma posed by renewal, then dozens of smaller but still significant dilemmas were posed by welfare, food stamps, Medicaid. One example was Patience Gromes's food stamp application.

"If it weren't for my handbag earnings, I'd be in the poor house, and that's a fact!" Patience sat in her rocking chair before the bay window of her middle room, sewing together handbags from strips of burlap. It was afternoon, and sunlight came through the window behind her. As a child Patience had cared for her grandparents when they were old. Her father and later her aunt had taken Lewis Armistead and his wife into their homes, fed them, served them, provided for them. Still, times had changed, and Patience seldom asked her children for help. She looked up. "I don't want Betsy to know," she said. "I never want her to know how tight things are for me."

As a matter of fact, Betsy did know and helped as much as Patience let her. "I come by after work and take mumma to the new supermarket up on the hill," Betsy told me later. "We make groceries, and at the checkout stand mumma puts down a couple old, spotted bananas. 'What you want those for?' I said.

" 'They're on special.'

" 'Come on mumma, I'm paying. Go get you some good bananas.' "

I sat at the dining room table and looked at Mrs. Gromes. She was sewing stars in green, red, and blue yarn on the burlap strips before assembling them. The winter before I had bought a handbag from her for five dollars and sent it to my mother. Handbag sales helped, but not much.

"Why don't you apply for welfare," I suggested. "I could help you get your receipts together and give you a ride uptown."

"I don't want charity," said Patience. "I don't want to be on no kind of relief."

"How about food stamps," I said. "You pay for those and they give you a better bargain on buying food."

"I've always worked for everything I've got," she said, "and I'm not taking handouts now."

It was hard to qualify Fulton residents for food stamps. And the few who were eligible, as often as not, decided that stamps weren't worth the bother or compromised their integrity. "This isn't a handout," I told one man. "The United States government is spending millions of dollars on this program to wipe out hunger, and it won't succeed without your help." I knew that Patience would never swallow this line, so I waited. She had spoken quietly without sputtering as she usually did when discussing the city. "Maybe," she said. "Maybe I'll get those stamps."

Acting as Patience's proxy, I visited the food stamp office and signed her up. A week later she received her food stamp card in the mail and rode uptown with her daughter to purchase the first month's allotment. Patience was pleased. She had not been insulted, demeaned, or aggravated. Now she could afford to drink fruit juice, which she dearly loved, in place of the Kool Aid she had been drinking as a substitute.

Unfortunately, the next month Patience did not receive her food-stamp card in the mail. I telephoned to find out why. The food-stamp bureaucrats had reviewed her case and cut her off. I traveled uptown to reapply on Patience's behalf, only to find that the food-stamp technicians were counting her roomer's income together with her own, thereby making her too wealthy to qualify. I could not understand why Rosie's earnings as an employee of Millhizer Bag Company should affect Patience's eligibility. Rosie was not related to Patience, did her shopping and cooking separately, and, other than rent money, did not share her income with Patience. Yet the food-stamp technicians insisted that they constituted one family. A tenant, by the definition of the food stamp office, was one who paid for use of a designated bedroom, a bathroom, a kitchen, and the passageways connecting these rooms. Due to the layout of Patience's house, Rosie was allowed to walk through the middle room to get to the kitchen. But Rosie was accustomed to sitting in the middle room to watch television. She was no longer using the middle room as a passageway, and therefore she was not a tenant but a family member.

Patience Gromes was saddened at the loss of her food stamps. She returned to drinking Kool Aid with a lemon squeezed in for flavor and pondered her situation. She could forbid Rosie to sit in the middle room or she could forgo food stamps. Did she want to regard Rosie narrowly, as a tenant, a customer? Would she have to become an entrepreneur who coolly broke rules of courtesy to observe the precise terms of a contract? The C&O Railroad had given its laborers such treatment, "according to the business." But this was Fulton, the neighborhood that had countered the cold attitude of city companies. To Patience Gromes the loss of food stamps was a small price to pay for continued freedom in the governance of her household.

A small lie, of course, would have solved the dilemma, but Patience would not hear of it. This solution seemed natural to the young welfare mothers of the neighborhood, but it was no solution at all to Patience Gromes, who was not trying to get food stamps, as such, but was trying to survive in this modern world without compromising her integrity. In the past her conception of good and evil had shown her how to interpret the world, how to act in order to succeed. Virtue had been rewarded. The virtuous family had worked hard, eaten well, and been able to provide for neighbors who were sick, out of work, or fallen on hard times. But now good and evil seemed fragmented and randomly mated to one another. In these odd times a woman who wished to treat a house guest with civility was forced to scrimp and go a little hungry.

When I explained to Patience, as the food-stamp technician had explained to me, that these particular regulations had been adopted to prevent hippies who lived in communes from receiving food stamps, she smiled a bit at the irony. "For all its brains," she said, "the city can't tell the difference between me and a hippie."

Another month Patience received a water bill for forty-five dollars and immediately began to worry. How could she pay it? If she fell behind this month, how could she catch up next month? The city would cut her water off for certain.

Charlie Barbour would not have worried if he were in such a predicament, for he was easygoing about financial obligations and often preferred to let bills go unpaid until it was time to change his address. Fulton had many other residents of Charlie's persuasion—so many, in fact, that a man named Congo Lee earned nearly as much money with his water key (which he used to cut on the water the city had cut off) as he did with his pushcart. But Patience was a homeowner, not a transient or tenant. She had always taken care to meet her obligations promptly and never to purchase more than she could afford. In this manner she had kept her property free of liens, paid her taxes, and never given the city a pretext for interfering in her life. But where would she find forty-five dollars?

At his sister's request Zach Armistead rode uptown to talk the matter over with the water company and discovered that the bill had been a mistake. "A mistake!" said Patience. "And how do I know that all my bills aren't mistakes?"

To a woman who had supported her family by washing diapers for a penny each, the implications were great. Patience had learned the secret, now generally forgotten and invalidated by inflation, that savings are an important source of income because they are untaxed and leave one's time free to earn money in conventional ways. With a program of severe thrift over fifteen or twenty years' time, Patience had accumulated pennies to the point where they held the power to purchase a house, to send a daughter to college.

But couldn't the same principle be applied in reverse? What if the city had been stealing a few cents from her on each water, gas, and light bill? Over twenty years' time the city could have stolen an enormous amount of money. And, more importantly, it could have deprived the residents of control over their lives. Patience and her people had never complained about discrimination, low wages, limited access to employment. What did it matter? They could work two or three jobs and could save. All along Patience felt that she and Frank were calling the shots, pursuing a chosen course.

What if the city had been picking their plums all these years, taking a little every month, never enough to be noticed, operating according to meters, printed numbers, and an aura of infallible authority that made it impossible for residents to verify, or even to doubt, the accuracy of their bills? Could it have been that the city was controlling things all along, deciding their lives for them, allowing them to advance a little this year, taking it back the next, and doing it all so smoothly that no one knew the difference?

After telling me this story Patience looked me square in the eye. "The city is rotten!" she said. " The city is rotten!" Patience could not wait with equanimity as urban renewal unfolded, for she knew that it controlled her future and there was nothing she could do about it. She could not challenge urban renewal or change it any more than she could her monthly water bills.

Third-generation residents had taken pride in the victories of civil rights, but they did not know how to respond to urban renewal and the anti-poverty programs that followed. Their ideals had become a hindrance. Jack Mosby obeyed the old axioms and lost his tax break. Patience Gromes did the same and lost her food stamps. Zach Armistead followed suit and threw $4,000 down a hole. Self-reliance had a way of backfiring in a welfare economy, and the old men and women in whom self-reliance had become ingrained found themselves unable to adapt, as though they were the last of a species that a sudden change in climate doomed to extinction. They refused to employ what they regarded as questionable techniques to promote their interests vis-à-vis the city bureaucracies and continued to insist on the old ways out of pride, loyalty, and a vain hope that their constancy would draw together a world that had come out of joint.

Fulton's old aristocrats were caught between their tried instincts and their pride in the facility and poise of urban renewal's citizen planners who were, after all, their children. Fulton's citizen planners talked as though Fulton could become a model for the nation. But still the old people were uncertain whether to welcome this glorious, new Fulton. Once the solid brick future had become a reality, would anyone recall what they had risked and won in their worn, frame dwellings?

Patience Gromes did not approve of the young men who hung out at the pool hall, but neither did she fret about them. She spoke with her daughter Betsy every day on the phone and may have known more about doings down Route 5, where her daughter lived, than she did about happenings around the corner on Louisiana, where the pool hall was located. Patience and most of her contemporaries were shocked at the criminal actions of neighborhood youth, but they usually found out about these incidents through the newspaper and tended to think of them as occurring in a distant world separate from the one in which they lived.

A few members of the third generation, however, lived closer to the street than Patience Gromes and responded to the wrongdoing of Fulton youth with far less restraint. The Reverend Squire Dowd, for example, lived cattycorner from Fanny and Chub's store. He did not have sons or daughters to talk to every day and talked instead with those who walked past his house, many of whom were customers of Fanny and Chub. The Reverend Dowd was well informed about happenings on his street and did not like much of what he heard.

One afternoon when Dowd was away from home, a young black man walked into Fanny and Chub's, pulled a gun, and cleaned out the cash register. According to Congo Lee, who lived a block down the street, the robber didn't get much because as soon as he pulled his gun on Chub, Fanny grabbed their sack of cash and ran out the back door and down the alley to the haven of another corner grocery. Congo Lee says that Chub fought with the robber, yelling, "Fanny I got him, I got him, Fanny, Fanny, Fanny," while the robber tapped him on the side of the head with his gun and laid him on the floor.

The robbery gave Fanny and Chub shivers. How could they continue in business if they could be robbed so easily? Fortunately, Chub was clever and devised a scheme to safeguard their store, a scheme involving the Reverend Dowd.

Dowd was one neighbor whom Fanny and Chub trusted. Everyone knew that he hated iniquity as much as he loved righteousness. In the afternoons he sat on his front porch and explained his views in great detail to all who would listen. He was known to call out to Fulton's more notorious revelers as they walked past, describing in a few sharp words the nature of their sin and its inevitable consequences. Fanny and Chub were not impressed with Reverend Dowd's credentials as a minister. ("If he's a preacher," Fanny told me later, "my cat's a preacher.") But they did not need a man of the cloth, they needed a security guard. Dowd was trustworthy and had a reputation as a man of action. He was good friends with Analiza Foster, Clara Jones, and others on Orleans Street who knew what trouble looked like close up. Jewel, Clara Jones's mother, who was full of philosophical insight when she was drunk, admired his toughness. "Reverend Dowd talk all smooth and easy," she said, "but when he's mad, he's something else."

A week after the robbery Chub offered Dowd a job protecting his store. Dowd agreed, and the following morning took his position in the back corner by the meat display. Here he sat in a chair, leaning against soda cases stacked atop one another, and let his chin rest comfortably upon his chest. Before the day was over a labor dispute had begun, for Dowd had his own ideas about how to foil miscreants. When such a person entered the store, he wanted to remain undercover until the crook committed himself. Then Dowd proposed to jump out and yell, "Reach for the sky or I'll blow your head off."

Fanny did not see the wisdom in Dowd's strategy but saw the risks all too clearly. She noticed that he had a tendency to snooze when he was hidden at the back of the store. In her judgment he was so thoroughly undercover that if a robbery did occur, he wouldn't wake up in time to make his move.

The Reverend Dowd acknowledged that he sometimes closed his eyes on the job, but he explained that this was all part of a ruse to lull potential robbers into complacency. Besides, the store was only three or four paces wide. In a space this small, how could he fail to notice a robbery in progress? And if he did notice, what could he do? How could he protect the store without a weapon?

One day Dowd came to work with his shotgun cradled over

his left arm. It made Fanny nervous. "You'll hit everyone in the store if you fire that thing," she said.

The turning point came one day when Dowd was hard at work in his corner and Fanny shouted, "There is a stranger comin', watch out for him."

"Don't call my name no kinda way," said Reverend Dowd. But he was too late, for Fanny had blown his cover. How could he be an effective guard if everybody knew he was there? Dowd turned in his resignation and retired to his accustomed post across the street.

Dowd knew Reginald Francis (who had been christened Tub of Lard when he was four months old), and so did everyone else in Fulton. By his seventeenth birthday Tub was bigger than most men and stronger than anyone in Fulton except for Snort, his father. Two weeks after Reverend Dowd quit his job at the corner store, Tub walked in. Fanny was at the cash register. "What do you want in here?" she said.

Tub picked up a bunch of bananas. Fanny came around the counter and stood facing him. She reached as high as she could and grabbed the front of his shirt with both hands. "Put those bananas down," she said, "and get out or I'll throw you out." Tub lifted her with one hand and held the bananas with the other. He walked out the door and dropped her on the sidewalk, then reached down and grabbed her again. At this moment Reverend Dowd placed his hands on Tub's shoulders and pulled him back. Dowd was gentle. "You don't want to do that son," he said, "you know that's no good."

Fanny picked herself up from the sidewalk and stepped into the store clutching her broken glasses. Tub walked down the street holding the bananas, Reverend Dowd returned to his porch.

As he was reaching for his chair, Reverend Dowd heard a bullet hit the side of the house a few inches from his shoulder. He turned and saw Tub with a revolver, a .45. Dowd grabbed his shotgun from inside the door, squeezed off a shot, and was right on target, but Tub was unhurt because he was behind a tree. Tub ran down the street. Dowd filled his pockets with shells and ran after him. Soon Tub was out of sight, so Dowd cut around and set up an ambush by the house where Tub lived with his aunt. Tub, however, did not come home but kept running until he got to Sugar Bottom, where he had friends and could hide.

Fanny called the police, and when Dowd returned home, empty handed, the police jumped him and took away his shotgun.

The Reverend Dowd had known Tub from the time he was a baby, had known his father and grandfather and all his family going back fifty years. Peggy Howell, Tub's great-grandmother, had known Dowd when they were both young and he was beginning to preach hellfire from the pulpits of this neighborhood. Fulton folk had been one tight family. But now they were gunning for one another in the streets.

At the time I worked in Fulton I regarded the showdown between Tub and the Reverend Dowd as well as the crimes of Charles Dowd and Sammy Fulkes as symptoms of black urban poverty, a collection of pathologies documented by white sociologists and popularized at the beginning of the war on poverty in the mid-sixties. But in fact I was witnessing something less clinical and more complex. The incidents I heard about and observed were like fragments of an exploded sun hurtling through space: I was witnessing the death of a culture.

8

FOURTH GENERATION
1968-1971

FULTON'S fourth-generation leaders had problems. Matte Curtis was one example. Matte and ten other NWRO ladies once pulled a demonstration in the food-stamp office while I watched. The women wore new pantsuits, wigs, makeup, perfume and high-heeled shoes and were accompanied by two white radicals, who wore dirty T shirts and jeans and had long, stringy hair. The demonstrators paraded around the reception area and sang "We Shall Overcome" when the reporters arrived.

Matte Curtis broke all the rules that governed public conduct. Tub had broken rules too, as had Charles Dowd, Sammy Fulkes, and Willy Cozart. Fourth-generation leaders did not have enough fingers to plug these leaks. Their impulse was to fight back, but what could they do? Jacob Pinckney could account for the transgressions of Sammy Fulkes and Grunt Curtis by narrowing the definition of Fulton to exclude them and their families. He could not exclude Charles Dowd and Tub Francis, whose people had been here for years, but he could choose to ignore them and their crimes. Betty Norton could strip Matte Curtis of her organized following in the neighborhood and remove the name "Poor People's Club," which had been chosen by Matte, from official usage. Jacob Pinckney could turn the firing of the old coach and the hiring of Willie Cozart into a hot issue that would keep the new director of the Bethlehem Center busy for months.

But none of these actions would impair or destroy the forces threatening Fulton. It was too late for such tactics, and I think Fulton's defenders knew it. They would have to resort to more radical means if the Fulton they knew and loved was to be restored. During the same months that Fulton's new poor and street youths stepped up their attacks on the old ideals, Fulton's defenders were beginning to understand an institution that had unbelievable power. Urban renewal was slow, unwieldy, and difficult to aim. Still, it was the nuclear weapon of neighborhood politics. Could fourth-generation residents harness this atom and use it to restore the governance of old ideals?

After the coup d'etat in March 1968, Fulton's leaders broke off contact with the housing authority. "We didn't know what was going on," one planner told me later. "Turned out to be a lot of infighting." But after the insurgents had consolidated their power they began to think about the crummy houses they and their neighbors lived in and about all that federal money sitting around in Washington with nothing to do. Before long the insurgents were pondering the same questions that Alford Stirling and Jacob Pinckney had been considering a year or two earlier: there must be some way to snag that federal money.

In May 1968, meetings between the residents of Fulton and the housing authority resumed. Daniel Brady and Stepney Waterman took the seats formerly reserved for Stirling and Pinckney, but the debate itself was unchanged. Brady and Waterman offered arguments against clearance that were identical to the ones Stirling and Pinckney had offered months earlier. The planners repeated their rebuttal. Brady and Waterman countered. The planners explained once again: it makes no sense to spend $10,000 rehabilitating a house that won't be worth more than $5,000 when it is finished.

By year's end Brady and Waterman, like Stirling and Pinckney before them, saw that clearance per se wasn't the issue. Fulton residents should instead be fighting for more acres of residential land in the renewal plan, and they should be fighting for this plan to be implemented in stages so that the community would stay alive during the process of renewal. In the staging scenario the people of one block would be moved to temporary housing, their houses and tenements torn down, new houses built. When construction on this block was completed the residents would move back and urban renewal would begin on another block. Staging would be complex, since one block in the old street pattern did not correspond to one block in the new street pattern. But it would allow Fulton to survive.

Fulton residents initially opposed clearance on the supposition that no compensation would be given for the houses or churches of this neighborhood. Alford Stirling had been restrained in talking about clearance because he understood that some compensation was certain and that generous compensation was a distinct possibility.

In the first months of 1969 Brady and other leaders learned that new federal relocation legislation would provide homeowners with cash payments to cover the market value of their houses and moving expenses, plus grants of up to $15,000 to allow them to purchase new houses with the same number of bedrooms as the old ones. Fifteen thousand dollars! A person could do something with that kind of money. At this time new houses in Richmond could be built for $25,000. If a family sold its old house to the housing authority for $5,000 and qualified for the maximum grant, they could build a new house for a debt of only $5,000. And if all the houses of Fulton were cleared and new streets, utilities, and sidewalks installed, Fulton would become a modern neighborhood, a good place to invest in a new house. The $15,000 grants could finance the rebuilding of Fulton.

Fulton's leaders sensed an opportunity here. They quickly agreed with the housing authority on a land-use scheme that would devote less than half of Fulton's usable land area to industry and would almost double the amount of land devoted to residential uses over the earliest housing authority proposals (according to Stirling). They took the plan to the neighborhood in a mass meeting, received the approval of the housing authority, and in January 1970 won the approval of HUD. The remaining hurdle was the city of Richmond, which would have to agree to provide its one-third matching money for the project's first year. In an event referred to ever after as the "March on City Hall," Fulton residents packed the council chambers. Patience Gromes was there, as was Mrs. B and most of their friends. Fred Fey, director of the housing authority, spoke, and was followed by Daniel Brady, Stepney Waterman, and Alford Stirling. The city council voted in favor: for the first time the people of Fulton had bested the city in a test of wills.

The victory at city hall in May 1970 opened a world of possibilities for the defenders of Fulton. Now they had the financial and technical means to stem the decay of Fulton's housing stock. Betty Norton knew that Fulton was a fine neighborhood, as good as any suburb. And now it appeared that her generation would give Fulton's merit a tangible expression. Stirling and Pinckney put their feud with Brady and Waterman on the back burner and applied themselves to the job of developing a detailed land use plan. They felt they were upholding and extending the old ideals of community service. Jacob Pinckney versed himself in the yearly process of obtaining federal and city funding, went on field trips to Columbia, Maryland, and Reston, Virginia, studied various construction systems upon which residents might draw to rebuild Fulton. I once asked Jacob about the possibility of using the modular housing that he had investigated at the suggestion of the planners. "We don't want any of that cheap, prefab stuff," he said. "We want brick. Only the very best."

Although housing authority staff members drew up the actual plans, they put the smallest questions to the citizen planners for decisions. For one thing, the citizens had to decide whether to install concrete or granite curbs. "Concrete is cheaper," said one planner, "but granite lasts longer." Jacob Pinckney and his fellow citizens chose granite. They also chose ranch-style, single-family dwellings with wide lawns and chain link fences. Houses would be grouped on curving asphalt streets, cul-de-sacs that fed a curv-

ing arterial, Admiral Gravely Boulevard. The new Fulton would
have the best of everything.

If urban renewal gave neighborhood leaders a means of bringing their neighborhood's physical appearance up to middle-class
standards, it also provided a tool with which to "purify" its social
makeup. I can imagine Jacob Pinckney, Betty Norton, and other
defenders of Fulton savoring the tactical advantages that clearance provided.

For one thing, the pool hall was situated in the path of the
realigned Williamsburg Avenue and would be among the first
buildings demolished. Citizen planners had made no provision
for a pool hall in the new Fulton, so it would have to move to
another neighborhood, as would its clientele. And what about
welfare mothers? At present 60 percent of the housing in Fulton
was rental housing, and rents were extremely low. This propor-
tion would be reduced to the 25-percent minimum required by
HUD. And these units would be located along Williamsburg
Avenue, where citizen planners felt they would be useful as a
buffer against that arterial and the industrial area beyond.

There would be fewer tenants in the new Fulton, and neighborhood defenders felt that the crime rate would go down accordingly. As one citizen planner told me later, "When you open
up to rentals, you don't know who you are bringing in. You are
going to invite in dope addicts plus other illegal activities."

Pool sharks and welfare mothers were not well represented
among the few Fulton residents who attended urban renewal
planning meetings each week, and neither were tenants generally. In one meeting the citizens had proposed eliminating rental
housing altogether. When the housing authority planners replied
that rental units were a condition of federal funding, the citizens
urged them, at the very least, to isolate rental units from the
rest of the community by placing them on swampy ground near
Gillies Creek and surrounding them entirely with industry.

Fulton's leaders seemed to think that deteriorated housing encouraged and concealed the people who were the cause of the
neighborhood's problems. Thus to Jacob Pinckney and his co-

horts, clearance was a godsend. Clearance was slow but all en-compassing. When Matte Curtis's house was torn down, she would have the choice of relocating to new housing within the neighborhood and giving up her trade in illegal whiskey, or mov-ing to a slum where the terrain lay more in her favor. Waddy and Nell Crowder would face a similar choice. When the project was complete, Willie Cozart would no longer live here, since he lacked the income to purchase a house yet was not poor enough to qualify for subsidy housing. The phenomena that threatened the traditional culture of Fulton could be considered temporary, whereas the buildings, streets, and playgrounds designed by the citizen planning committee could be thought of as permanent. Neighborhood leaders intended to clear and remake this neigh-borhood in the image of the most prestigious suburbs. They thought of their work as a tribute to the men and women who had founded Fulton and as a practical means of cleansing it of those who were uncouth, poor, or rowdy.

Chief among the citizen planners were the four men who figured most prominently in the power struggle of March 1968. Of these four leaders, Daniel Brady might have been expected to represent Fulton's tenants in renewal planning meetings, for he was a tenant himself, had been poor as a child, and had spent time in prison alongside the sons of tenant families from Fulton and other Richmond neighborhoods. But this was not to be. As soon as Brady secured his own position he quickly shed any ties he might have possessed with the rougher and poorer residents of Fulton.

In the months following the March on City Hall, Brady and Waterman consolidated their positions of leadership and met frequently with housing authority officials to put together the details of how and where government money would be spent in Fulton. In these days immediately following their victory, things appeared to be progressing smoothly, and Brady thought he was doing an intelligent job of distributing the spoils of battle. As the months passed, renewal planning progressed in ways that were intangible to those who lived here. Brady and other leaders spent most of their time in meetings and, as they grew better educated on the subject of urban renewal, became progressively more isolated from the neighborhood as a whole. Unfortunately for Fulton, Brady's style of leadership reinforced this isolation. Casting himself in the role of champion, Brady achieved some remarkable successes but did little to give residents a sense of their own power. He did not show Fulton folk how to use urban renewal to reshape their lives.

Brady liked to give the impression that he had contacts, that he could make anything happen. When Betty Norton's unnamed civic group decided to sponsor a cleanup campaign, it was Brady who negotiated with merchants uptown and downtown to donate sodas. A cleanup campaign is impossible without sodas with which to reward the workers. Brady got to know the people at an Easter egg wholesale house. Nothing to it! Every Easter for years afterward he distributed crates of free Easter eggs to Fulton kids. But that's not all. Only a month after becoming Fulton's official leader in the eyes of the housing authority and on the golden paperwork they submitted to Washington, Brady landed a $3,300 planning grant from the Richmond Community Action Program. And a few months later he negotiated a $7,500 grant from St. Stephens Episcopal Church. Nothing to it! The wider culture had plenty of sodas and Easter eggs to give, and Daniel Brady was happy to serve as the conduit for these riches. He was a generous man, and although his way of outfoxing the city world and living by his wits was similar to that of Fulton's bootleggers, members of all classes were happy to receive the benefits.

Brady was ill-equipped to make Fulton's staging program a success, however, for he did not know how to develop a constituency, how to bring forward the real needs of Fulton residents who had an interest in seeing the project progress. Brady's style tended to reinforce patterns of dependency. Fulton's poor were used to taking what they were given. What they needed was a leader who would encourage them to develop skills, to take better care of themselves and their families, to use urban renewal as a way of improving their circumstances. Although the staging program appeared to have considerable momentum in May 1970, without a real constituency demanding results that it could see and understand, the momentum would soon be lost. Then Fulton's leaders would be vulnerable, for the housing authority was "thinking of its own image," as Stirling put it, and had little incentive to enter into a venture such as staging, which was complicated and risky.

Still, Brady's personal style, in itself, was only the beginning of the problem with his leadership. The heart of his difficulties had to do with a choice he made, a choice between using his position to attain personal success and using it to implement a successful staging program. In March 1968 he did not have a wife, a house, or a job. A year later the man who had sworn never to move from Fulton had married, moved to a nice house in Richmond's West End, and taken a full-time job as the citizen coordinator of urban renewal. The man whose rage had recommended him to Fulton residents now was working alongside housing authority planners, his former antagonists. At first Brady's position was funded by the grant from St. Stephens Church, but by 1970 he was on the housing authority payroll. In either case, Fulton residents could see that he was benefiting personally from his position as leader. Alford Stirling had rallied people during the civil rights movement by appealing to their sense of pride, but Daniel Brady could not do the same. He lost his authority the moment he took his first paycheck.

Fulton's first families never fully accepted Brady as neighborhood leader. Other residents backed him in March 1968 but began to withdraw their support a year later when he started making money. Robert Lumpkin, the white grocer, had admired Brady for his initial outspoken attacks on the housing authority. But when I talked to him several years later he accused Brady of "two-timing" the people of Fulton. "Brady was fighting the redevelopment and housing. All of a sudden they offered him a job paying an enormous amount of money, and he switched sides in the middle of the stream."

Fulton's recent immigrants from the country and failed working folk concurred with Lumpkin. They thought Brady ignored them and curried the favor of Fulton's old families in an attempt to rebuild his reputation. And, more to the point, they judged that he had sold out to the housing authority for a little money, professional status, and a desk of his own. As Minnie Fulkes told me later, "He ain't did nothing but take the money."

Minnie Fulkes frequently saw Brady walk past her wooden shack to Richard C. Moring's brick mansion. She admired Moring but was jealous and once referred to him as "that bigshot man living on the corner." Minnie assumed that Brady was explaining to Moring the details of renewal, how and when and how much he would get for his house. Still, Minnie resented the fact that Brady never stopped in to counsel her about the few pennies in moving expenses that would be coming her way. "As far as Brady's coming out to us, the little poorshot, to get us our little money, we ain't got none. He just go around to the ones that he going to get a dollar or two out of the deal."

Brady did not have control of renewal funds and therefore had little opportunity to be dishonest, but the public perception, particularly on the part of "poorshots" like Minnie Fulkes, was quite the contrary. "Brady and Moring were two crooks together," she told me later. "You take two crooks together you know they ain't doing nothing right."

During 1970 and 1971 angry black leaders were in demand on the lecture circuit. Brady traveled to Detroit and Baltimore to display his rage to admiring audiences. He traveled to Washington to confer with HUD officials.

In the meantime, the staging program still lacked a constituency and was going nowhere. Dozens of neighborhood residents attended planning meetings and seminars at the site office in the old liquor store on Williamsburg Avenue. The housing authority's project director kept the doors of this office open four evenings every week simply to answer questions. Even so, renewal was being planned in isolation. Those residents who visited the site office to ask questions never saw anything to be gained through renewal and never moved or pushed or pressured their leaders who were making the plans. Urban renewal was being handed down from above. It was the gift of a small group of fourth-generation leaders to their neighborhood. But their "neighborhood" did not include Fulton's tenants. Ironically, Fulton's leaders were planning urban renewal on behalf of neighborhood homeowners, even though these homeowners were not particularly interested in continuing to live here, given the alternatives.

Nearly all the homeowners of Fulton belonged to the third generation. They had made their great effort at community building decades before and were now concerned to protect what they had gained. And that value resided in their houses. Federal relocation benefits and $15,000 grants made it possible for them to move to another neighborhood if they chose and thereby transfer their investment to a place where there was little or no crime, where parents disciplined their children. Why should these homeowners stay in Fulton? The purchase of a new house in a new Fulton would be a wise investment only if the renewal project was completed successfully. If federal funds ran out when the project was half finished, the savings of a lifetime would be put in jeopardy. No one trusted the government to make good on its promises.

Neither did homeowners trust the staging plan developed by their own leaders. Ophelia Whitley's daughter was one. "Frankly, I could never see it," she told me. "How were you going to move people from one area and where were you going to put them? You have to build your sewer lines and electricity and all that, and to me you couldn't do that in stages, not unless you were going to keep the same street pattern."

Fulton residents hesitated to bring up controversial topics in public. Dozens of homeowners attended the March on City Hall, yet this action was not an accurate gauge of their loyalties. Many of them, like Ophelia's daughter, never expressed their true feelings. "I never talked against the plan to anyone outside of my home," she said, "because I didn't want anyone to say I was against what the [citizen planning] committee was doing. But

within our home we just couldn't see it working." Fulton's homeowners would have to see results to believe in the renewal plan.
They would have to feel the momentum. But they were not the
ones to generate that momentum.

On the other hand, Fulton's tenants (many of whom had
moved here after World War II) included men and women who
felt they had not yet succeeded in life. If their aspirations had
been awakened, they could have exercised more control over
their children, reduced crime, or at least the fear of crime, and
supplied the push to force neighborhood leaders and the housing
authority to address the real problems of real people. Alford
Stirling had reached out to Fulton's tenants during civil rights.
If Daniel Brady could have done the same in 1970 and 1971 the
staging program might have succeeded, and Fulton might have
survived. As it was, neighborhood leaders were drifting off into
ethereal visions of Fulton's future, while the housing authority
was pursuing a different agenda altogether.

In the lull following the March on City Hall in 1970, it appeared that the major battle for the restoration of Fulton had
been fought and won. But behind the scenes, the housing authority was probing, penetrating Fulton more deeply, and extending its control over every block. Neighborhood leaders had
stood before the television cameras and spoken on behalf of the
urban renewal plan, and their endorsement gave the housing
authority carte blanche in the neighborhood. As the months
passed, the endorsement of Fulton leaders would remain an
undeniable, historical fact. But the conditions on which that
endorsement was gained—namely, that Fulton would be maintained as a community during the renewal process—became
blurred, eminently deniable.

In the fall of 1970 a new project director moved into the
renewal site office. He was quick to argue the impracticality of
staging: large parcels of land needed to be packaged so that construction prices could be kept low; trunk lines for water, sewer,
and gas had to be put in place before construction could begin;

maintaining utilities to houses that were still occupied during construction would be difficult if not impossible. But if staging was impractical, how could Fulton survive? The obvious answer, the project director pointed out, was not staging but temporary relocation: residents would move en masse to other neighborhoods, then return to Fulton a year or two later when houses had been constructed here.

Ezra Whitley had moved from Fulton on his own. I think he was self-conscious about having abandoned ship so early and was disconcerted at the talk about residents who had relocated returning to Fulton. His response to the temporary relocation scheme went something like this: "One move is all I can handle!"

Ezra Whitley was a community-spirited man, a member of the Bel Aire Club who had served as a citizen planner in designing the staging plan. If he found it too great a burden to move twice, what could be expected of homeowners like Jack and Abby Mosby who were oblivious to renewal, or to those like Patience Gromes who were too old to carry cardboard boxes packed with dishes? Did anyone really believe they would move back to Fulton once construction had been completed?

The $15,000 replacement housing grants were the tool that would enable a staging program to rebuild Fulton, yet they were also the chief threat to staging. These grants provided an incentive for Fulton's homeowners to purchase houses in more exclusive neighborhoods, for a house in the suburbs would always be worth more than one in Richmond's old, unfashionable East End. No matter how deftly curved its cul-de-sac, a new house in Fulton would be only a few blocks away from the public housing required by HUD. How could Fulton, as a location, compete with Heckler Village? Did anyone really expect Fulton residents to move twice when they could move once and get more for their money?

In the months following the March on City Hall, it became more and more clear that the housing authority did not favor staging and would do nothing to implement it unless forced to do so. Neighborhood leaders were at a loss as to how to proceed. Brady responded by pacing back and forth before the television

cameras, hosting more black dignitaries on limousine tours of
Fulton, serenading the city council with lengthy, rasping
speeches. It was all to no avail. His partner, Stepney Waterman,
was equally stymied. He told me later of one run-in with the
housing authority:

"I met with them in the evening and Mr. Fey told me the law
was one way, but when we met at 10:00 the next morning, he
told me the law was something else. 'You lyin' sons of bitches,'
I told them. 'Congressmen in Washington, D.C., don't work at
night, you all don't work at night.' "

Waterman complained to me that housing authority officials
would make concessions in one meeting, then, weeks later, bring
out drawings that showed no sign of change and continue their
discussion as though nothing had happened. At the time Waterman felt that the housing authority and, more to the point,
unidentified figures behind this agency, still wanted to take Fulton for industry. The planners and their bosses thought this reasoning was foolish and they said so. Still, Waterman was
convinced that the housing authority was deliberately trying to
disorient Fulton residents and cut off city services in hope that
residents would become discouraged and leave.

Alford Stirling agreed. "In the beginning they wanted to railroad us. Then that stiff fight was put up, and they slowed down,
just like North Carolina University do when they get ahead,
what they call 'pull a slowdown' and wait the residents out. If
they are able to wait people out, they usually get their way."

How could Fultonians deal with this kind of slipperiness? A
well-delivered curse sometimes had proven decisive in disputes
among themselves. But the housing authority was immune. As
Waterman put it, "You can't just walk into the Man's office and
bless him out." What could a person do?

For one thing, Brady and Waterman could have lit a fire under
the city council and enlisted it to put pressure on the housing
authority. But here Brady's tactics prevented his being as effective
as he needed to be. The council listened to his speeches, counted
his troops, but never put the screws on the housing authority.

When it came to more substantial, private conversation, Brady lacked the requisite ability, or clout, or both.

But Brady's political style was only the first obstacle to motivating the city council. Civil-rights litigation prevented city council elections in Richmond for seven years, from 1970 to 1977. The city council had no reason to come to Fulton residents for their support; consequently, Brady and other leaders had little leverage. Fulton had demonstrated ability to get out the vote and might have used the media to influence the votes of others.

But even if elections had been held, I doubt Fulton's leaders would have gained active council support for staging since they still could not demonstrate that staging was feasible. No amount of political pressure, it appeared, could negate the expert opinions on which the housing authority rested its case. Neighborhood leaders lacked an expert who could define the possible in their own interests, as the housing authority had done for itself. Staging had seemed feasible several years earlier when officials first mentioned it in connection with their plan to take most of Fulton for industry. Why was it that now, when staging would serve the residents' interests, it was quite out of reason?

Staging was stuck in a bog, and no one could see how to rescue it or knew how long it would take to do so. In the meantime, Fulton's leaders tried to minimize the impact of renewal by spending the first two years' money acquiring vacant land and houses and relocating ahead of schedule residents like Ophelia Whitley who could demonstrate special need. The citizen planning committee spread funds so thinly that residents could not see progress and began to doubt that the promises of renewal ever would be kept. For staging to succeed the renewal agency should have concentrated its money. It should have purchased a solid block of land, demolished the houses, and begun work on new structures.

By 1971 everyone in Fulton who thought about it knew that staging was in trouble. But the implications for the survival of Fulton were obscured. Renewal floated all considerations in a kind of mist. The project director and his associates in the site office were patient and helpful. The drawings of the sports complex, the park, the lots, and the houses were seductive. It was difficult to believe that urban renewal could make things worse than they already were. What did Fulton have to lose? How could all that federal money hurt? As Alford Stirling observed later, "Everybody was sort of lulled to sleep."

A year had passed since the "March on City Hall." And now it was time for the citizens of Fulton to repeat their earlier performance, to lobby the city council to include the city's one-third matching money in the coming year's budget. This meeting, like the one a year earlier, was televised live on the public station. But this meeting never found its place in neighborhood memory, never was given a name or distinguished in any way from dozens of other renewal meetings. The speeches were pro forma. Daniel Brady was no longer the fire-breathing orator of the early rallies. He followed Mr. Fey of the housing authority at the microphone to endorse the renewal proposal Fey had outlined. Brady did not mention staging:

> Mr. Mayor, City Manager, and Members of Council, my name is Daniel Taylor Brady, a resident of Fulton and a member of the Fulton Ad Hoc Committee.
>
> At the risk of being repetitious I would like to say to members of Council which have not been here before that this is a plan which has been in the making since nineteen hundred sixty-eight. That the people of Fulton worked on the plan, carried the plan before the city planning commission, and the city planning commission approved it.
>
> This is a plan that the mayor and each department head of the city of Richmond saw and eventually approved. This is a plan that was brought before city council and up until today it has been approved by city council.
>
> We are coming here tonight asking members of city council, if you will, to approve the presentation that the housing authority has presented. We know what is in the plan. We know what is going into the plan, and the reason we know it is because we helped to create it to date.

And I think there is no doubt in the back of the minds of any of you as to what Fulton will do if anyone, any organization or bureaucracy or whatnot, should go against the will of the people of Fulton.

Heretofore we have worked closely with city council, the planning commission to get what we want. We are very grateful that we've got this far, we are grateful to God. We hope you will let us continue.

A year earlier Fulton residents had gone to the city council to fight for an idea. But now the issues had grown more complex. Neither Brady nor anyone else could see the end toward which the neighborhood and the housing authority were drifting, and the idea itself was in doubt.

Urban renewal was supposed to revitalize Fulton, and no one knew for certain whether it would or would not. But the facts that slowly came to light following the March on City Hall suggested only that it would divide and scatter those who lived here. The men and women of Fulton wanted to believe their neighborhood would survive. Neighborhood leaders kept talking about staging, discussing plans for tearing down this section first, that section next. No one looked too hard at the facts. As Stirling told me later, "Everybody kept hoping it would come out the way they wanted it to come out."

In April 1971 I saw Harrison's drugstore going down. Black men with wrecking bars pried loose the floor joists. A truck hauled loads of brick to the M&M Wrecking Yard at the edge of Fulton. Here I saw an old black man sitting on a wooden box amidst the piles of rubble. He handled one brick at a time, smacking the mortar with a hatchet, placing cleaned bricks in six-foot stacks. These bricks were in demand for expensive houses being built in the other end of town.

The loss of Harrison's drugstore was an unpleasant reminder to Fulton residents that their neighborhood was indeed undergoing urban renewal. Harrison's had occupied one corner of Fulton's main intersection for decades, standing two stories above the

street, and now this block, which once had been the main block
of Fulton's business district, had lost one of its walls. Harrison's
had been closed for a couple of years. Now, suddenly, it was no
longer here at all, the block looked different, and residents wondered uneasily what was next.

Since the March on City Hall, visible progress had been nil.
The housing authority slowly began to purchase land and houses
while the detailed plans according to which the neighborhood
would be destroyed or reborn were drafted, fought over, drafted
again. Nothing was happening that anyone could see. Urban
renewal was going on but mostly in an abstract realm far removed
from the streets and alleys of Fulton, the way events in the
newspaper sometimes seem far removed from reality. A few people followed the developments with a curious interest, like that
of people who check the stock market each evening just for the
sake of poking into the financial section. Urban renewal was
diffuse and dreamlike, spinning a fine web around the neighborhood. A person could never quite understand it or pin it down.
Then one day it hit like a freight train coming around a corner.

Abby Mosby owned her own house, but she did not know
much about urban renewal. She was a mother first and last. She
had never been to the urban renewal meetings, although she
heard a few rumors. To her it was all just a rumor.

The rumor spread through Fulton. Printed leaflets strewn in
the gutter announced it. So did one or two houses in each block
that were vacant and boarded up and displayed yellow signs.

Fulton people talked about urban renewal and embellished the
rumor a bit every Wednesday evening when the planners brought
their maps and charts to the site office in the old liquor store.
Sitting inside on metal folding chairs were a few Fulton residents,
working people who could understand and endure the endless
talk of the planners. Passersby knew something was afoot. They
could tell it was not a lodge meeting, for women were present.
And they did not mistake it for a crap game, because the lights
were bright and the shades were up. They knew it was not a
raiding party preparing for an evening of grand larceny on Church

Hill, because where were the tough guys in red pants? But it was hard to understand, looking in the great windows of the old storefront, that this gathering would decide the fate of Fulton.

The Wednesday evening meetings went on like rain in winter: they were interminable; they stopped after a few hours, but began again days later; they never built up to a crescendo, nor did they ever disappear entirely. There were twenty-five hundred people still living in Fulton. Eight corner groceries extended credit for preferred customers, and seven churches, not counting storefront churches, held services each Sunday. Fulton still had its own undertaker's parlor, and, when funeral time came, Fulton folk wearing dark clothes crowded close in the street and watched silently as black, polished cars drove past. Henderson's store still had coal sacks stacked in front, and its hand-painted sign advertising for sale the meat of coons and possums still hung above the door. According to rumor, urban renewal was taking place in Fulton, but a woman I met in Rocketts whose ceiling fell in a little more with the rain each winter knew only that things had not gotten better: a neighbor had died, another had moved, the future was dim—as it always had been.

Fitfully the rumor tightened its grip on Fulton. For months there was nothing but winter cold and stories about one's neighbors. And then, unannounced, the heavy bulldozers and dump trucks took a house, quickly—a house that had stood for sixty or eighty years. On Nicholson I saw a flat-bed truck and two dump trucks backed up across the curb. In the lot itself was a Caterpillar tractor crawling over the stubs of the front walls and using its scoop blade against the splintered wood as though it were an animal chewing at the innards of this house.

In each block were houses where men and women still slept and cooked and received mail. But among them now one could see other houses, wrecked houses, and it seemed as though the dead had appeared among the living.

On Louisiana Street I saw a wooden tenement that had housed twenty families at the time of my arrival in Fulton. Now, a year later, the tenement was empty with the exception of the Stokes family. Mr. Stokes was sick and bedridden. Sometimes I saw his daughters tending their plants in the small, square front yard, its wooden fences still upright while neighboring fences had been smashed down. One day I noticed that the Stokes family had moved.

The tenement was empty now and workmen nailed plywood over the windows and doors. But a month later new inhabitants arrived, broke open a back door and ripped the plywood from a window. Cast-off syringes joined the wine bottles and beer cans in the yard. As the months passed the more civilized elements of Fulton began to deposit their tailings here as well. I saw broken baby carriages, bent tricycles, old dishes, kitchen tables, ironing boards without legs.

Around the corner on Williamsburg, Queen's store had a fire. The firemen broke out windows, hosed the place down, and it was black and full of smoke. After the flames were gone, the firemen went at the store with axes and shovels, clearing the debris. When they were gone I saw the wet guts of Queen's store piled on the sidewalk. In the center of another block a dozen dogs were chained to trees and ran on packed earth and howled. In a workyard beside a wooden house lumber grew wet and the rounded bodies of washing machines glistened white and wet. A refrigerator missing its door rested sideways on the ground as though for some purpose and was wet and slick in the rain. I saw a narrow house that stood alone in a field with curtains in the windows, a chair on the front stoop, and a great, ragged wound where weatherboards had been ripped and torn from its side, leaving odd strips hanging.

Fulton was a place that was wed to an idea, and it was breaking apart in the hands of those who lived and worked here. It happened piece by piece, so that I never perceived the larger trend until, at year's end, I thought back and realized how different this community had been twelve months before. A little more had been lost, never to be recovered. A powerful, mysterious force was loose all around, and no one could pin it down or call it to account. Fulton residents never could see what it was they were trying to fight. Perhaps it was only a rumor after all. How much better to forget the whole thing and take a good-paying job with Philip Morris.

9

LOW LIFE
1968-1972

BEGINNING in 1968 Fulton's defenders tried to use urban renewal as a weapon. Their efforts were to no avail. Renewal was powerful but indiscriminate. Although it would move the rougher type of people from Fulton, it threatened to move everyone else as well.

Renewal was an apparatus without a soul of its own. It could never serve good ends unless governed by a vision. Only a vision could convince neighborhood residents to endure months of inconvenience, to move twice or live in a construction zone, or to take the risk that the program would collapse before federal grants arrived. Only a vision could motivate neighborhood leaders to find experts of their own who would overrule the technical imperatives of the planners. Patience Gromes had come in from the country with such a vision. Neighborhood civil rights leaders had had a vision. But the urban renewal project of Fulton's citizen planners did not. It began as an effort to stop the housing authority cold. Then it jumped to the goal of building new houses and getting rid of tenants. The citizen planners had a material goal, but it was not inspired by anything higher. They pulled down the vision of their parents and tried to fit it within the program. Needless to say, ideals developed in the country for people who lacked political power or government help lost their meaning when put into a package that included bureaucrats, federal regulations, politicians, and wads of federal cash.

These days Fulton's leaders spent more and more time in meetings, burrowed deeper into the technicalities of urban renewal. They left the task of evangelizing on behalf of the old ideals to the Reverend Squire Dowd and a few other fearless souls.

If the old virtues now were poorly represented on the street corners of Fulton, the opposite was true for the old evils. After the advent of urban renewal the influence of neighborhood bootleggers like Waddy and Nell Crowder grew in unexpected ways. During the long hot summers, neighborhood youth had begun to be radicalized. After the murder of Martin Luther King, Jr., they looked for an alternative to traditional virtues and found it in the example of Waddy Crowder. Waddy was a plain man, not a philosopher like Willy Cozart, the vet who spent his time talking about life in the ghetto. But Waddy had succeeded in living outside the law for fifty years. And his plainness made his example powerful. If a little man like Waddy Crowder could make his million, street youths figured they would have little difficulty doing the same.

Although public evangelists such as the Reverend Dowd had grown scarce, bootleggers and other sinners still met resistance from their immediate neighbors. On the 800 block of Orleans Street five women occupied three wooden row houses that looked directly across the street at the dwelling of Waddy and Nell Crowder. Three of these women solidly opposed Waddy and Nell, one of them was an ally, and the last was a woman who turned both directions.

The first house belonged to Analiza Foster, a heavy-set woman who wore flower print dresses, and her mother, a mild, white-haired woman who had come from the country about the same time as Patience Gromes. Analiza had strayed from the straight and narrow in her youth and, by rights, should have been an ally of Waddy Crowder. Hammer, the baseball player who had been her lover, had been a customer of Waddy's. Nowadays her son Snort was a regular at Waddy's and her grandson Tub dropped in occasionally. But motherhood had changed Analiza. Twenty years on a welfare budget was a steep price to pay for good times that, in retrospect, weren't all that good. She mourned the lost opportunities of her youth. These days Analiza lived for her sons and daughters. She fed and clothed them, sent them to school each day, took them to Mt. Calvary Baptist on Sundays. She tried to equip them to make better choices than she had made. When Analiza looked across the street at Waddy Crowder and the drunks who decorated his front porch she didn't see anyone who would help her children lead good lives. Alcohol disgusted Analiza, and people who sold alcohol illegally made her angry.

Analiza's mother had settled the right and wrong of Waddy Crowder's bootlegging operation long before and elevated her thought to the point where she could look across the street with perfect equanimity. From early morning until midday she sat in a metal chair on her porch and rocked gently. It was quiet across the street, and she rested in the day's new light. Morning traffic on Orleans Street was slow, but occasionally a neighbor woman paused a few moments to pay her respects.

"How you doin', mumma?"

"Kinda so. Kinda so."

Analiza's mother did not approve of Waddy and Nell but did not fuss about them. She seemed to trust the example of her life and her well-kept house to argue silently in her behalf.

The second house was rented to Clara Jones and her mother. Clara was a bony woman with thick glasses who, I imagined, never had enough to eat. She was a teetotaler but Jewel, her mother, had different tastes. Jewel craved corn liquor. She had a potbelly and lay snoring in bed until noon, then arose and prepared a heavy meal. She ate well, thanks to her daughter, who spent hours scrawling budgets on the backs of envelopes, saving pennies from her welfare allotment toward the purchase of food. In late afternoon Jewel would wander across the street to Waddy and Nell's, where she became, in her own estimation, the life of the party.

The third house was rented to Hattie Rogers, who drank on

the sly. Hattie was a withered woman in her eighties who wore a synthetic wig over her matted, white hair, and who frequently poisoned herself by eating food cooked in lard. She loved the taste of that "grease," even though it made her "some kinda sick," Clara told me, and it was hard for her to go two weeks without it. When she was healthy, Hattie sat on her front porch in the afternoons and kept track of doings on Orleans Street, never hesitating to ask neighbors to repeat portions of conversation she had been unable to overhear. When the drunken arguments of late afternoon began, Hattie walked down from her porch and "stood right up in the face" of the disputants, prodding them for explanations where their logic grew confused.

Clara accused Hattie of "nosin' and dippin' " into other people's business, but that was not the true cause of her enmity. Clara was death on Waddy and Nell, whereas Mrs. Hattie was a woman of divided loyalties.

Clara feared for her mother. How long could Jewel live, drinking the way she did? Clara accused Waddy and Nell of exploiting her mother's weaknesses for their own profit, and they in turn accused her of "doggin' Jewel around" and otherwise badgering and scolding her to distraction. Analiza Foster backed Clara all the way, and Analiza's mother provided spiritual leadership to their cause. But the more vigorously Clara pressed the attack, the more openly Jewel sided with the enemy. Nothing could turn Jewel around. In fear and sorrow for her mother, Clara Jones found the behavior of Hattie Rogers distasteful, to say the least.

At dinner time, when neither Clara nor Analiza was out front, Hattie would sneak over to Waddy and Nell's. Once inside, she would purchase a drink, usually on credit.

"This is just for my arthritis," she'd say. "Don't tell anyone."

Back on her front porch once again, Hattie would look out with a dignified air. If Clara walked past after dinner Hattie would stop her and nod in the direction of Waddy and Nell's. "They ought to call the Man on them," she'd say.

Every summer Hattie Rogers looked forward to the Fourth of July and, most particularly, to the Fourth of July party at Waddy and Nell's, to which she was not invited. Jewel was invited, although she minimized the importance of her invitation and consciously declined to prepare herself for this event any more than she did for the night-long parties held the first and third of every month to celebrate the arrival of welfare and Social Security checks. For her part, Analiza's mother was happy to be excluded, although she was sad about the inconvenience, since her daughter would not allow her to sit out front on the Fourth.

Upstanding citizens of Fulton regarded the Fourth of July as the anniversary of their country's birth, but it was a very different kind of anniversary to Nell Crowder. One Fourth of July many years before she had parted from her husband in a last, decisive argument. He was her first husband, the father of her children, and, although she left her second husband on equally unfriendly terms, it was that first dissolution that came back to haunt her.

Invariably the Fourth started out well enough, much like any day, but with more men and more drink. Waddy and Nell rose late and ate a meal at the kitchen table, then Waddy came out front to warm his blood a little and Nell walked to Lumpkin's Supermarket to purchase supplies. Their first customers were middle-aged men who came in late afternoon to buy drinks, sit on the front stoop, and share the wisdom that drink brought forth in them. In the beginning these men spoke civilly, but later they began to quarrel, shouting and making violent, unbalanced gestures. At dinnertime a somewhat younger and tougher crowd of men came to visit. Chief among them was William Francis— Snort. He and his comrades went inside to purchase drinks, then came out front to shoot craps. Snort was huge and never seemed to be in a good mood. The middle-aged men became subdued when he appeared, and shortly before dusk they returned to their homes in Fulton where faithful, sober wives waited to bathe them and put them to bed.

The tough crowd stayed until late, or stayed an hour, then drove to Roach's Store, the saloon with apartments above where one tenant, an amputee, hung his artificial limb out a back window to air. Sometimes Snort and his followers stopped by the poolroom to play cards with gamblers at the round table, but usually they did not, for this was the hangout of younger men.

The wisdom of afternoon and the quarreling of evening were succeeded on this day with a crescendo of fights. By now a "spell" had come over Nell, the product of bad drink and worse memory perhaps, but according to Clara it was simply the "devil in her" coming out. Nell possessed the sole key to the gun closet. She left the party for a moment, then came out shooting. Drunken men stumbled and ran to get out of the way. Some jumped from the windows, others dove from the porch, everyone scrambled to find cover. Nell may have grazed one or two before she cleared the place, but she didn't hit anyone—not that they would have felt any pain if she had. Except for Jewel, who had earlier refused her daughter's rescue mission and now lay blissfully unconscious on a bedroom floor, Nell was alone. After a night of solitude she became her old self again and welcomed Waddy back home.

Analiza and Clara did their best to uphold traditional virtues against the example of the Crowders. Once the old ways had been unassailable, but now they needed every advantage to hold their own. Without knowing it, I ended up tipping the balance of power decisively in favor of these fourth-generation defenders.

By the beginning of my second year in Fulton, the Poor People's Club, which Betty Norton had stolen from Matte Curtis but had never gotten around to naming, became known as the Fulton League. Although Betty Norton still attended, she had resigned as president in favor of Analiza Foster, who held meetings next door in Clara Jones's kitchen. We still helped residents apply for food stamps, or found free lawyers for residents who had been victimized by door-to-door salesmen, or called the health department to force a landlord to make repairs. The Fulton League also invited city officials to speak at public meetings held at the Bethlehem Center. On one such occasion a representative from the water company explained how bills were calculated.

Analiza Foster was proud to serve as president of the Fulton League. Clara Jones was proud to serve as hostess. Waddy and Nell Crowder watched the comings and goings from across the street and sneered at the whole affair. Secretly, however, they were jealous.

Nearly every week I came to visit Analiza or Clara on business, but the residents of this block felt I came as an ally. For their part Analiza and Clara were quick to exploit the advantage I conferred. In conversation with neighbors they left the impression that their faction had contacts in the world beyond Fulton. People had been fussing about water bills for many a year, they pointed out, but Analiza and Clara were the "onliest somebodies" who had ever done anything about it. Analiza and Clara did not say that Waddy and Nell were crude, backward, and ignorant. They simply provided evidence of their own sophistication and allowed neighbors to draw their own conclusions.

As far as Waddy and Nell were concerned, the antics of Analiza and Clara were bearable, even humorous. But that was before the television episode.

Analiza Foster had led the fight for a food-stamp purchase station in Fulton. The women of the Fulton League drew up petitions and collected signatures. Each meeting they delivered speeches across the kitchen table explaining the need for the purchase station, and at each go around their speeches became more polished. Finally I drove three of them uptown to speak with the city's director of welfare. Against the advice of his staff, he granted their request. Two months later, the station was installed in a corner of the Bethlehem Center's quonset hut. This occasion deserved television coverage, of course. That evening when Waddy and Nell turned on their TV, who should be looking out at them but Analiza Foster.

One day shortly after that I passed Nell Crowder on the sidewalk in front of her house. She gave me a quick look. "Come visit *us* some time," she said.

During my work in Fulton I was oblivious to the gradual decline of traditional virtues and to the rearguard actions being fought by defenders such as Analiza Foster and Clara Jones. I did not know much about the ideas of neighborhood patricians, and neither did I realize the significance of neighborhood bootleggers. To the parents and grandparents of Fulton's patricians, slavery was the classic definition of evil in this world. And Fulton residents found a little of the same evil in the Crowder's nip joint.

I did not think of bootleggers as evil. Matte Curtis, for example, seemed a type of revolutionary who broke the routine of day-to-day life. Of course, I had just graduated from college in the San Francisco Bay Area, where the prevailing wisdom held that we had long ago surpassed such categories as good and evil.

I never had the opportunity to visit Waddy and Nell during my two years' work in Fulton, but several years later I interviewed Clara Jones, who spoke more freely now that she lived at a distance from her old adversaries. One Fourth of July years before, Clara said, Nell Crowder stabbed her first husband to death with an ice pick. A few years later she threw lye in the face of her second husband and, later still, shot him to death. Nell had given the police a line to escape punishment for her first offense and did only a few years' time for her second. The police didn't pick up much evidence about the other people she killed. One man owed Nell money. She shot him to death on her front porch.

According to Clara, Waddy Crowder killed Smokey, an eighty-five year-old man, and also shot Charlie Crump, a "young boy" of perhaps thirty-five, who was carried to the hospital, where he died. Murdering people was bad enough, in Clara's view, but even worse was the spirit of meanness and disrespect with which Nell regarded her victims. "Nell never goes to the funerals of the people she kills," Clara said.

What had Waddy and Nell done to inspire such bizarre stories? I spoke with Thomas Arrington's daughter-in-law, who had lived a block from the Crowders for ten years. She was a generation younger than Clara Jones and was a teacher, so I could trust her to be more objective. "They have killed several over there," said Mrs. Arrington. "I haven't seen any get killed, but that's what I've heard."

The real problem with the Crowders, Mrs. Arrington said, wasn't bullets but alcohol. They sold bootleg whiskey on credit to dozens of pensioners, who gradually became dependent upon it. Many of them signed over their entire checks to Waddy and Nell each month to pay for the previous month's drink. Clara Jones's mother, Jewel, was but one example. The real crime of Waddy and Nell, to Mrs. Arrington, was not in shooting one or two of their cronies, but in playing upon the weaknesses of dozens of men and women simply for money. A few died from bullets, but many more died from alcohol.

I wanted to know more about Fulton's bootleggers. I thought my story of this community otherwise would be incomplete. Yet few residents would discuss the subject, even in generalities. I needed specifics. At length I decided to ask Waddy and Nell themselves.

Although I didn't realize it at the time, I was making a mistake. Waddy and Nell had blood on their hands. They were jittery. They had informed on dozens of their neighbors and never knew when the favor might be returned. Waddy and Nell had secrets to keep. I could sit in their house all day and observe liquor being sold without a license, but the moment I asked a question about their past, I became suspect. This is the kind of behavior they associated with plainclothes police. Under the circumstances, they could never believe that I wanted nothing more than a few anecdotes for my book.

I drove into Fulton on a Saturday afternoon in December. I saw blocks near the river that had been cleared and were now overgrown with weeds. Up from the river, dozens of houses were vacant and boarded, with only scattered dwellings still occupied. Fulton was eerie. No one was on the streets except Snort and his followers. They seemed more ominous than before because they had the place to themselves and could do whatever they pleased.

I parked my car around the corner from Waddy and Nell's. This side street had been cut away for the construction of Admiral Gravely Boulevard; my car faced a steel barrier. I locked up and walked into the street. When I was twenty paces from the Crowders' front porch I saw Nell coming toward me. She carried a shopping bag and appeared to be returning from the market. "Hello Chris," she said.

Nell always called me Chris because I looked like Chris, the VISTA who had worked in Fulton the year before I arrived. To her we were one and the same. She invited me to come inside.

The front hallway was dark. I walked forward, then a door opened and I saw two dozen men standing and sitting in a room, old and cavelike. Walls were rough and covered with soot. I saw a huge cast-iron stove glowing red and white and heard a fire sucking and rumbling inside. A man sat before the stove, arms crossed on his chest, and stared into the fire. I recognized Waddy Crowder.

Nell proceeded into a back room, the kitchen, and seemed to forget I was there. I sat down in a chair near an open door to the kitchen. There were men everywhere, but no one seemed to notice me. A man entered wearing a shooting vest with cartridges. He sat by the stove and felt the heat. Another man walked in and began to joke about hunters who can never kill a rabbit. I could hear a door opening and closing behind me. I turned and saw that there were two refrigerators in the kitchen. On a table were paper cups. Men walked in and out. They put dollar bills down on the table, took change, and returned with an amber liquid in their cups. In the corner opposite me, beyond the cast iron stove, a shotgun leaned in a corner. I wondered if it was loaded.

A dog the size of a large rat scampered at my feet, then ran into the kitchen. I followed. The door of one refrigerator was open and I could see inside. Where are the earthen jugs of corn whiskey, I thought? I saw clear, tall bottles with new labels. The bottles had black caps that had not been sealed with a tax stamp. Inside the bottles was an amber liquid.

Nell walked into the other room. A short man came into the kitchen, pulled a grape soda from the refrigerator and a bottle of vodka from a lower cabinet. Waddy walked in. Now was my chance. "Say, Waddy," I said, "do you know anything about stills and bootlegging in Fulton?"

Waddy looked at me with the expression of a man who has drunk too much lead-poisoned corn whiskey over the years. He grunted. Nell appeared from the other room. "Why don't you sit down in here, Chris?" she said and motioned me out of the kitchen.

I returned to my chair with nothing to do now that my attempt at rational inquiry had been thwarted. My thought drifted. I remembered the stories Clara had told me about this house, these men, and about Nell Crowder. The murders were real. I had never visualized them before, but sitting here I seemed powerless to exclude from my mind images of Nell's victims bleeding to death on her front porch.

I had always thought of this as Waddy's business, for he had founded it decades before when he arrived from North Carolina. But now he was dull-witted and seemed to fill the role of the heavy or trigger man. Nell, on the other hand, had a calculating intelligence. She missed nothing. Apparently she had become the mastermind of Waddy's operation, the one who schemed, negotiated, and enforced contracts with suppliers in Charles City County, bribed the police, cut out competitors. She was the one who prevented outsiders from learning too much, dealing with them swiftly and mercilessly if they came too close. The men she killed had probably caught her at a bad moment. On the other hand, they may have known too much, talked too freely.

I heard Nell's voice behind me in the kitchen. But this was not the folksy, charming Nell who used swear words with offhand familiarity. Nell was interrogating Waddy, speaking quickly and sharply in a low voice, a Gestapo voice, and her tone was one of cunning and evil such as I have never heard before. I could not quite make out her words.

"Yeah, something like that," Waddy mumbled.

Suddenly I realized that Nell was questioning Waddy about what he had said to me. Had Waddy given them away? I didn't need to hear Nell's words to understand what she was saying. I could feel her thought like a great stone blocking my escape: does Chris know too much?

I felt uneasy, to put it mildly. I wanted to run for the door. Why had I parked on a dead end street? If I ran out the back door I would have to climb the high back fence, for the gate was nailed shut. That fence would slow me up long enough for someone to unload a shotgun into my back.

I looked for the shotgun, but could not see it. It had been there; I knew it had been there. The hunters were still talking, but not about rabbits. One of them gestured with his hand across his head and shoulders. "Shot it clean off, man. Shot it clean off."

Nell Crowder stopped talking. Waddy walked into the living room. The hunters stood up and left as though by some signal.

I stood, turned, and entered the kitchen. Nell had returned to her jovial self. But she seemed over-friendly, as though trying to put me off guard. She opened the lid of a blue enamel pot on the stove. Inside I saw stewed meat falling away from bones, small and long. I suppose they were ribs, but they seemed to me like the fingers of her victims. "Would you like to stay for dinner," Nell said.

"I think maybe I should be going now, Mrs. Crowder," I said.

"Come by anytime," said Nell.

I walked into the other room. Waddy was stoking the fire, and I could see the shadows of fire moving on his face. I passed him and drew near the door, which was scarred from use and hung unevenly on its hinges. I closed it behind me. The hallway was dark, and I could not see. Was I alone? I opened the front door.

A car pulled up. There were a dozen men standing across the street and in their midst was a huge figure. It was Snort. I know too much, I thought.

The men came at me. I could see revolvers tucked, nose down, beneath their belts. I walked to the sidewalk to meet them, twenty paces from my car.

"How about a game of craps?" Snort said. He was talking to someone on the porch behind me. I got into my car and looked at the unmailed letters there, the Christmas present I had intended to send to a friend in another city. Let's get out of here, I told myself.

The notion that the social problems of poor, urban blacks are disorders that will disappear if they are given sympathy, government money, and a dose of technical expertise is based on illusions. It does not recognize the existence of evil—withering, bone-crushing evil like that of Nell Crowder.

Food stamps did nothing to free Jewel from Nell's influence (although they did prevent malnutrition and an early death). Welfare checks to Sammy Fulkes's mother allowed her family to have a place to live, but did not prevent Sammy from losing control of his life, taking drugs, committing crimes, going to prison. In themselves anti-poverty programs and urban renewal were useful in some ways but never reached to the mental and moral realm where the issues of life and death are decided.

I now think that Patience Gromes had more to offer her neighbors than anti-poverty experts such as myself. We had been to college, but she knew the difference between good and evil. In her own life she had turned this knowledge into power.

Patience Gromes thought of good as industry, chastity, love of family and church, and charity toward one's neighbors. She understood that good nourishes a family, gives it steadiness, assurance, and the ability to withstand the dulling influence of company work. She thought of evil as adultery, theft, lying, smoking, drinking, and gossip. And she knew that indulging evil inevitably brings sorrow, fear, and sickness.

Patience was raised and educated in a country setting only a few years after slavery. Patience and her family used images and scenarios drawn from slavery to interpret the data of their lives, to discern the powers beyond themselves, to devise a strategy for avoiding or overcoming obstacles. After the experience of slavery they recognized the practical importance of legal wills and deeds, legal contracts for their labor, legal marriage. They understood that outright confrontation with white authority could only prove disastrous, but that by avoiding conflict, developing skills, and purchasing property, they could gradually improve their lives and weaken the prejudices against them. To the family of Patience Gromes, slavery was a conclusive statement about the working of good and evil in the world.

Looking back on the situation of their race before 1865, the Armisteads discerned strengths of character that had enabled blacks to withstand the deadening effects of slavery. Love of family and a willingness to entrust their lives to a larger spiritual power gave them resilience and an ability to look past the provocations and hardships of the present. The Armisteads saw how master had played upon the weaknesses of black men and women to erode their will to resist. In some ways master encouraged sexual license and drunkenness and undermined stable family life. Master sometimes preferred to see his slaves dissipate their moral energy rather than use it to develop skills and intellect. Under slavery blacks were tempted to steal from master, to "live by their wits," in order to get due compensation for their labor. Yet stealing and then lying about it or playing dumb afterward corrupted them, reinforced their dependency, and discouraged them from challenging the system directly by rebelling or escaping.

The Armistead family and others of their race learned mental tactics in the years following the Civil War. Their memory of slavery gave them a convenient means of grasping elements of thought, distinguishing those that strengthened their cause from those that weakened it. As blacks assumed control over their own minds, they were able to improve their skills as farmers and entrepreneurs and thereby to alter their day-to-day lives. The object lessons of slavery enabled blacks to orient themselves, gather confidence, focus energy on the precise point where it would be most effective. To a people living in a hostile world with no hope of government assistance, an understanding of good and evil was the key to advancement.

When she came to the city, Patience Gromes saw drunks, gamblers, and thieves. To her these were blacks who had not advanced from slavery. Waddy Crowder was not the equivalent of a slave owner, exactly, but he preyed upon human failing. He destroyed an individual's character in order to control him. To men and women like Patience Gromes, these techniques hearkened back directly to the practice of the most unscrupulous slave owners.

As a member of the third generation, Patience Gromes worked to civilize a city neighborhood. And, as one who lived within a stone's throw of bootleggers and gamblers for sixty years, she knew that the prizes of civilized life are always in jeopardy and must be achieved again by each generation or they will wane and be lost. To her way of thinking good and evil are the primary distinction upon which the complex demarcations of a civilization depend.

Patience Gromes was convinced that good and evil are not the arbitrary designations of a class, a generation, or a culture. Her convictions were natural to one of her background. But now, after visiting Waddy and Nell and seeing with my own eyes, I can say more. Patience Gromes was right. Good and evil are not arbitrary conceptions. They are part of the nature of being in this world. They describe actual forces and conditions of life that we ignore at our peril.

Urban renewal was a perplexing variation on an old theme of evil. It was a new evil that never quite showed its colors, never provided an exact comparison to Waddy Crowder's bootlegging operation, or the gambling dens of this neighborhood, or the institution of slavery which lay in the background. Patience Gromes and her contemporaries knew in their hearts that renewal was wrong. Still, it was something they could not separate from themselves. It had caught the imagination of their sons and daughters, and it called upon the loyalties of all Fulton folk. In some ways it was a civic responsibility, like voting drives. Each year when the time came to march on city hall and ask the city council for next year's funding, Patience and her neighbors set aside their doubts, donned Sunday clothes, and waited by their front doors for a ride uptown.

Patience and her friends did not know what to think or do

about renewal. Neither did fourth-generation leaders, for all their new-found expertise. They beat the subject to death in private conversation but never came to a conclusion. Then an event occurred that broke through the mists and allowed all the people of Fulton to see where this project was headed. Urban renewal was moving slowly but steadily like an immense ship that takes hours to get up speed, that can't turn very well, and that requires twenty or thirty miles to come to a halt. Urban renewal was like a ship steaming through the fog. In June 1972 the fog cleared and everyone could see that it was heading for a rock.

10

FLOOD

June 1972

PEOPLE who live on low ground beside the James River expect summer spells of "hotsticky," as they call it, but this one had lasted too long. The sky was overcast, the air humid, and heat had been with us for days. It was night when the heat broke. Lightning struck, rain fell. The air was cool now, and the children of Fulton could sleep.

In the morning, fog moved up the James and ran over its banks, filling the bottom where the creek lay, funneling through streets and alleys. When I looked for Fulton from neighboring bluffs I could see nothing but fog, the top of the big stack at Sternheimer's, and the water tower with "Richmond Cedar Works" painted on its side. I heard a train down there. Its warning call sounded like a voice, and I could hear its engines, amplified on the elevated railway that bridges Gillies Creek and the industrial area beyond. The engines sounded dull and massive on this trestle, and I thought of ocean waves beating on a lost, fog-covered strip of land.

The following day the fog lifted. The sky was gray, and at first the rain was fine, like spray. But by noon rain was coming down hard on streets and sidewalks and vacant lots. Rain fell on the painted tin roofs of the houses on State, on the slate roofs of houses on Denny, and on the tar roofs of the new apartments and the school and the Bethlehem Center. Rain fell on the rooftops of the brick building where Simon's department store had been and the brick building where Charlie's pool room had been and on bare dirt and scattered brick where Harrison's drugstore had been. Rain fell on the wooded flanks of Clay Hill and drained down to make streams flowing in the street, creating eddies behind the wheels of parked automobiles, filling storm sewers to overflowing, finding its way through alleys and culverts to Gillies Creek in the swampy bottom beyond the school and playground and the last line of houses on Centre Street, beyond the bleak, modern apartments standing there, and carried forward in Gillies Creek, beneath three bridges, winding through the auto salvage yard and the M&M Wrecking yard, and passing the gas works and oil tanks to join the great James River, the magnificent, muddy James River, on its journey to the sea.

Rain came hard, in salvos, carried by the wind and driven by it, punishing the land, beating upon it. Water puddled on front and back stoops, ran under doors, drained down chimneys. Fulton folk kept within their houses and stayed dry the best they could. Homeowners took satisfaction in their tight, freshly painted tin roofs. Tenants ran back and forth with pots to catch the drips and could not sleep for the plop plop of leaking water. Folk could hear rain in their sleep, and once, when the bottom of heaven seemed to drop out, they awoke from what they thought was a train crash—but it was only rain slamming down on their roofs.

Rain fell for three days and three nights. It was all Fulton would get of Hurricane Agnes. And now the rain stopped, the sun dried rooftops, and steam rose from yards and from the wet sides of Clay Hill. The roads were dry and sewers contained themselves once again. In midday heat the radio told us that a flood was coming.

That afternoon all manner of people stood on East Main Street above the river to watch the water rise and old tires and pieces of outhouses and whole trees float past. At the Bethlehem Center we cleared the quonset hut, opened the double doors, and soon were labeling and stacking sofas and dressers and queen-size beds.

Most of this furniture belonged to welfare mothers who lived in cinderblock apartments in the Bottom. They had gotten wet two summers before when Gillies Creek flooded, so they needed little encouragement to evacuate now. By dinner time the hut was full, and the official evacuation had begun.

The houses in the Bottom were the first to be evacuated, followed by those near the trestle, those on Lewis with their back yards already getting wet, and then the first blocks of Fulton Street before it crosses the creek.

People moved during the evening and into the night—moved in cars of their own or in cars of friends or in the Greyhound Bus the Fire Department had commandeered or the bus the Bethlehem Center owned. They came holding blankets, glass vases, and paper bags of food and carrying children and grandchildren. The red lights of fire trucks and police cars gave a strange illumination to the scene. Men and women were wild with excitement as though this were the kickoff of a football game or the crescendo of a party or the immediate aftermath of an auto accident. And within their excitement was fear. The old people were afraid, the very young were afraid, and those who owned their houses were unhappy and afraid.

Some of the evacuees moved in with friends who lived on higher ground on Louisiana or State, but most moved to the Red Cross shelter at East End Middle School. Low life and first citizens came bunched together and sat on cots and opened bags and suitcases in old classrooms with high windows where blackboards had been cleaned and made ready for the first lesson of the following school year.

Water rose and entered the oil company building, where windows and doors had been left open, so that the building drank in the river. Water backed up under the bridge where East Main Street crosses Gillies Creek and rose over the bridge and poured over East Main where it runs low and parallel to the river. It sucked against the silver-colored oil tanks, moving through brush and woods beneath the trestle, entering the first houses on low ground, edging closer to the house of Minnie Fulkes and the house of Richard C. Moring, which stood on higher ground beyond. Water moved across the brickyard where many of Fulton's houses lay dismembered, their bricks assembled into six-foot stacks waiting to be sold, and covered the first layer of brick and the second layer. It moved into the junk yard, covering the rusting hulks of automobiles stacked there—Oldsmobiles, Pontiacs, and Chevrolets that had been sold for scrap and were waiting to be flattened and loaded on flatbed trucks for their last trip.

We thought the water would stop here, as it had two years earlier, but it kept coming, pushing its way up Gillies Creek, entering the row of M&M-owned houses along Lewis Street and filling them ankle deep, then knee deep. The old man who owned the house with the thickly painted screen enclosing the front porch came to the door and left. Later water moved past his shed in the backyard and his garden. Soon it was beneath his house, surrounding the brick footings on which his house rested and rising until they were like pilings in the water and continuing to rise until it was washing the girders and the joists and the planking of the floor and then rising and running in the doors and washing over linoleum and carpet and working its way up the walls, soaking into plaster and lathe, then covering the coffee table and sofabed, covering the kitchen chairs and table and the long white freezer with its cache of fish.

Water came into the cinder-block apartments in the Bottom and filled them to the ceilings of the first floor. It flooded the houses of the whites living on Government Road, forcing traffic to detour up hollow, past the P.L. Farmer Company, the city dump, and the great, old graveyard on the hill.

Lucy Beazley, the president of the Nicholson Street Civic Association, was a strong-looking woman who spent most of her time caring for half a dozen old or sick people on her block including Charlie Barbour, retired lady's man and tippler. Her house stood in the section of Nicholson where water had never come before. That afternoon she ignored the advice of her neighbors to leave, and that evening she helped Charlie Barbour onto the bus but declined to join the evacuation herself. Later she said no to the request of the Fire Department and the Red Cross and the police, who wanted her out. Much later, in the dark of night, as water slowly rose along Nicholson Street, entering houses it had never touched before and filling houses that had barely gotten wet before, she chose not to leave with the National Guard but stayed on alone, not intimidated by the red lights of the evacuation that evening or the troops with their rifles and helmets later that night. Mostly she was not intimidated by the river, the old river she had known as a girl and her mother had known, the river she loved.

The evacuation was nearly completed by ten, the National Guard had taken their positions by midnight, and the river still rose, only more slowly now. Guardsmen expected a lonely night in Fulton, but they found that this neighborhood had considerable night traffic. Not an hour passed without the rumble of low-slung cars in the alleys and streets. The onset of waters did not deter the customers of Matte Curtis and Waddy Crowder and other entrepreneurs, for whom Friday night is Friday night.

In the morning I visited Nicholson Street and came to the house of Lucy Beazley, the woman who had refused to move. The water had stopped its advance at her picket fence and by now had receded a few feet, leaving behind tokens of its esteem— old tires, pieces of stove wood, a plastic bottle.

The water stayed high all day Saturday, and from the bluffs overlooking the river I could see brown water spreading out over Southside. The flood took out Richmond's sewage treatment plant, fouled the city water system, and cut off power. It cracked the concrete bridge where East Main crosses Gillies Creek, lifted huge oil tanks from their foundations, and caused a leak at the Fulton Gas works that filled the air with the smell of gas. So far only those Fulton residents in the floodplain had been evacuated, but now the Red Cross uptown, acting on higher authority, said to evacuate everyone from Fulton, since the gas leak posed an imminent danger. But the men at the renewal site office, which had become a local headquarters for the disaster operation, had other information and decided that the leak did not pose a danger and that no further evacuation would take place. Fulton residents heard rumors one way, then another, and no one was comforted when the total evacuation never came.

As the waters receded, Fulton was overcome with another kind of flood: disaster voyeurs. These were middle-aged white men who carried flashlights and first-aid kits and wore recently acquired Red Cross patches. The amateur voyeurs were followed by the professionals: journalists, television cameramen, photographers. The national media got their feet wet and put Fulton on the screens of televisions as far away as Seattle, Washington, where my parents saw Fulton's houses sitting waist deep and chin deep in water.

To people whose decency and intelligence had been scarcely recognized in years past by the local media, this national television coverage was a dream come true, or at least it would have been if the professionals hadn't bungled the job. For the media portrayed Fulton residents as victims, whereas the story that Fulton folk longed to tell was of their self-sufficiency under all hardships. The irony doubled when Spiro Agnew, our vice president, visited Fulton in what was intended as a gesture of concern but was too little too late for people who had not had the government's ear when they needed it, in the twenties and thirties, and whose neighborhood at present was being dismembered by a federally funded renewal program.

By Sunday morning the waters had retreated from Fulton's residential spaces, leaving a water line within and without all the dwellings it had touched. On Monday morning young white volunteers came forth en masse to scrub down the houses with Lysol and wash them out with water from garden hoses. No one knew for certain whether the authorities would allow residents to move back.

Monday morning also saw the invasion of relief workers, who set up shop in the cafeteria of Webster Davis School. Food stamps and welfare were well represented, along with the Red Cross, Salvation Army, and Small Business Administration. The river bank had been congested on Friday afternoon when the water began to rise, but now it was Webster Davis School that drew crowds; everyone in Fulton who could walk was here. Since Fulton had been declared a national disaster area, residents who suffered only marginally from the flood were eligible for food stamps and other benefits. I hurried from house to house, making application for a month's food stamps for Patience Gromes and a dozen others who couldn't make it to Webster Davis and who were technically ineligible under normal circumstances. They needed and deserved food stamps for reasons that had nothing to do with the flood, but now they happened to be eligible. I had long since learned to take what the bureaucracy would give.

No one could accuse Spiro Agnew of making promises he couldn't keep. The food-stamp largesse was surpassed by SBA loans to those whose belongings had been destroyed in the flood. Later these loans became outright grants. Flood victims were grateful for federal help. But about the time they learned the good news of food stamp and SBA benefits, they learned the bad news that their houses in Fulton had been condemned by the health department.

The flood took fifty families from Fulton, and even after the water subsided and the river flowed within its banks, the flood continued to drain this neighborhood in ways not apparent to the eye. The flood drained the will of Fulton's third generation to continue living here. In its wake dozens of elderly homeowners decided to take the $15,000 grants and move. They went to the housing authority site office and put their names on the list.

As the list grew longer, neighborhood leaders worked more and more feverishly to save their neighborhood. The flood had awakened them, and now they knew that no agency beyond Fulton, least of all the housing authority, would save Fulton if they did not save it themselves. Brady and Waterman led a busload of residents on a sit-in at housing authority headquarters. Patience Gromes and forty of her neighbors sat all day on metal folding chairs in the housing authority meeting room. The chairs were arranged in a circle. They waited in silence. No one came to talk with them until late afternoon, and by then they were happy to leave.

Next, Brady and Waterman invited housing authority bigwigs to a roast at Rising Mt. Zion. Doug Wilder, black lawyer and politician, was the featured speaker. "I am like Thomas," he said. "I want to see the proof, the prints of the nails." The renewal officials had no proof, but needed none. Still, the audience was glad to see them on stage, like condemned men, sweating in the heat. When the entertainment was over everyone went home, knowing that nothing had changed.

Brady and Waterman were under pressure now and attained clarity of vision: if the housing authority says staging is too complex to be practical, they reasoned, why not simplify it by retaining the existing street pattern and building first on vacant lots? Brady and Waterman found the hole in the housing authority's anti-staging argument, and now they had the intellectual ingredient they needed to make staging work. But it was too late. A critical momentum had been lost. The confidence of Fulton residents, especially the old folk, had eroded during two years of inaction, and now it would be impossible to convince them that the staging plan could succeed.

In November, Richard Nixon won reelection and announced a moratorium on urban renewal. Residents who had not already done so rushed to the renewal site office to put in for early relocation. Those who had applied earlier rushed over once again to try to move their names up higher on the list. No one wanted to be left in a shack in Fulton when relocation money and $15,000 grants ran out. Neighborhood leaders attempted to rally the neighborhood, but it was like trying to hold water in one's hands. Fulton was over. Fulton was lost. And now people were looking out for themselves.

In the first months of 1968 the housing authority jarred Fulton loose from its cultural foundations. For four years Fulton's patricians and the housing authority had offered competing conceptions of the world. No one could say for certain who would prevail.

But the flood carried away the old and made way for the new. And if the flood began in June 1972, it did not end, to my mind, until six months later. In January 1973, Fulton residents conceded defeat and formally turned their neighborhood over to the housing authority's governance. They voted in favor of the housing authority's land use scheme, which Fulton's leaders had spent two years helping to detail. No one mentioned staging.

The meeting was held on a Sunday afternoon. About two hundred residents sat in the auditorium of Webster Davis School. The atmosphere was subdued, not at all like the mass meetings five years earlier. As the assembly was called to order, I saw Lindsay Faucette, the crippled woman who lived on Fulton Street. She was sitting in her wheel chair, down front and to the side.

It took only a few minutes to present the land use plan: new streets, new houses, new everything. When the planners finished talking, the audience sat quietly as though their suspicions of five years earlier had been confirmed. The man who operated Honey's store turned around and said to me, "Well, that's fine, but when they get done what are the they going to call it?"

The plan did look fine. Industry down in Rocketts, houses above Williamsburg Avenue, apartments in Happy Hollow. The neighborhood depicted on the planners' maps, however, was not Fulton, not at all.

The housing authority's project director asked for questions.

"Question!" Lindsay Faucette waved an arm. "Are you goin' to take away Fulton Street?"

"Yes ma'm, we are."

"You can't take away Fulton Street. I live on Fulton Street."

Until the flood, Charlie Barbour also lived on Fulton Street. The early sun filled his front porch, and often I saw him sitting here in a worn chair, eyes closed, receiving the sun as though it were his life. I liked Charlie. He knew things. To take one example, he knew the real reason that the astronauts went to the moon. "Moongals," said Charlie. "Couldn't get enough of those moongals."

When he was young Charlie had lived a life of freedom and excitement. He had worked at American Tobacco and spent his free time gambling, drinking, and womanizing. Charlie had been handsome. He had moved from one tenement apartment to another, lived with one woman after another. He never married, for to him love and marriage were two different things.

Charlie's middle years marked a long slide into debauchery. His job at the tobacco factory had been dull from the first, but he loved the work because it gave him money and respect. Nowadays Charlie did not care whether his neighbors thought of him as a working man or as a bum. He realized that men who work are really no better than those who do not. Charlie no longer loved his women as before. He drank more heavily. The tobacco company fired him for coming to work drunk, but he did not mind. Now he had full days of freedom to pursue his interests. He hung out at Waddy Crowder's and spent hours standing at the corner of Williamsburg and Louisiana begging coins from married women as they passed by on their way to market. One day a woman walking at the edge of the dump found a body lying face down in the weeds. It was Charlie Barbour, unconscious but not dead. His life of freedom and excitement, however, had come to an end.

Charlie awoke in the apartment of his niece. At first he could not speak. Over the months his niece cared for him. Slowly his health returned. Although he never regained full use of his right leg, Charlie discovered other capacities which were more important to him than physical mobility. For the first time he appreciated family life.

Charlie and his niece shared household tasks. She cooked, he cleaned; she shopped, he did the wash. Mornings they sat out front together, and evenings they worked in back, beating down the weeds. The third of each month Charlie's niece cashed their checks at Grubb's Supermarket. They pooled their money, taking out for rent and groceries, setting aside for clothing and bus fare. In winter they bought coal and wood. In the summer they opened windows and set screens. Charlie Barbour and his niece might have taken rooms with strangers, but they chose to keep the family together.

"Lord help me, if I ever get out of this one." Charlie's niece lay sick in the darkness of their middle room and was afraid and felt as though she was trapped in a maze from which there was no exit. Her sickness was like ropes tying her down, drawing tighter each day. I visited her, sat beside the sofa where she lay, and listened to her talk. Fever came, and she could see her former life before her like a vision. Fever left, and her forehead was cold and wet to the touch.

When his niece died, it shook Charlie Barbour to the depths of his soul. Now he was alone. His life was drifting out of his control. How could he put his family back together? In a gambling mood Charlie made a play for the allegiance of a child. Two houses up the street a family broke apart when the woman left her husband and moved to Church Hill. She had ten children. On Charlie's suggestion one of them, a boy of nine, stayed behind. The mother would keep the child's welfare allotment, Charlie would provide the child's food, shelter, and clothes.

It looked as though a balance had been struck. Charlie Barbour had a child who was like a nephew, someone he could protect and provide for, someone to keep him company at night when he sat in the middle room with the television going. Here was a child to raise the ruckus for which children are famous.

Charlie wanted to speak to his new charge, to share the wit of an old man and an old man's sorrow. But he knew that boys speak a language of their own. So one day Charlie hobbled over to the bus stop and rode uptown to Sears. He chose a bicycle, a low-slung model that handled the way a Ferrari would handle if it were a bicycle, and asked them to please deliver it. He handed the cashier six ten-dollar bills that had been filling a hole in his mattress for years. Charlie Barbour spoke to the child, and the new bicycle was the first thing he said.

After a month passed the boy's mother knocked on Charlie's front door. Her caseworker had discovered the switch and threatened to reduce her welfare check if her son did not return home. When the boy stood to go, Charlie Barbour looked at him. "Leave the bike," he said.

The flood came into Charlie's house. It covered the new bicycle and the couch where Charlie's niece had died and the front porch where Charlie had sat alone for a year airing his grief in the morning sun. Flood waters came to the low end of Fulton Street and forced Charlie to leave. He would never again see the wooden row house where he had taken the greatest risk of his life, where he had dared to make a claim upon the affections of a nine-year-old boy.

Charlie moved into temporary quarters at East End School, then to the housing authority highrise uptown. Thanks to relocation expenses provided under urban renewal and to SBA benefits, Charlie was wealthy for the first time in his life. Still, he was lonely. He had lost his niece, his adopted nephew, and now his house. His life was sliding away, and Charlie was desperate to shore it up or at least to slow the inevitable, downward movement.

Charlie telephoned Lucy Beazley, the president of the Nicholson Street Civic Association, and pleaded with her to let him return to Fulton and live at her house. She said no. He telephoned again and again to beg rides to the bank to check on his money. I visited him once. Charlie showed me the appliances in his kitchen; all were in the color harvest gold. I stayed an hour, but it was not long enough. I got ready to leave. "Come back," said Charlie.

I did not come back. And Lucy Beazley busied herself helping others who still lived in Fulton. Charlie was alone with his money, and, although he was not an educated man or a churchgoer, he knew that he could not take it with him. He began to purchase the affections of a young woman. His life was spinning now, farther and farther from his grasp, yet a little of the old excitement returned. Wealth can compensate for the lost charm of youth, Charlie learned. His gal accepted big checks from him, fifty and seventy-five dollar checks. When his money ran out, however, she stopped coming to visit. The excitement was gone, and Charlie Barbour died. Lucy Beazley had to scrounge money from welfare with which to bury her former neighbor. "Charlie Barbour was the type of person who wanted someone else to do everything for him," she said. She had shopped and cooked and banked for him from the time his niece took ill, and so she had a right to her complaint. But I think of Charlie differently.

Charlie was never a first citizen of Fulton. He never visibly contributed to neighborhood institutions, never owned a house, never felt any great obligation to pay his rent on time. Even so, Charlie's life was redeemed and nurtured by the charity of this neighborhood. For the ideal of racial advancement, which sounds cold and ineffectual when put into words, was charity, forgiveness, and forbearance in practice. It was the companionship of Charlie's niece, the patient help of the president who lived around the corner, the eager glance of a young boy.

What was lost when Fulton acceded to the governance of the Richmond Redevelopment and Housing Authority? Charlie Barbour boarded the Greyhound on the night of the flood and within a week was living at the housing authority's highrise uptown where everything was lovely. Six months later he was dead. Charlie Barbour, like half the other old people who moved from Fulton at the time of the flood or in the months that followed, depended upon this neighborhood and could not live without it.

In the months following the flood the people of Fulton moved in four directions. Sammy Fulkes, as I mentioned, went to prison, and his crime partner, Grunt Curtis, moved to New York City, where he was killed on the street. Their mothers, Minnie Fulkes and Matte Curtis, moved to the projects on Church Hill. Matte Curtis went into retirement from NWRO and bootlegging. Minnie Fulkes received her daughters back from their foster homes. After several years Sammy was released from prison. The whole family was together at last. Minnie went to work each day but her sons stayed home and spoke moodily with their women friends. Sammy fathered a child. At last Minnie made a difficult decision: she told her sons that they were grown and to get out of her house and find jobs and pay their own rent. "It's a hard thing for a mother to tell her boys to leave out from home," she told me. Within a year Sammy was back in prison.

Fourth-generation defenders of Fulton like Jacob Pinckney, Alford Stirling, and Stepney Waterman purchased modern houses in the suburbs or in the Montrose area behind Fulton. Betty Norton couldn't see the advantages of homeownership, however, and rented a place on Church Hill. Daniel Brady died and was widely praised by his enemies after his passing. Three years later, however, the move to name one of Fulton's new housing clusters in his memory met stiff resistance. "My brother scrambled and worked hard for you all," his sister replied to his detractors. "He gave you nice houses. All you give him is a bad name."

Richard C. Moring, the magnanimous bootlegger, moved to a modest ranch-style house on Montrose Heights. He made a trip to Las Vegas where, I am tempted to speculate, he went to spend some of the money he couldn't spend anywhere else, thanks to the IRS. He died in Las Vegas.

Fanny and Chub moved to a modern house in a white neighborhood of Richmond, where they were comfortable and bored. When I visited in 1976, they complained about their years in Fulton, then told me of their love for their old store and for the storekeeper's life. "When business is slow," said Chub, "you can always eat food from the store." I tried to telephone them recently but they are gone, and Fulton residents say that they are dead. Few people knew them outside of Fulton. They left no children or other relatives. They had insisted that they belonged to the wider white culture, but that culture carries no mark or memorial as witness to their lives. Fanny and Chub have left no trace except in the memory of a poor, black neighborhood.

Charles Dowd and his three friends went to prison for killing Pinto the bootlegger. Fulton folk still have difficulty understanding how he got in trouble. Many wish him well in life. "He got his disruption from his father's side," says one former neighbor, who agreed, however, that Charles had chosen his companions unwisely. "You get with the wrong people," she says, "and it cost you like the devil."

Tub Francis, the son of Snort, moved to Church Hill and was laid up with multiple gunshot wounds the last I heard. The wounds were not inflicted by the Reverend Squire Dowd, however, for the city haled Dowd into court. "You could hurt someone, running around with a gun like that," the judge told him.

"Your Honor," said Dowd, "if you were in my shoes, if some kid took a shot at you, wouldn't you have grabbed your gun?" The courtroom audience broke into laughter, for this judge happened to be wearing a handgun under his robes even as he spoke. (Richmond's blacks had chafed under the judge's announcement, some months earlier, of his intention to arm himself.) The judge let Dowd off without a fine but confiscated his shotgun.

The court could not take away the Reverend's righteous anger, however. And there was one woman in Fulton of whom he thoroughly disapproved. She was the niece of Waddy Crowder, a notorious bulldagger (lesbian), and spent her time drinking, gambling, and shouting obscenities in the streets. One afternoon she strutted past Reverend Dowd's porch. "Leave your evil ways," he said, among other things.

That night she returned, poured stove oil on his porch and lit it. As the flames rose around the house she chanted, "Burn Dowd, burn. Burn damitall, burn." The house burned quickly, but Dowd escaped injury because he had moved to Church Hill a few hours before. His words to her were intended as the final pronouncement from the pulpit of his front porch.

The residents of Orleans Street were some of the last to move. Mrs. Hattie Rogers, the snoopy woman who took drinks on the sly, started a fire in her back room upstairs and came running out front hollering, "Fire! Fire!" In the adjoining house Clara Jones was awakened by the commotion. She heard Mrs. Hattie shouting but did not move out of bed. "Mrs. Hattie's always exaggeratin' anyhow," Clara told me later. Then Analiza Foster started hollering and Clara got the message and came out through the smoke a short time before flames burned the wall down. Afterward nothing was left of their two houses but the blackened shells. Still, a week later Mrs. Hattie led Jewel, Clara's mother, back into the house. They poked among the cold ashes and found two dinner plates, a Sunday dress, a woman's shoe.

The fire and the prospect of quick relocation did not dull Jewel's taste for bootleg whiskey. She kept up her association with Waddy and Nell while housing authority technicians were filling out papers, but one morning she did not come home to her daughter, who had found temporary quarters next door with Analiza Foster. Clara discovered her mother's body across the street at Waddy and Nell's. It lay in an upstairs bedroom, "beaten in her privates," as Clara put it.

Clara grieved for her mother and fretted that she had not done enough to save her from her fate. But always she came to the same conclusion. "Jewel lived drinking, and she died drinking," Clara said.

Eventually Clara moved to Church Hill. She was bitter because she felt that the housing authority had not given her the relocation benefits to which she was entitled. Her Church Hill apartment suffered a small fire, and only two weeks later the downstairs apartment was gutted when some drunken tenants set a blaze going and then decided to seek lodgings elsewhere. Clara's health was poor, and she went to the hospital for operations. "I feel like I'm agoin' to die," she told me.

"It's God's revenge for the way she treated her poor mother," said Nell Crowder.

Waddy and Nell Crowder had accumulated more cash than anyone in Fulton except Richard C. Moring. They were wealthy, and their neighbors did not understand why they didn't buy a nice house in the suburbs and hire someone to run their business for them. Of course these neighbors had not considered the way the IRS calculates unreported income from expenditures or the

way absentee owners can be betrayed by their underlings. At
length Waddy and Nell relocated to a comfortable house over
in Northside. Fultonians are not saying whether they have resumed business in their new location.

When I returned to Fulton in December 1975, State Street
was gone in the block where Patience Gromes had lived, although
houses on her side of the street still stood. The other houses had
been torn down, and the sidewalks and the cobbled street itself
had been ripped up to make way for Admiral Gravely Boulevard.
Houses were demolished all along the route of this new arterial,
which would cut diagonally across the old street pattern. Cicely
Tallman and Jack Mosby were some of the first residents in the
right of way to be relocated, to lose their houses to the bulldozers.
Mrs. Tallman was unconcerned about moving until a few weeks
before she had to go. Then she said she wasn't moving and would
rather die right here. Eventually, a white woman who lived on
Fulton Hill spoke with her, gained her confidence, and got her
to accept her fate. The renewal agency relocated her to Southside, the white woman helped her move, comforted her, and
nowadays looked in on her several times a week. When I visited
Mrs. Tallman in her new house, she seemed little changed. She
still sang, stamped her foot, and spat tobacco juice. Many of her
neighbors, the old ones, died after being relocated from Fulton.
One woman said they died from "worriation." But Cicely Tallman didn't let things worry her, and she survived.

Jack Mosby's wife, Abby, did not make the adjustment as
easily, however, for her mind was weak to begin with. Although
she had worked in a tobacco factory to help Jack pay for their
house, she was a mother first and last. Her children grew, left
home, then all but one died of sickness or accident. Some say
that Abby's mind snapped. In any case, she never was able to
accept their deaths and spoke to neighbors as though her children
were still alive. The renewal agency relocated Jack and Abby to
a comfortable house about half a mile from Fulton, but Abby ran
away twice. Jack called the police, who searched. Both times

they found her down in Fulton, pacing back and forth on the bare earth where their house had been, as though she were trying to find her way home.

The houses of Cicely Tallman and Jack Mosby were gone, but the dwelling of Patience Gromes still stood. It was vacant now. Unlike other vacant houses, however, it had not been vandalized. When I walked through, it seemed small and empty. Suddenly I understood the dignity which the furnishings and the presence of Patience Gromes had given this little box of wood and plaster.

Two doors down, Patience's friend Mrs. B still inhabited her house, although the adjoining unit was vacant and boarded. Mrs. B didn't like living in a ghost town but had no choice. The urban renewal agency wouldn't relocate her until it got the paperwork straight, and who could say how many months that might be? Mrs. B was retired after forty years at the tobacco factory and spent her days listening to the great machines moving back and forth across her front yard, five paces from her porch. The dust was worse than the noise, she said, but worst of all was the loss of her fence. It had been a kind of moral barrier, her first line of defense against the unknown. Now the public spaces of Fulton mingled freely with her private domain. "At night," she said, "men stand on my porch tryin' to get at me."

Since it was growing dark when I came to visit, Mrs. B demonstrated her strategy to foil these men. She locked her front and back doors, then moved from window to window, drawing each shade and thumbtacking it flat against the window casing, two tacks to each side, four to each shade. She felt safe now, for no one could see inside, no one could get a fix on her position. "They don't nobody even know I'm in here," said Mrs. B. "If somebody knock on the door, I don't answer."

Since then, Mrs. B has moved to a new ranch house on Fulton Hill that has the convenience of bedrooms, bath, and kitchen on a single floor. "I jump up all night and come in the kitchen for a snack," she told me. "I gained ten pounds in the first month."

Stepney Waterman's new house on Fulton Hill was just within the boundaries of the renewal project and was one of several single-family homes at the edge of the hill built under the plan. When the time came to build in Fulton proper, construction costs had risen so that private construction of single-family houses was no longer possible with $15,000 grants. The choice was between government-financed apartments and no housing at all. Projects were built here, subsidy apartments of the type that citizen planners had hoped to exclude, and a number of former residents returned. These were low-income residents such as Willie Cozart, the reformed addict and ideologue, not a favorite of the citizen planners. Willie preferred to philosophize about the Black Experience rather than work and had, it turned out, no trouble qualifying for an apartment in his old neighborhood.

In February 1971, during my first few days in Fulton, I explored the edges of this neighborhood. I walked along the river, beneath trees that grew thick and dense against its banks, following paths made by animals. I lifted aside some branches, crawled beneath others, and climbed the bank a little on the slippery footing of last year's leaves. I stepped out on an earthen pier, restrained with rotting pilings and timbers, the remnants of loading slips to each side that once had been large enough for skiffs to tie up but now were silted in and forgotten in the brush.

I saw slender trees, sad trees. Their limbs were coated with silt and bent downstream in a strange, suppliant gesture. Bicycle tires hung casually in their branches where the river had placed them in the previous year's high water.

The mother of Moses had brought her child from the village to the river. She had placed him in a basket of reeds and set it adrift. She knew that his well-being was now beyond her own control, subject to the will of the river itself. The river flowed from its own, unseen sources. It could not be shaped or measured or enclosed. For the river was more than plain water. It was a way of imagining an infinite, spiritual substance and the flowing line of its expression in human life.

Patience Gromes was not a leader like Moses. But she had an

idea of the travail of her people which reminds me of him. She entrusted her life to a power beyond herself. She was an activist. "She was for right and doing the right things and all that kinda stuff," says her daughter.

Patience believed in the ability of black men and women to overcome obstacles and make something of themselves. For her, life had a governing morality beneath the surface of falsehood and hate. She acted upon the world, expected truth to prevail, and invariably it did so. She and Frank reared eight children, supported a church, paid off two mortgages. Neither Patience nor her family fought to take what was theirs from a jealous world. They did not attempt to outwit the world but were more concerned with improving their own skills. They expected the world to respond appropriately to the real value of their products and labor. Patience and her family thought their qualities of character, not objective conditions in the world, ultimately would determine their happiness and success. I think Patience intended her life as an object lesson, an encouragement to others. That's what the preacher said later. "She was still uplifting her fellow man when she died."

In the year following the flood, Patience Gromes moved to a ranch-style house in the suburbs. A week later she went to the county building to register to vote. When she raised her right hand to repeat the oath, she dropped dead.

Even through the frustrations of her last years in Fulton, Patience Gromes was optimistic, convinced that the line of accomplishment and progress that had distinguished her family and her people would continue despite the present confusion. Beneath her dedication to hard work and thrift, beneath her understanding of good and evil, was the vision of a benevolent force acting upon history in her behalf, impelling progress, destroying obstacles, uplifting her family, her neighborhood, her people.

To Patience Gromes, life was a river of divine pleasures continually unfolding a spiritual bounty.

Flood came upon Fulton and filled fifty of its houses and receded and left Fulton with flood stench as it baked in the sun.
Fifty houses lost their inhabitants and stayed empty awaiting
vandals and wrecking crews. Fifty houses died in the flood; in
some way they were the life of their inhabitants, the body of
their dreams and remembrances, the full evidence of all they had
accomplished with their lives. And the inhabitants of those fifty
houses were part of the life of Fulton. The flood took from Fulton
a portion of its last life when it took people like Charlie Barbour
and Minnie Fulkes. The flood forced them and their neighbors
to move from Fulton and take up lives in different neighborhoods
all over town. They did not all die, but their old roots died; their
old garden vines got covered with flood wash and turned yellow
in the sun. Some of the old ones lived, others did not. Fulton
lived and died with the flood, but mostly it died—the spirit died.
The final end began with the flood.

A woman who lived on Williamsburg Avenue owned a chest
of drawers that floated in floodwater for a day but was still good,
she thought. Later the housing authority got her a house on
Fulton Hill, and she moved and settled in. Much later, four months
later, she pulled open a drawer: the whole chest fell in pieces.

Fulton floated in river water for a day but most houses did not
get wet and still looked all right. Yet something was at work in
them beneath the surface, some wetness that had not been here
before. Fifty families moved out, and those who were left felt
suddenly as though "everysomebody" was leaving and it was time
to get out. A kind of glue had held Fulton together, made it
more than a chance collection of wood and brick and people
strewn about in the hollow by the river. After the flood the glue
was weakened and began to lose hold. It would be only time now
and the last stores would close, the last people would leave, the
last houses would splinter before the bulldozers. The Fulton I
had known would soon be gone, the land prepared for whatever
community might be the next to settle in this place. Fulton would
be gone, but the river would stay.

The river is an image for an idea and the flowing line of its descent through six generations. At the turn of the century men and women came in diverse strands from the country to Fulton. They brought with them an idea of their own power, a vision of attainable grace. Following the flood, Fulton broke apart. The community of Patience Gromes had lived and now one could say that it died. But the men and women moved on and in some ways took their community with them. Their vision continued to flow and could not be channeled or divided or contained, any more than floodwaters could be contained by the earthen dikes that city trucks built at the edge of the James River. If Patience Gromes and her contemporaries died after leaving Fulton, others would rise to take their place. Younger men and women would corner the children of a new generation, look straight at them, and leave them with words of advice: "Be somebody."

BIBLIOGRAPHY

THIS BOOK is based on interviews with former Fulton residents, their relatives, and urban renewal officials.

I have also been helped by the insights of other writers. Some have made general observations about black life that have had particular application in Fulton. Cloward and Piven, for example, drew my attention to the period of tension that began with the long hot summer of 1967 and ended with the assassination of Martin Luther King, Jr. the following spring. Other writers, notably Bruce, Moger, and McDonald, have documented the life and times of freedmen in Virginia and North Carolina, a subject which for the most part was beyond the reach of my interviews. I have also used City Directories to tabulate black and white population totals from 1885.

PRIMARY SOURCES

Fulton Ad Hoc Committee. Minutes of meeting, March 6, 1968, Fulton RCAP Center, Richmond, Va.

Fulton Improvement Association. Minutes of special meeting with Mr. Robert Gray, Urban League, February 26, 1968, Bethlehem Center, Richmond, Va.

————. Minutes of monthly meetings, March 3 and 26, 1968, Bethlehem Center, Richmond, Va.

Fulton Project Area Committee, Detail Planning Committee. Minutes of meeting, May 27, 1970, Bethlehem Center, Richmond, Va.

————. Minutes of meeting, June 10, 1970, Fulton Planning Office, Richmond, Va.

Friedman, Molly. *Poor White Trash.* Richmond, Virginia: privately published, 1948.

Richmond City Council. Tape recording of regular meeting, July 12, 1971. Tapes 2B-3B.

Richmond, City of. *Community Renewal Program.* Richmond, Va., 1966.

————. Planning Commission. *Master Plan.* Richmond, Va. 1964.

Richmond Redevelopment and Housing Authority. Advisory Committee [a group of citizen planners who lived in Fulton]. Excerpts from minutes of meeting, February 20, 1968. Bethlehem Center, Richmond, Va.

————. *Fulton General Neighborhood Renewal Area.* April 4, 1968. [Summary of estimated cost, acreage, number and condition of buildings, and of families to be relocated, in Fulton.] Richmond, Va.

————. *Fulton Structural Survey Data.* February 20, 1968. Richmond, Va.

————. Minutes of a meeting between Mr. Howell of the Richmond Redevelopment and Housing Authority, and the Vice President of the Fulton Ad Hoc Committee, March 27, 1968, Wright's Inn, Richmond, Virginia.

————. *Redevelopment Plan for Fulton Urban Renewal Area as Amended by Amendment No. 4.* March 1970 as amended July 1974. Richmond, Va.

Rising Mount Zion Baptist Church. *History of the Church.* Richmond, Virginia Rising Mount Zion Baptist Church, 1969.

Federal Writers' Project. *Slave Narratives: A Folk History of Slavery in the United States, from Interviews with Former Slaves.* St. Clair Shores, Mich.: Scholarly Press, 1976.

SECONDARY SOURCES

Anderson, Charles P., and Anderson, Dorothy D. *The Montrose Baptist Church: From the Valley to the Heights, 1870-1970.* Richmond, Va. Keel-William Corp., 1973.

Aptheker, Herbert. *Nat Turner's Slave Rebellion.* New York: Humanities Press, 1966.

Armstrong, M.F., and Ludlow, Helen W. *Hampton and Its Students.* New York: G.P. Putnam's Sons, 1874.

Armstrong, Samuel Chapman. *Education for Life.* Hampton, Va.: Press of the Hampton Normal and Agricultural Institute, 1914.

Ballagh, James Curtis. *White Servitude in the Colony of Virginia.* Johns Hopkins University Studies in Historical and Political Science, Herbert B. Adams, ed. Baltimore: Johns Hopkins Press, 1895.

Bancroft, Frederic. *Slave Trading in the Old South.* Baltimore: J.H. Furst Co., 1931.

Bitting, Samuel T. *Rural Land Ownership among the Negroes of Virginia.* Phelps-Stokes Fellowship Papers. Charlottesville, Va.: University of Virginia Press, 1915.

Bonekemper, Edward H., III. "Negro Ownership of Real Property in Hampton and Elizabeth City County, Virginia, 1860-1870." *Journal of Negro History* 55, no. 3 (1970) 165-81.

Bremer, Fredrika. *The Homes of the New World.* Translated by Mary Howitt. New York: Harper & Brothers, 1868.

Brown, W.H. *The Education and Economic Development of the Negro in Virginia.* Phelps-Stokes Fellowship Papers, No. 6. Charlottesville, Va.: University of Virginia Press, 1923.

Bruce, Phillip A. *The Plantation Negro as a Freeman.* New York: G.P. Putnam's Sons, 1889.

Bullington, Ann. *Vignettes of the James.* Richmond, Va.: Richmond Press, 1941.

Campbell, Sir George. *White and Black.* New York: R. Worthington, 1879.

Chamberlain, Bernard Peyton. *The Negro and Crime in Virginia.* Phelps-Stokes Fellowship Papers, No. 15. Charlottesville, Va.: University of Virginia Press, 1936.

Cloward, Richard A., and Piven, Frances Fox. *Poor People's Movements: Why They Succeed, How They Fail.* New York: Random House, 1979.

————— and —————. *Regulating the Poor: The Functions of Public Welfare.* New York: Random House, 1971.

Commonwealth of Virginia. *Calendar of Virginia State Papers, and Other Manuscripts.* Richmond, Va. 4 (1884): 302; 6 (1886): 538; 7 (1888): 58, 110, 446; 8 (1890): 293, 305; 9 (1890): 36, 48, 165, 189, 200, 230, 239, 288.

—————. *Hening's Statutes.* 10 (1779-1781):459, 475; 11 (1782-

1784):210, 235, 237, 238; 12 (1785-1788):66, 67, 258, 281, 435, 455, 581, 582, 667; 13 (1789-1792):479. Facsimile reprint. Charlottesville: University Press of Virginia, 1969.

Cope, Robert S. *Carry Me Back.* Pikeville, Ky.: Pikeville College Press of the Appalachian Studies Center, 1973.

Dabney, Virginius. *Richmond: The Story of a City.* New York: Doubleday & Co., 1976.

Davidson, Basil. *Black Mother.* Boston: Atlantic-Little, Brown, 1961.

Dixon, William Hepworth. *New America.* Philadelphia: J.B. Lippincott & Co., 1867.

Drewry, William Sidney. *The Southampton Insurrection.* Washington, D.C.: Neale Co. 1900. Reprinted Murfreesboro, N.C.: Johnson Publishing Co., 1968.

DuBois, W.E. Burghardt. *The Negroes of Farmville, Virginia: A Social Study.* Bulletin of the Department of Labor, No. 14. Washington, D.C.: 1898.

————. *The Souls of Black Folk.* New York: New American Library, 1969.

Frazier, E. Franklin. *The Negro Family in Chicago.* Chicago: University of Chicago Press, 1932.

————. *The Negro Family in the United States.* Chicago: University of Chicago Press, 1966.

"Fulton: Community Spirit Grows in Ailing Area of City." *Richmond Times-Dispatch.* February 9, 1969.

Genovese, Eugene D. *Roll, Jordan, Roll.* New York: Random House, 1974.

Glanz, Rudolf. *Studies in Judaica Americana.* New York: KTAV Publishing House, 1970.

Gray, Lewis Cecil. *History of Agriculture in the Southern United States to 1860.* Washington, D.C.: Carnegie Institution of Washington, 1933.

Gutman, Herbert George. *The Black Family in Slavery and Freedom, 1750-1925.* New York: Pantheon Books, 1976.

Hampton Normal and Agricultural Institute. *Forty-Eighth Annual Report of the Principal.* Hampton, Va.: Press of the Hampton Normal and Agricultural Institute, 1916.

Handlin, Oscar. *The Uprooted.* 2nd ed., enlarged. Boston: Atlantic-Little, Brown, 1973.

Harlan, Howard H. *Zion Town: A Study in Human Ecology.* Phelps-

Stokes Fellowship Papers, No. 13. Charlottesville: University of Virginia Press, 1935.

Herskovits, Melville Jean. *The Myth of the Negro Past.* Boston: Beacon Press, 1958.

Higgs, Robert. *Competition and Coercion: Blacks in the American Economy, 1865-1914.* Chicago: University of Chicago Press, 1977.

Huhner, Leon. *Jews in America in Colonial and Revolutionary Times.* New York: Gertz Brothers, 1959.

Jackson, Luther Porter. "The Early Strivings of the Negro in Virginia." *Journal of Negro History* 25 (January 1940): 25-34.

————. *Free Negro Labor and Property Holding in Virginia, 1830-1860.* New York: D. Appleton-Century Co., 1942.

————. "The Virginia Free Negro Farmer and Property Owner, 1830-1860." *Journal of Negro History* 24 (October 1939): 390-439.

Klein, Herbert S. *Slavery in the Americas: A Comparative Study of Virginia and Cuba.* Chicago: University of Chicago Press, 1967.

Knight, Charles Louis. *Negro Housing in Certain Virginia Cities.* Phelps-Stokes Fellowship Papers. Richmond, Va.: William Byrd Press, 1927.

Langhorne, Orra. *Southern Sketches from Virginia, 1881-1901.* Charlottesville, Va.: University of Virginia Press, 1964.

McConnell, John Preston. *Negroes and Their Treatment in Virginia from 1865 to 1867.* Pulaski, Va.: B.D. Smith & Brothers, 1910.

McDonald, James J. *Life in Old Virginia.* Norfolk: Old Virginia Publishing Co., 1907.

Mannix, Daniel P., and Cowley, Malcolm. *Black Cargoes.* New York: Viking Press, 1962.

Marcus, Jacob R. *The Colonial American Jew, 1492-1776.* vol. 1. Detroit: Wayne State University Press, 1970.

Moger, Allen Wesley. *Rebuilding the Old Dominion.* Ann Arbor: Edwards Brothers Publishing Co., 1940.

Mullin, Gerald W. *Flight and Rebellion.* New York: Oxford University Press, 1972.

Negro Welfare Survey Committee. *The Negro in Richmond, Virginia.* Richmond: Council of Social Agencies, 1921.

Olmsted, Frederick Law. *A Journey in the Seaboard Slave States in 1853-54.* New York: G.P. Putnam's Sons, 1904.

Phillips, Ulrich B. *Life and Labor in the Old South.* Boston: Little, Brown, 1929.

Polanyi, Karl. *Dahomey and the Slave Trade.* Seattle: University of Washington Press, 1966.

Pope-Hennessy, James. *Sins of the Fathers: A Study of the Atlantic Slave Traders, 1441-1807.* London: Weidenfeld and Nicolson, 1967.

Raines, Howell. *My Soul Is Rested.* New York: G.P. Putnam's Sons, 1977.

Randolph, E.A. *The Life of Rev. John Jasper.* Richmond, Va.: R.T. Hill & Co., 1884.

Raywick, George P., ed. *The American Slave: A Composite Biography.* Westport, Conn.: Greenwood Publishing Co., 1972.

Richmond Council of Social Agencies. *The Negro in Richmond, Virginia: The Report of the Negro Welfare Survey Committee.* Richmond, Va., 1929.

Robert, Joseph Clarke. *The Tobacco Kingdom: Plantation, Market and Factory in Virginia and North Carolina, 1800-1860.* Durham, N.C.: Duke University Press, 1938.

Rosengarten, Theodore. *All God's Dangers: The Life of Nate Shaw.* New York: Alfred A. Knopf, 1974.

Russell, John H. *The Free Negro in Virginia, 1819-1865.* Baltimore: Johns Hopkins Press, 1913.

Russell, Lester F. *Black Baptist Secondary Schools in Virginia, 1887-1957.* Metuchen, N.J.: Scarecrow Press, 1981.

Sowell, Thomas. *Race and Economics.* New York: McKay Co., 1975.

Stampp, Kenneth M. *The Peculiar Institution: Slavery in the Ante-Bellum South.* New York: Random House, 1956.

Sterling, Dorothy, ed. *The Trouble They Seen.* New York: Doubleday & Co., 1976.

Swem, E.G. *Virginia Historical Index.* Vol. 1. Gloucester, Mass.: Peter Smith, 1965.

Taylor, Alrutheus Ambush. *The Negro in the Reconstruction of Virginia.* Washington, D.C.: Association for the Study of Negro Life and History, 1926.

Thom, William Taylor. *The Negroes of Litwalton, Virginia: A Social Study of the 'Oyster Negro.'* Bulletin of the Department of Labor, no. 37.

Trelease, Allen W. *White Terror: The Ku Klux Klan Conspiracy and Southern Reconstruction.* New York: Harper and Row, 1971.

Tyler's Quarterly 5:45. Richmond, Va.: Richmond Press, Inc., 1924.

Wade, Richard C. *Slavery in the Cities, 1820-1860.* New York: Oxford University Press, 1964.

Walker, T.C. "Development in the Tidewater Counties of Virginia." *Annals of the American Academy of Political and Social Sciences* 50 (1913): 28-31.

Washington, Booker T. *Up from Slavery.* Garden City, N.Y.: Doubleday, c. 1963.

Weber, Gustavus A. *Report on Housing and Living Conditions in the Neglected Sections of Richmond, Virginia.* Society for the Betterment of Housing and Living Conditions in Richmond. Richmond, Va.: Whittet & Shepperson, 1913.

Weinstein, Allen, and Gatell, Frank Otto, eds. *American Negro Slavery: A Modern Reader.* New York: Oxford University Press, 1968.

William and Mary Quarterly. 1st ser. 15 (1907):58, 69.

Williamson, Joel. *After Slavery: The Negro in South Carolina during Reconstruction, 1861-1877.* Chapel Hill: University of North Carolina Press, 1965.

Woofter, T.J., Jr. *Negro Problems in Cities.* New York: Doubleday, Doran & Co., 1925.

Writers' Program of the Work Projects Administration in the State of Virginia. *The Negro in Virginia.* New York: Hastings House, 1940.

Wynes, Charles E. *Race Relations in Virginia, 1870-1902.* Charlottesville: University of Virginia Press, 1961.

Yetman, Norman R. *Life under the Peculiar Institution: Selections from the Slave Narrative Collection.* New York: Holt, Rinehart and Winston, 1970.

ACKNOWLEDGMENTS

I WOULD like to thank the people of Fulton whose stories, anecdotes, and opinions are the basis of this book. To preserve their privacy I have not acknowledged them as individuals. Needless to say, their attitudes toward urban renewal have mellowed since the years of confrontation that are the subject of my narrative.

The planners and consultants of Richmond Redevelopment and Housing Authority and Mr. Fred Fey, the former director, have been generous in their help. They made a strong case in favor of the course that renewal took in Fulton. In the end I have come to a different conclusion but my writing has benefited from their views.

This book developed slowly over ten years' time. I am grateful to those who offered critical readings and helped in other ways: Mike Agather, John Anderson, Diane Benedict Gill, James Britain, Lillian Britain, Kay Bullitt, Kathy Burger, Knox Burger, Marie Cantlon, Ann Close, Alan Crabb, Jean Davis, John M. Davis, Sally Davis, Peter Davis, Marceil DeLacy, Marianne Dusenbury, Charles Drekmeier, Margot Drekmeier, John Egerton, Earl W. Emerson, Sandy Emerson, Delores Ettress, Mary Evans, Larry Friedlander, Sal Garcia, Carolyn D. Geise, Susan Green, Gus Garber, Natalie Greenberg, Jan Hale, Bob Hermer,

Bud Krogh, Laura Lee Krogh, Richard C. Locke, Joegil Lundquist, Lance Matteson, Jon McLaughlin, Merri-Jim McLaughlin, Alberta Moore, Kathleen Mulcahy, Dan Mulcahy, Pat Murray, Otis Pease, Dawn Reed, Alan Siff, Diane Solvang-Angell, Linda Thorne, John M. Turner, Greg Vette, Dave Weaver, and Peter Womble.

Special thanks go to my parents, Don and Lyn Davis, and to my wife, Mary McConnel Davis.

The Author

Scott C. Davis was born in 1948 in Seattle
and graduated from Stanford in 1970.
He served as a social worker in Richmond,
Virginia, in 1971 and 1972 and now
supports himself and his wife as a building
contractor in Seattle. His writing has
appeared in *The Christian Science Monitor*
and has been read nationally on public radio.